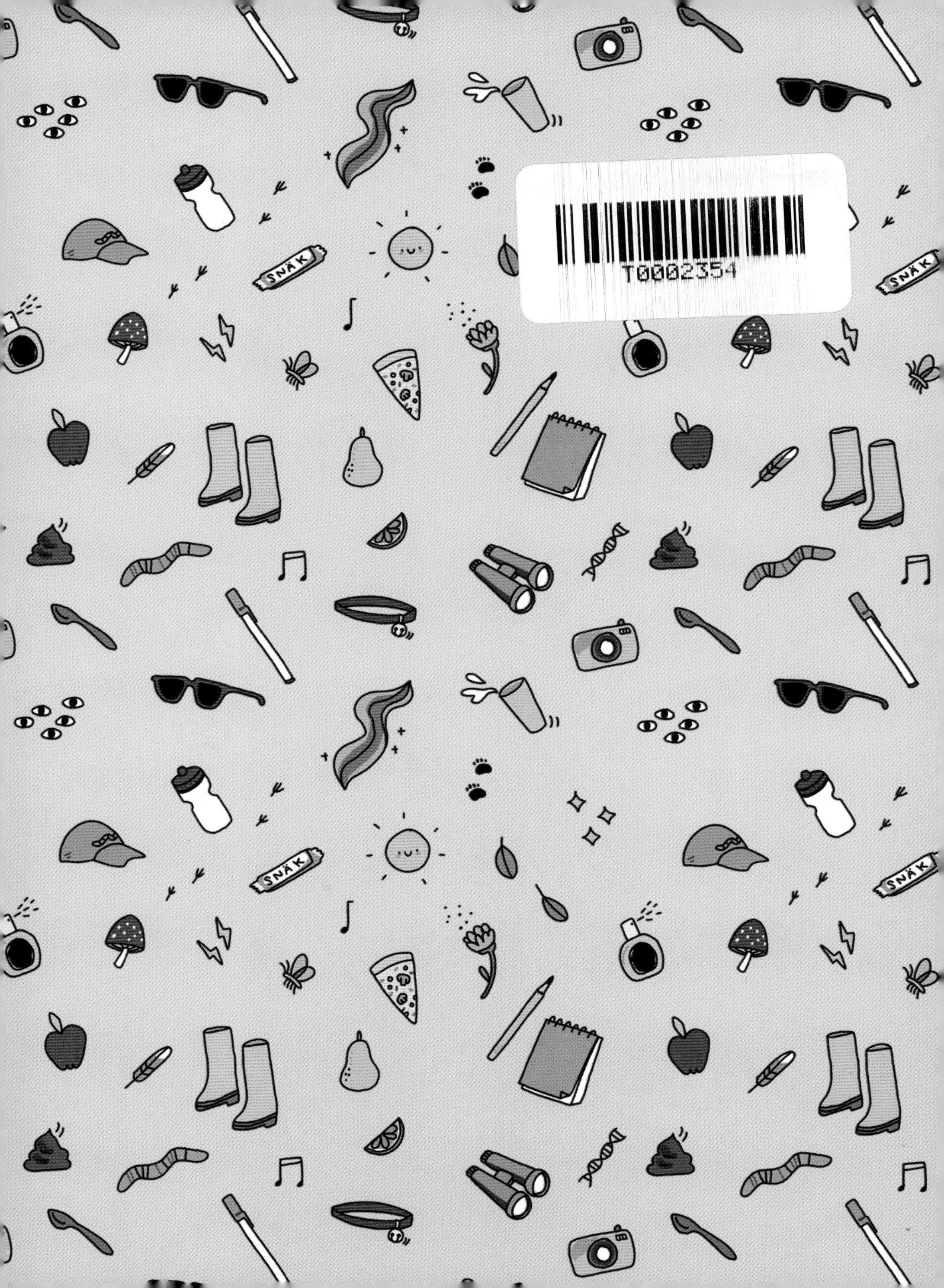
SNÄK
SNÄK
SNÄK
SNÄK

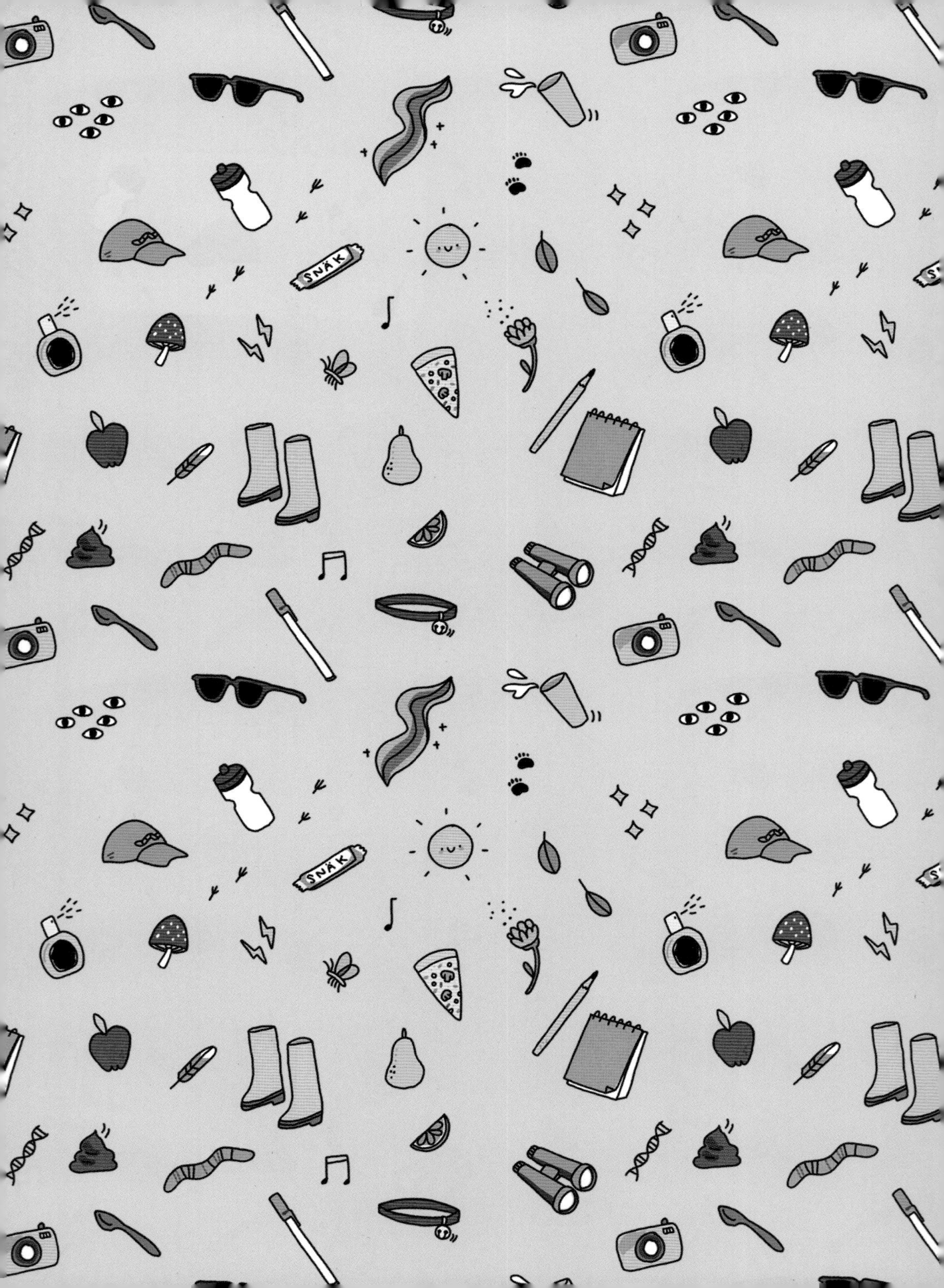
SNÄK

THIS BOOK BELONGS TO:

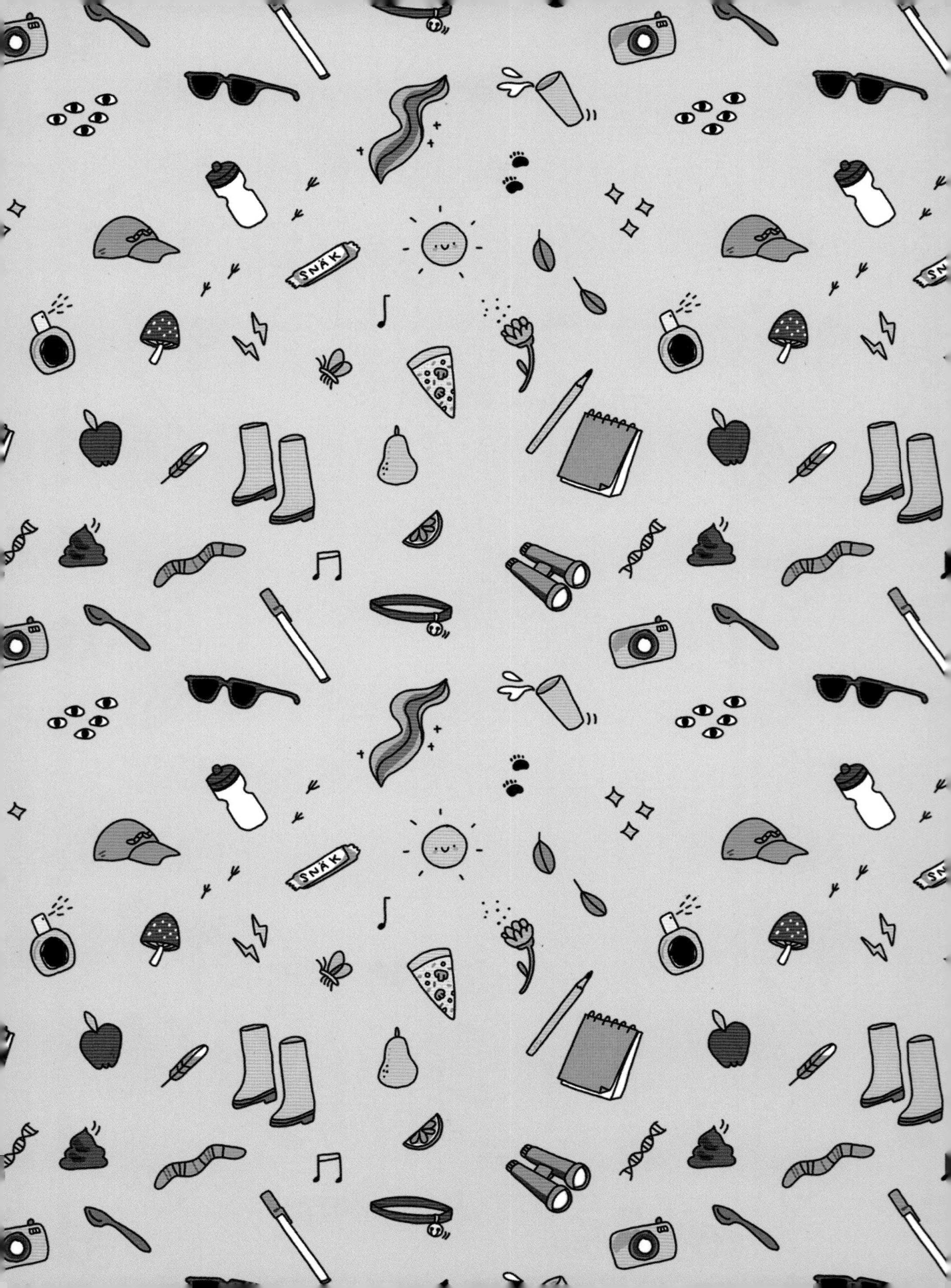
SNÄK

How Do Meerkats Order Pizza?

Wild Facts about Animals and the Scientists Who Study Them

BROOKE BARKER

Simon & Schuster Books for Young Readers
New York   London   Toronto   Sydney   New Delhi

SIMON & SCHUSTER BOOKS FOR YOUNG READERS
An imprint of Simon & Schuster Children's Publishing Division
1230 Avenue of the Americas, New York, New York 10020
© 2022 by Brooke Barker
Book design by Lizzy Bromley © 2022 by Simon & Schuster, Inc.
SIMON & SCHUSTER BOOKS FOR YOUNG READERS
and related marks are trademarks of Simon & Schuster, Inc.
For information about special discounts for bulk purchases, please contact
Simon & Schuster Special Sales at 1-866-506-1949 or business@simonandschuster.com.
The Simon & Schuster Speakers Bureau can bring authors to your live event.
For more information or to book an event, contact the Simon & Schuster Speakers Bureau
at 1-866-248-3049 or visit our website at www.simonspeakers.com.
Also available in a Simon & Schuster Books for Young Readers hardcover edition
The text for this book was set in Brandon. • The illustrations for this book were rendered digitally.
Manufactured in China • 0623 SCP
First Simon & Schuster Books for Young Readers paperback edition October 2023
2 4 6 8 10 9 7 5 3 1
Library of Congress Control Number: 2022938949
ISBN 9781665901604 (hc)
ISBN 9781665901611 (pbk)
ISBN 9781665901628 (ebook)

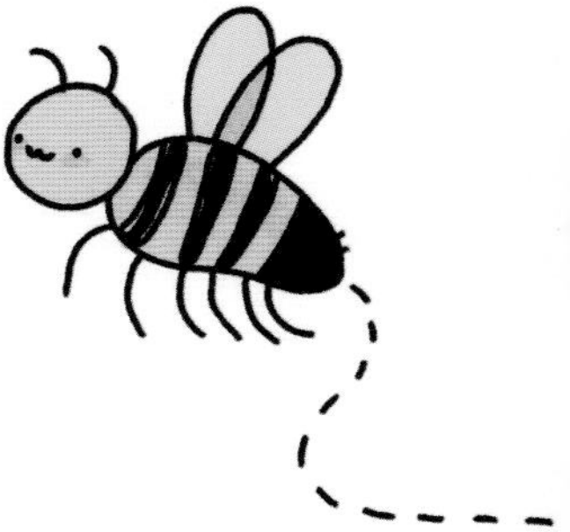

For Avery, George,
Harris, James, and Miles.
Earth is amazing—
I'm so glad we all live here.
—B. B.

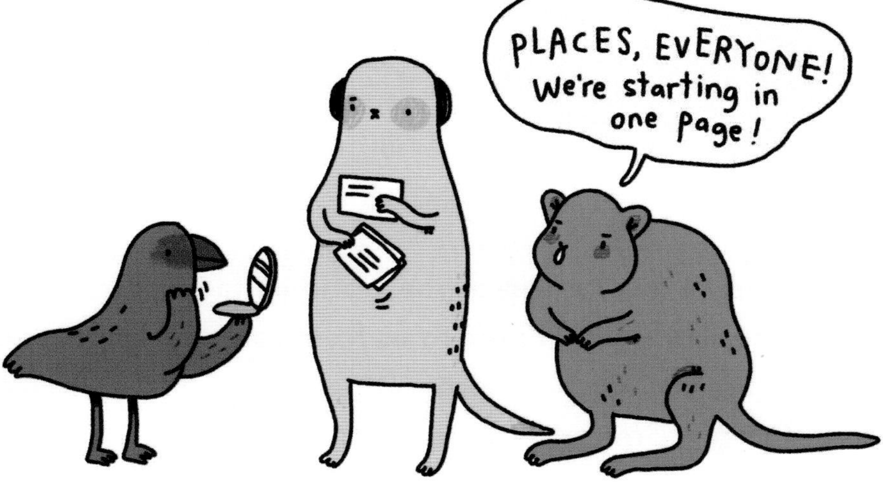
PLACES, EVERYONE! We're starting in one page!

What's your favorite animal fact?

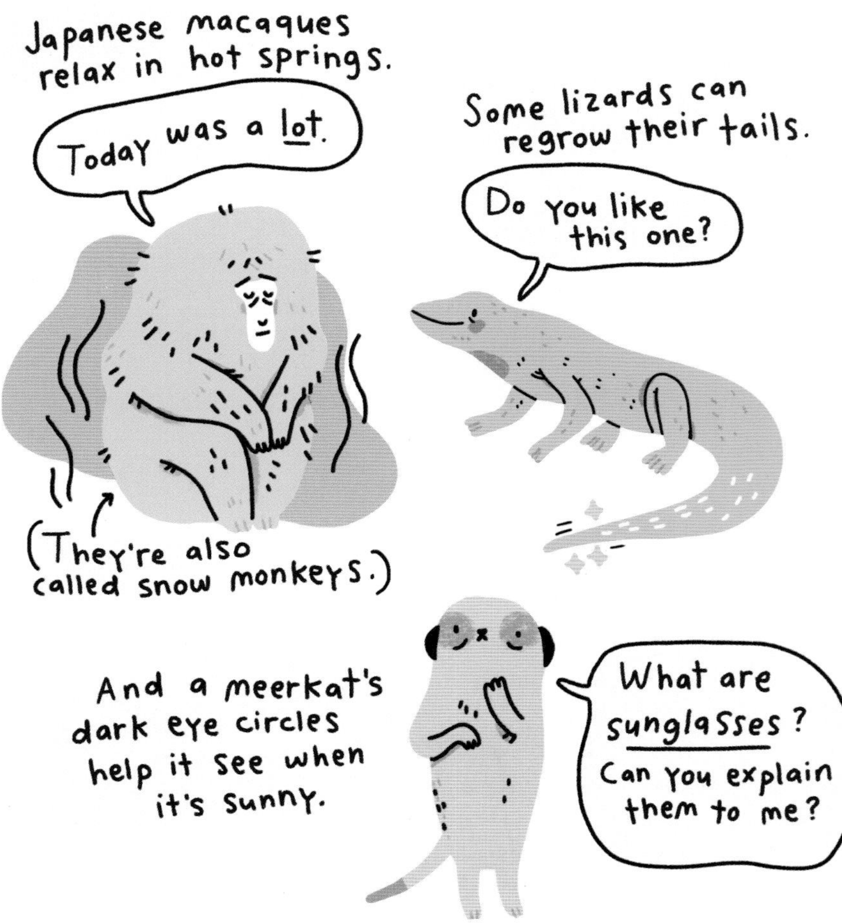

Japanese macaques relax in hot springs.
Today was a lot.
(They're also called snow monkeys.)
Some lizards can regrow their tails.
Do you like this one?
And a meerkat's dark eye circles help it see when it's sunny.
What are sunglasses? Can you explain them to me?

Have you ever wondered where animal facts come from? Most often, they come to us from scientists—people who are studying and protecting animals and learning more about them all the time.

But here's a fact: sometimes, how the scientists learn about animals is even wilder and weirder than what they learn. The stories of these scientists are full of:

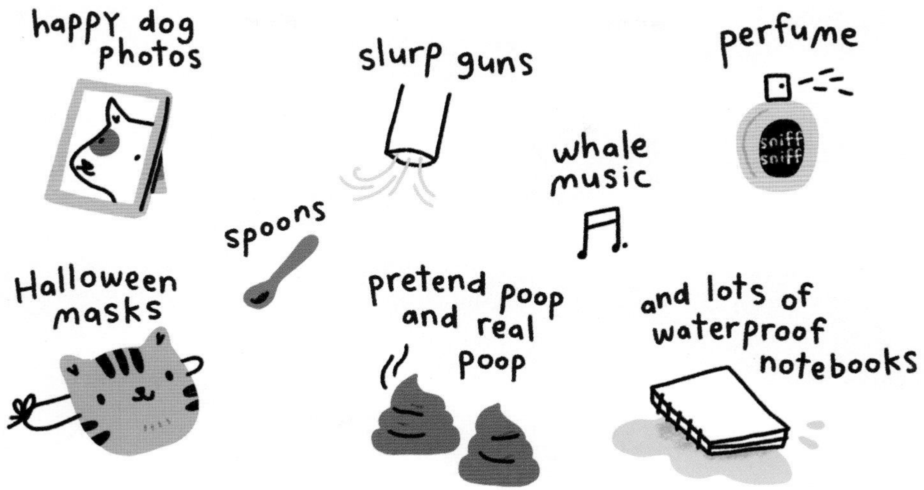
happy dog photos
slurp guns
perfume
sniff sniff
whale music
spoons
Halloween masks
pretend poop and real poop
and lots of waterproof notebooks

To find out more, get ready to meet some scientists and the animals they follow around all day.

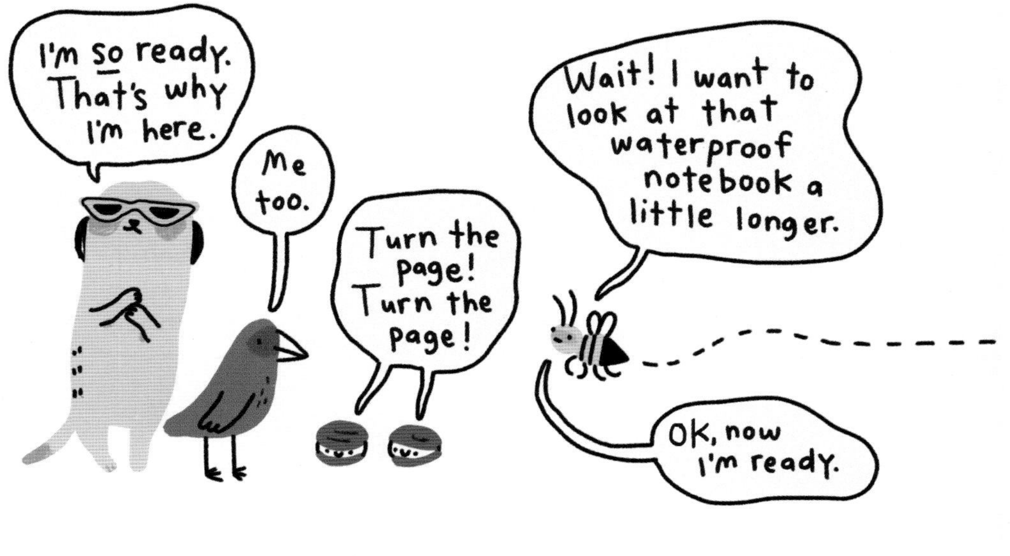
I'm so ready. That's why I'm here.
Me too.
Turn the page! Turn the page!
Wait! I want to look at that waterproof notebook a little longer.
OK, now I'm ready.

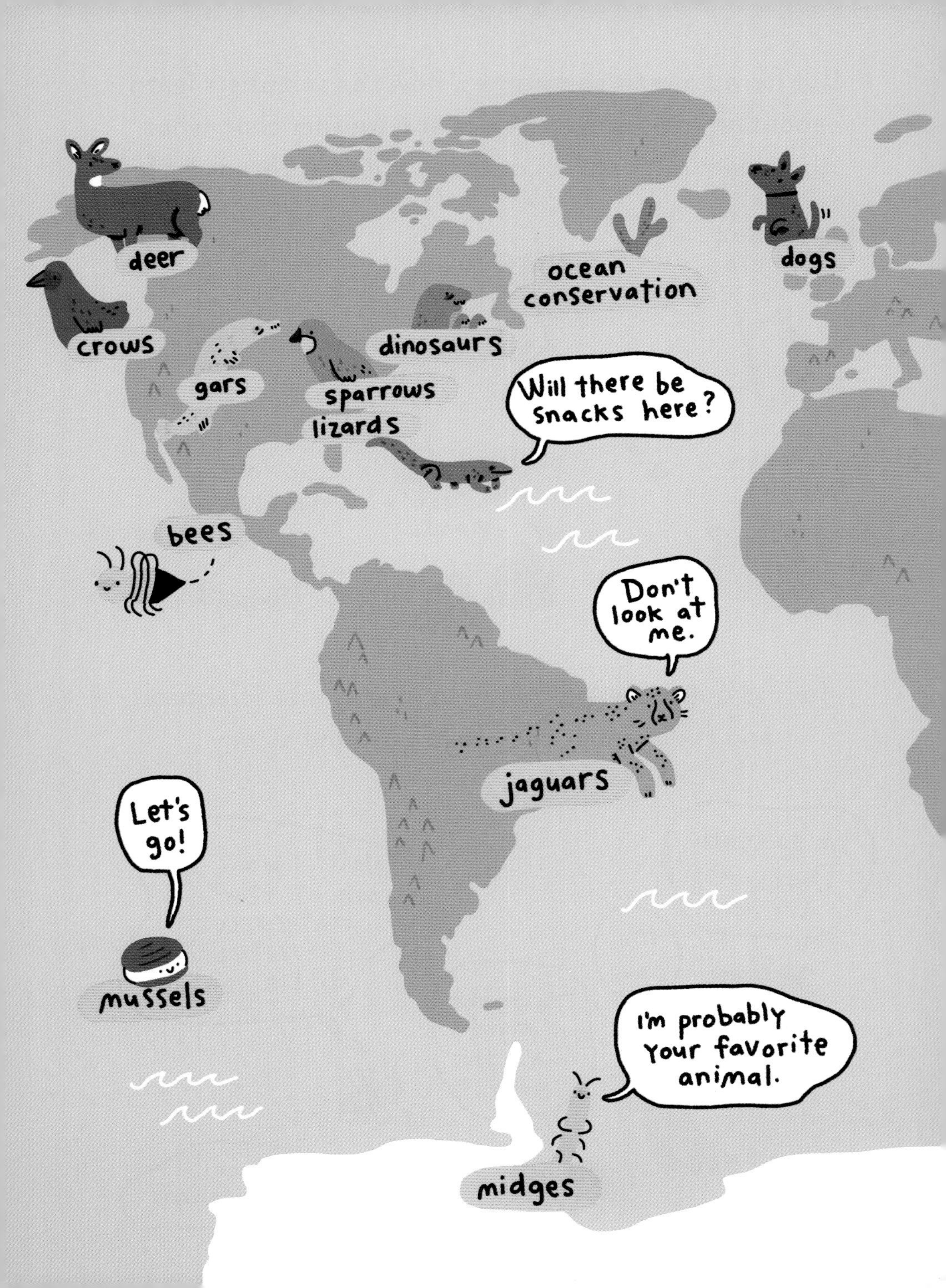
deer
crows
gars
sparrows
lizards
dinosaurs
ocean conservation
dogs
Will there be snacks here?
bees
Don't look at me.
jaguars
Let's go!
mussels
I'm probably your favorite animal.
midges

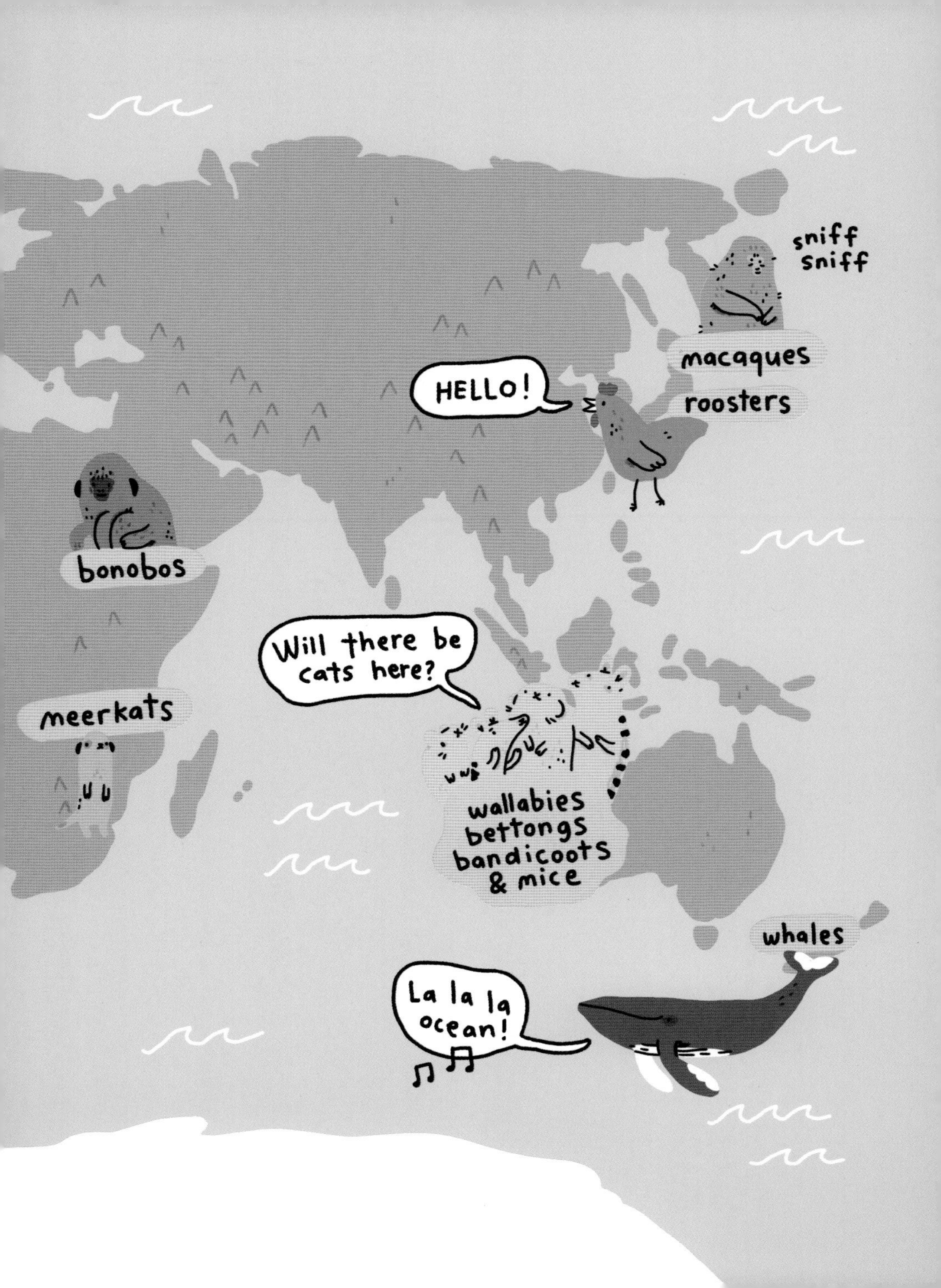
sniff
sniff
macaques
HELLO!
roosters
bonobos
Will there be cats here?
meerkats
wallabies
bettongs
bandicoots
& mice
whales
La la la ocean!

Dr. Marta Manser studies meerkats.

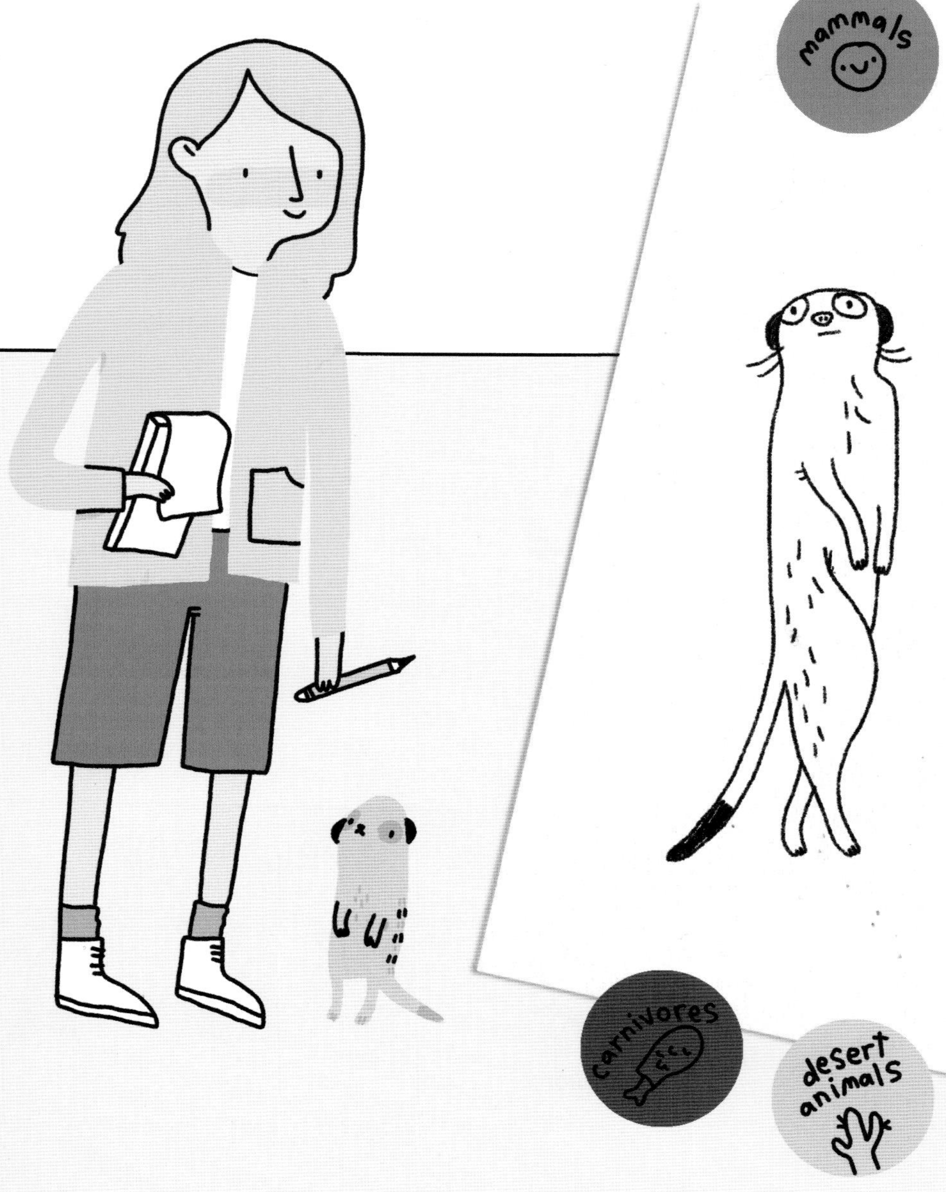
mammals
carnivores
desert animals

MEERKATS

Meerkats live in the Kalahari Desert
in southern Africa.

- 10–14 inches tall
- weigh 1–6 pounds
- covered in fur (and sand)

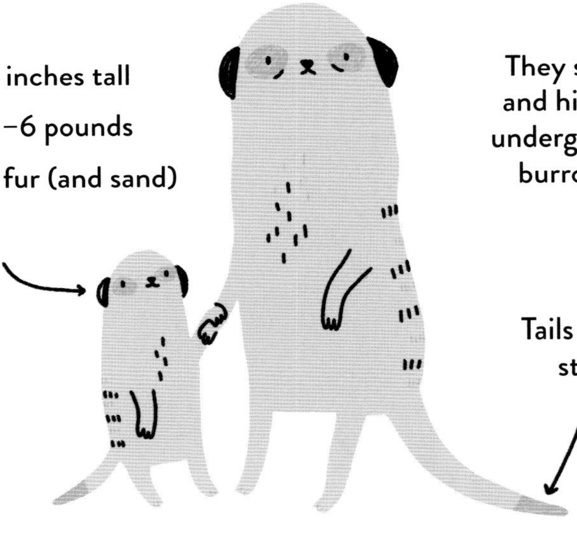

They sleep and hide in underground burrows.

Tails help them stand up.

FAVORITE FOODS

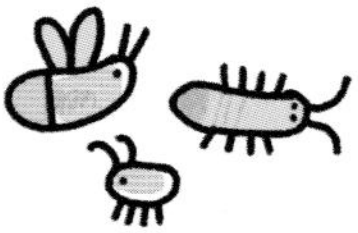

insects

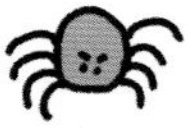

spiders

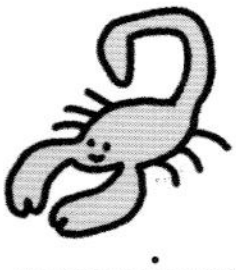

scorpions

PREDATORS

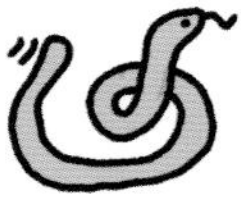

snakes

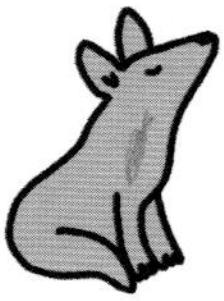

jackals

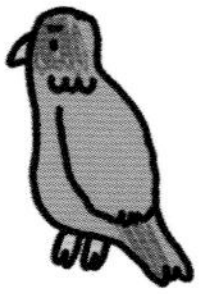

birds

Meerkats live in groups of up to fifty and spend every day with their family and friends. Communication is important—they need to work together and cooperate to stay safe.

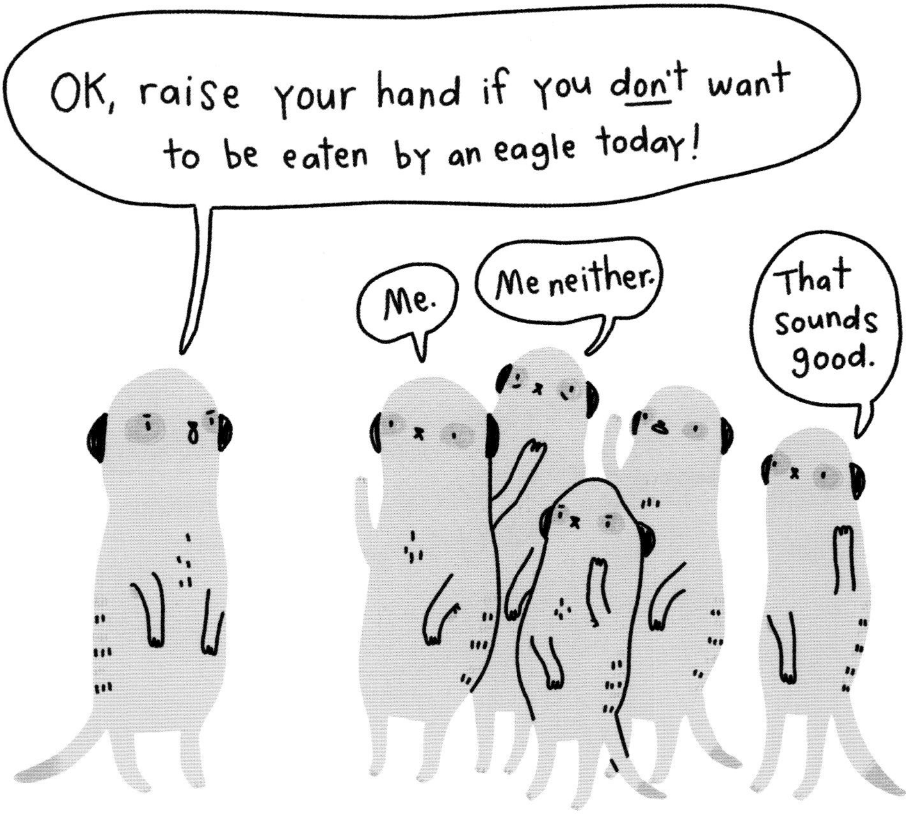
OK, raise your hand if you don't want to be eaten by an eagle today!
Me.
Me neither.
That sounds good.

Dr. Manser decided to study meerkats so she could learn more about how they communicate and get along.

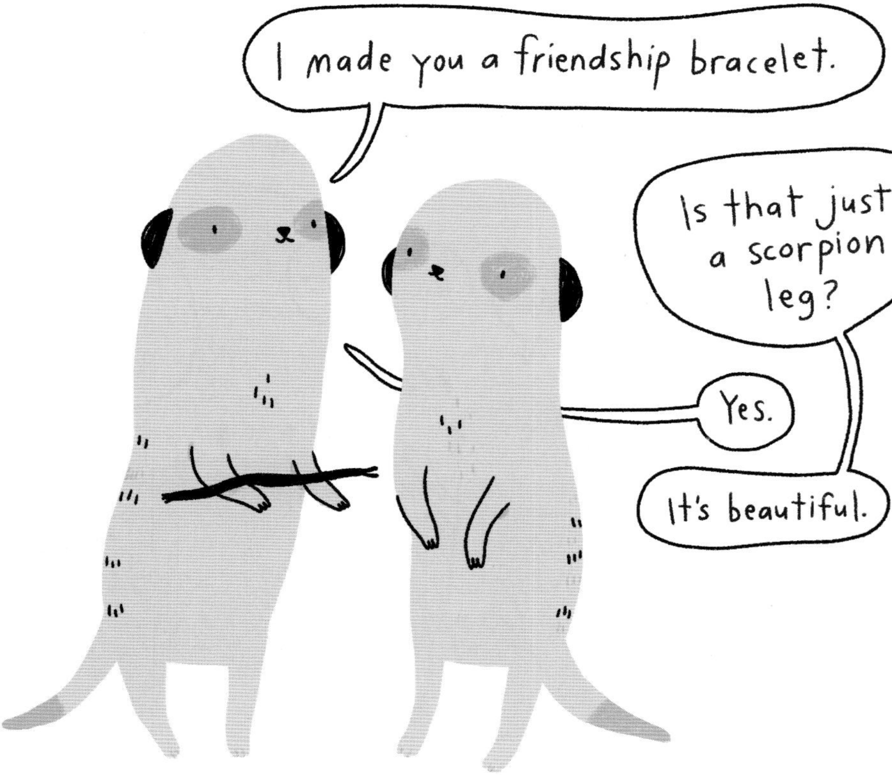
I made you a friendship bracelet.
Is that just a scorpion leg?
Yes.
It's beautiful.

She observes the meerkats for an hour at a time and takes notes on everything.

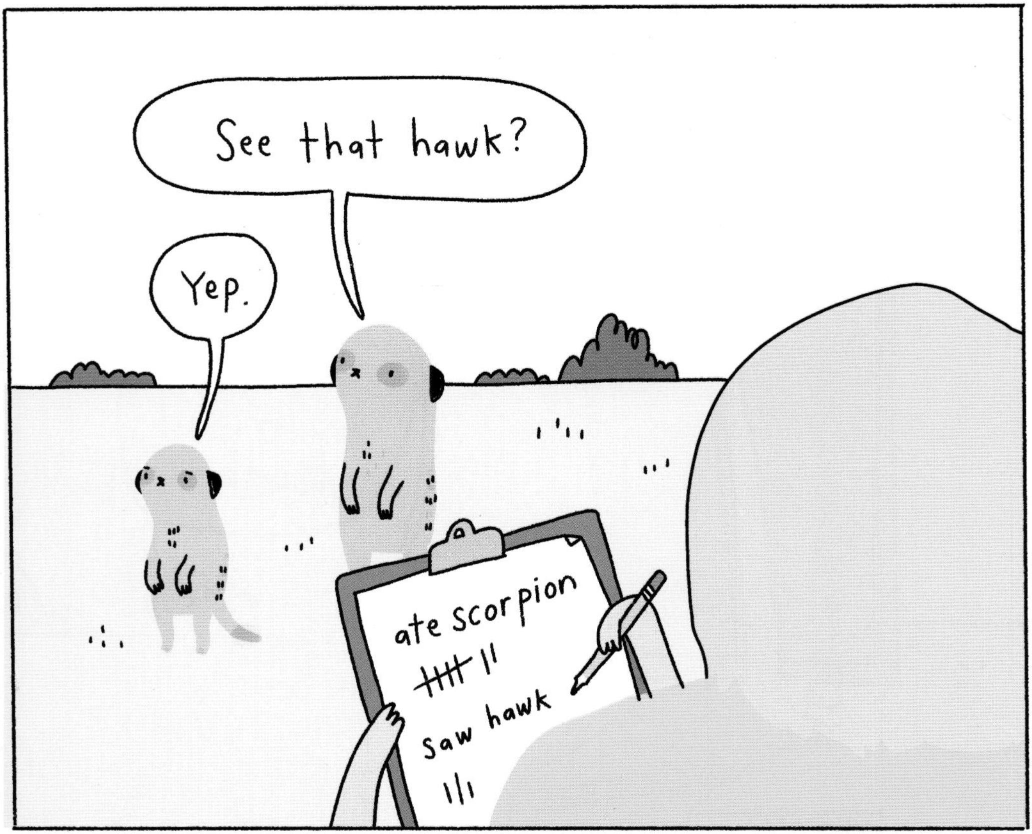
See that hawk?
Yep.
ate scorpion
saw hawk

She and her team have been watching the same group of meerkats for twenty years.

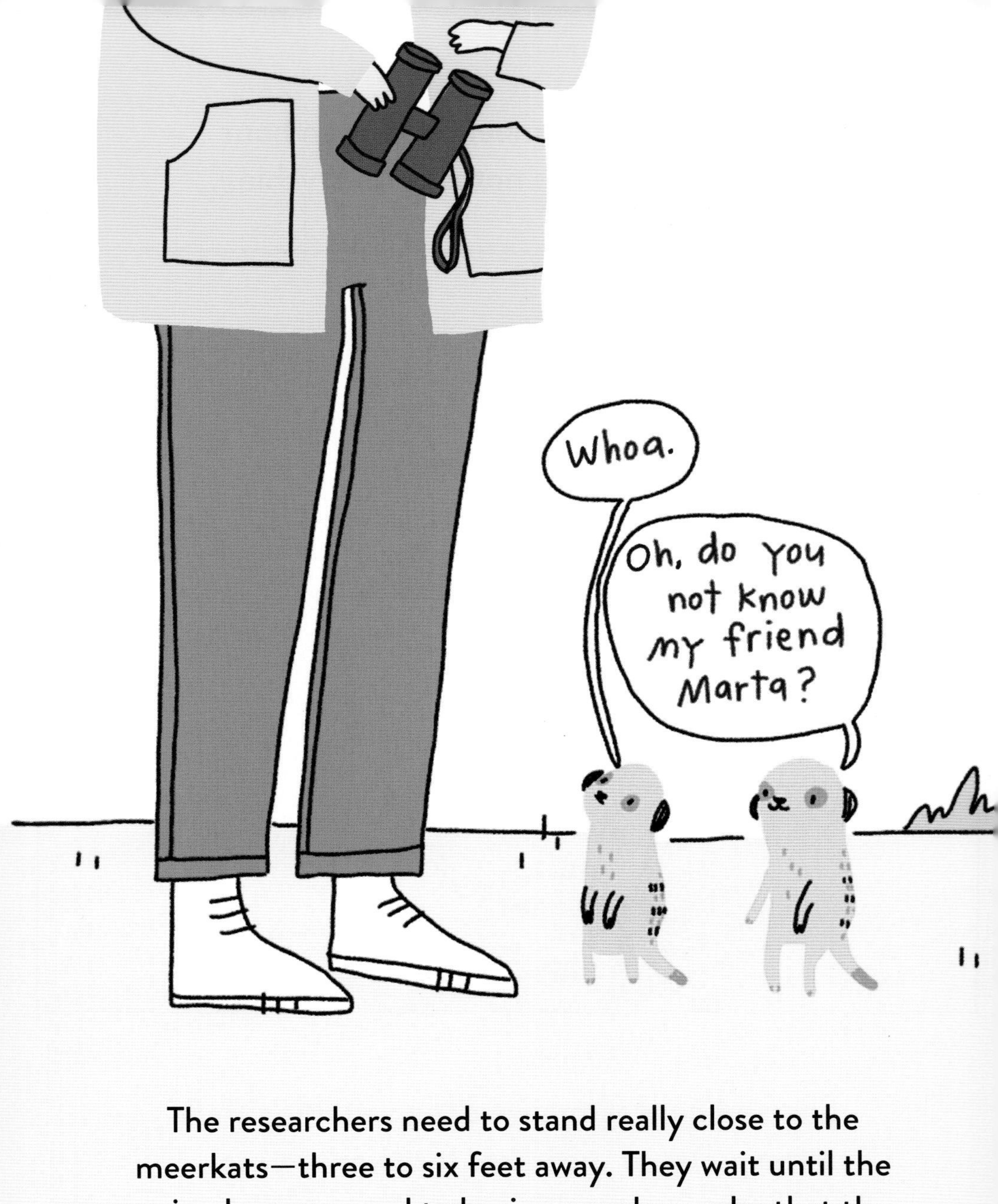
Whoa.
Oh, do you not know my friend Marta?

The researchers need to stand really close to the meerkats—three to six feet away. They wait until the animals are so used to having people nearby that the meerkats act like the scientists aren't there.

Here's what scientists who study meerkats bring to work:

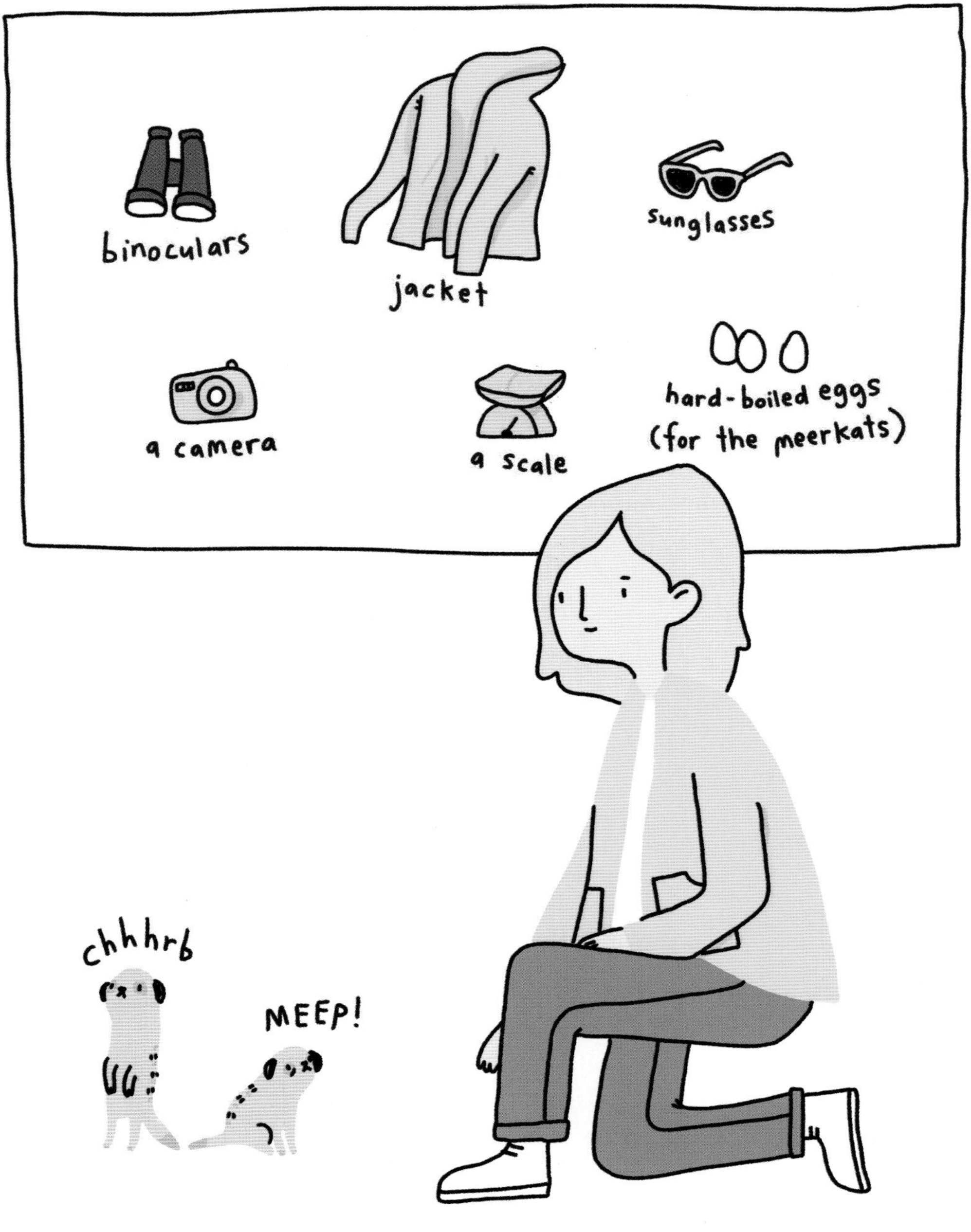
binoculars
jacket
sunglasses
a camera
a scale
hard-boiled eggs (for the meerkats)
chhhrb
MEEP!

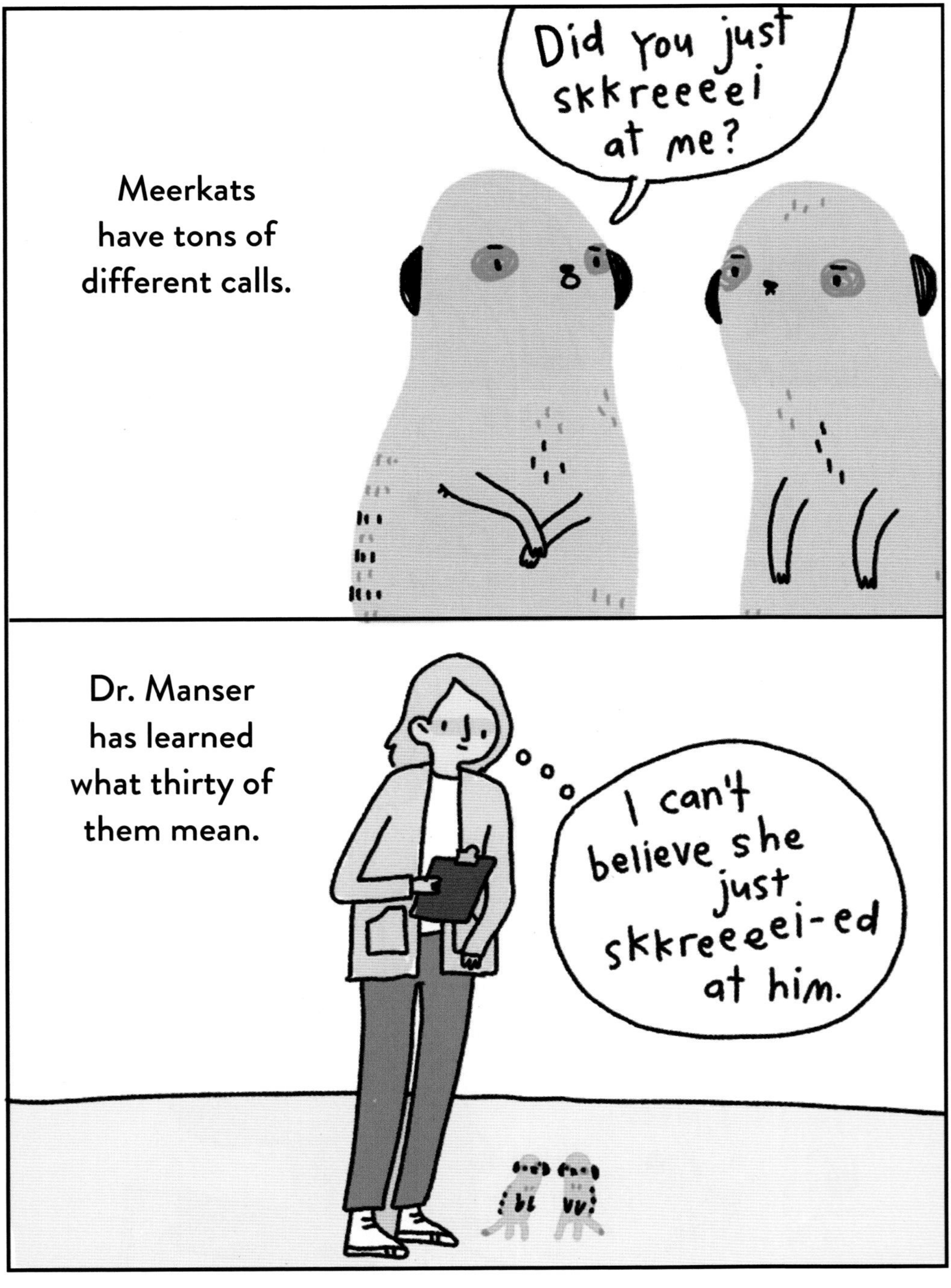
Meerkats have tons of different calls.
Did you just skkreeeei at me?
Dr. Manser has learned what thirty of them mean.
I can't believe she just skkreeeei-ed at him.

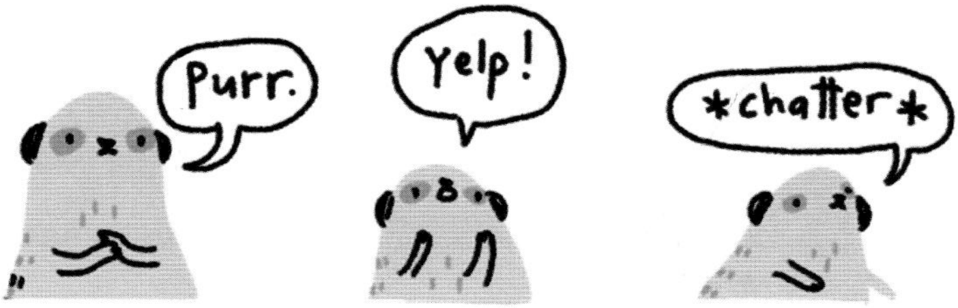
Purr.
Yelp!
chatter

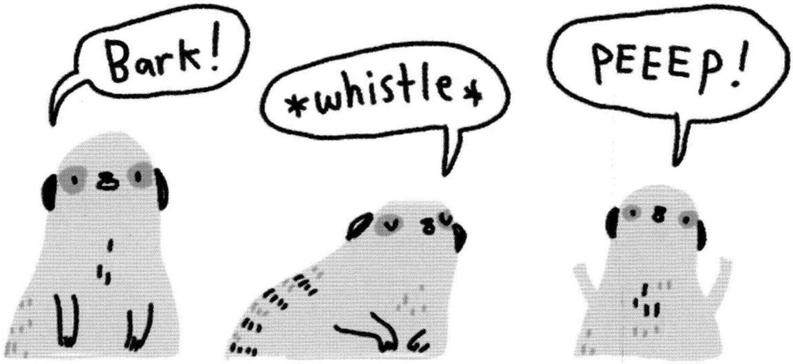
Bark!
whistle
PEEEP!

They also communicate by:

mobbing
(gathering around a threatening object) . . .

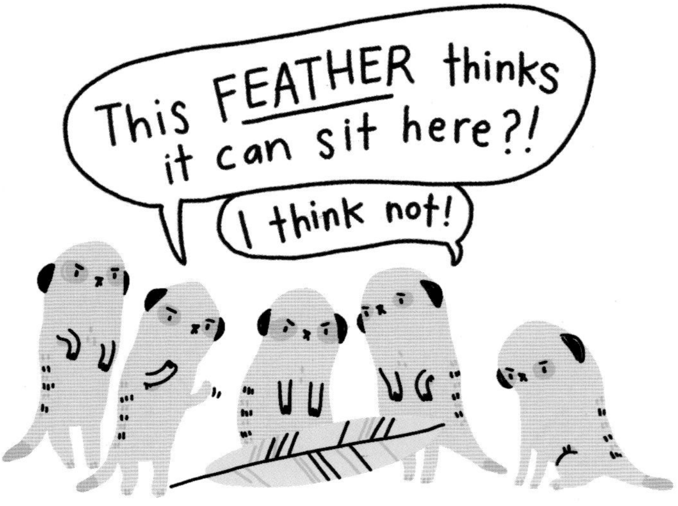
This FEATHER thinks it can sit here?!
I think not!

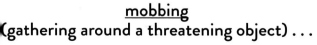

standing guard and staring at dangers . . .

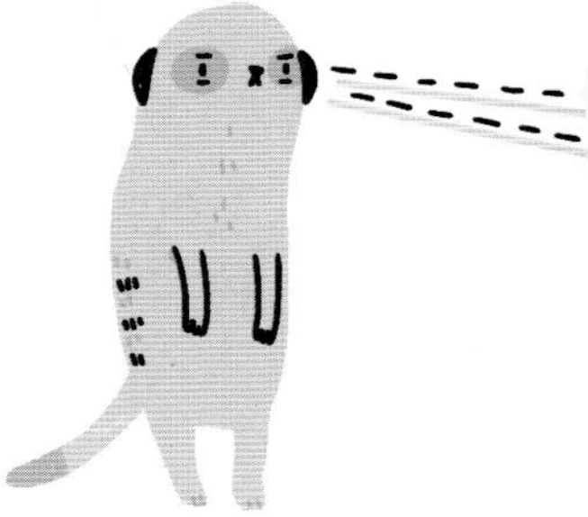

and smelling.

What do meerkats talk about?
The team discovered that
meerkats vote:

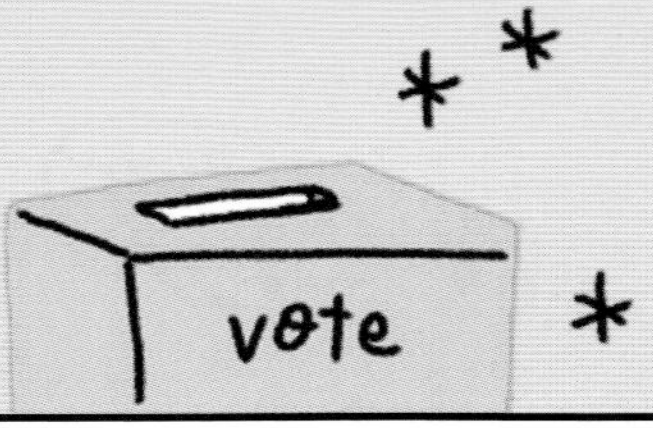
vote

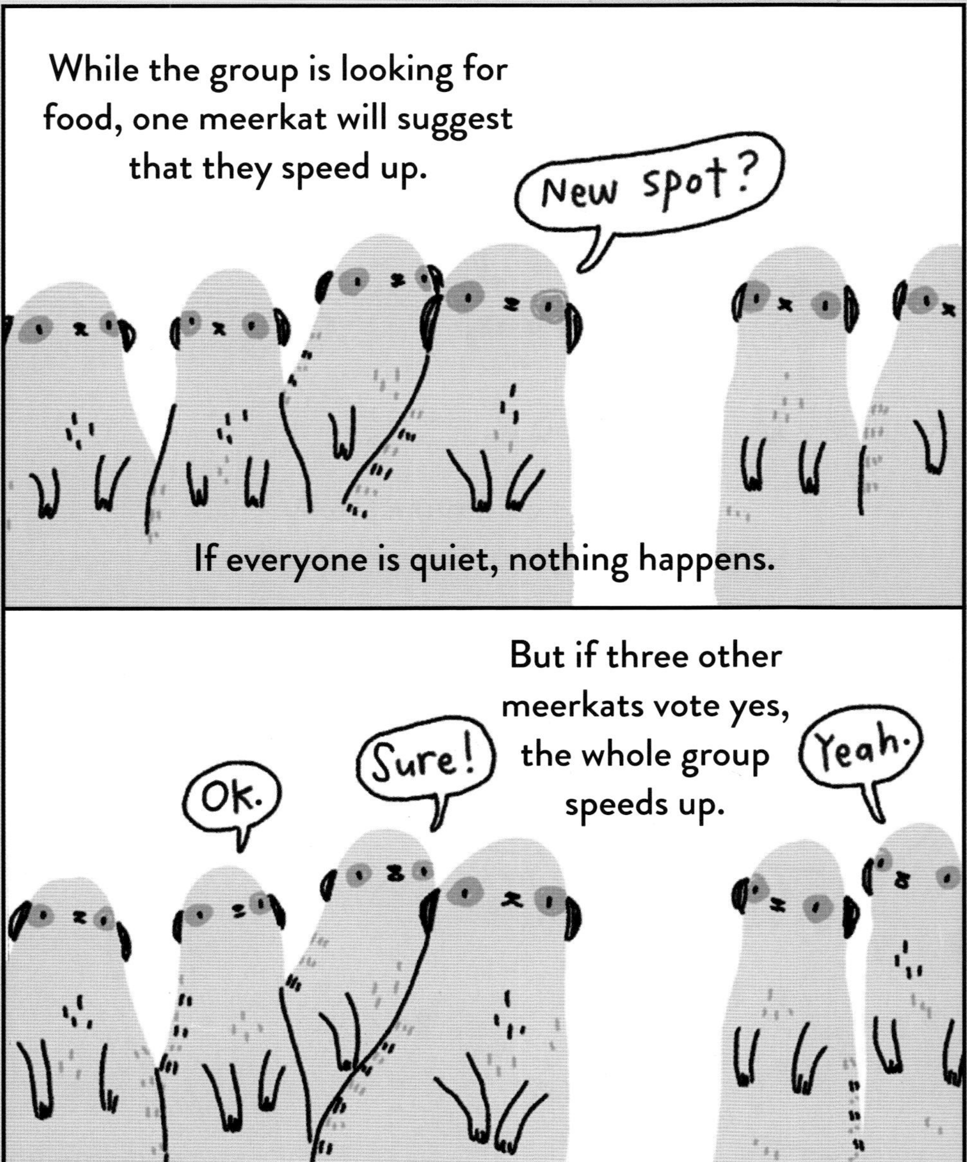
While the group is looking for food, one meerkat will suggest that they speed up.
New spot?
If everyone is quiet, nothing happens.
But if three other meerkats vote yes, the whole group speeds up.
Ok.
Sure!
Yeah.

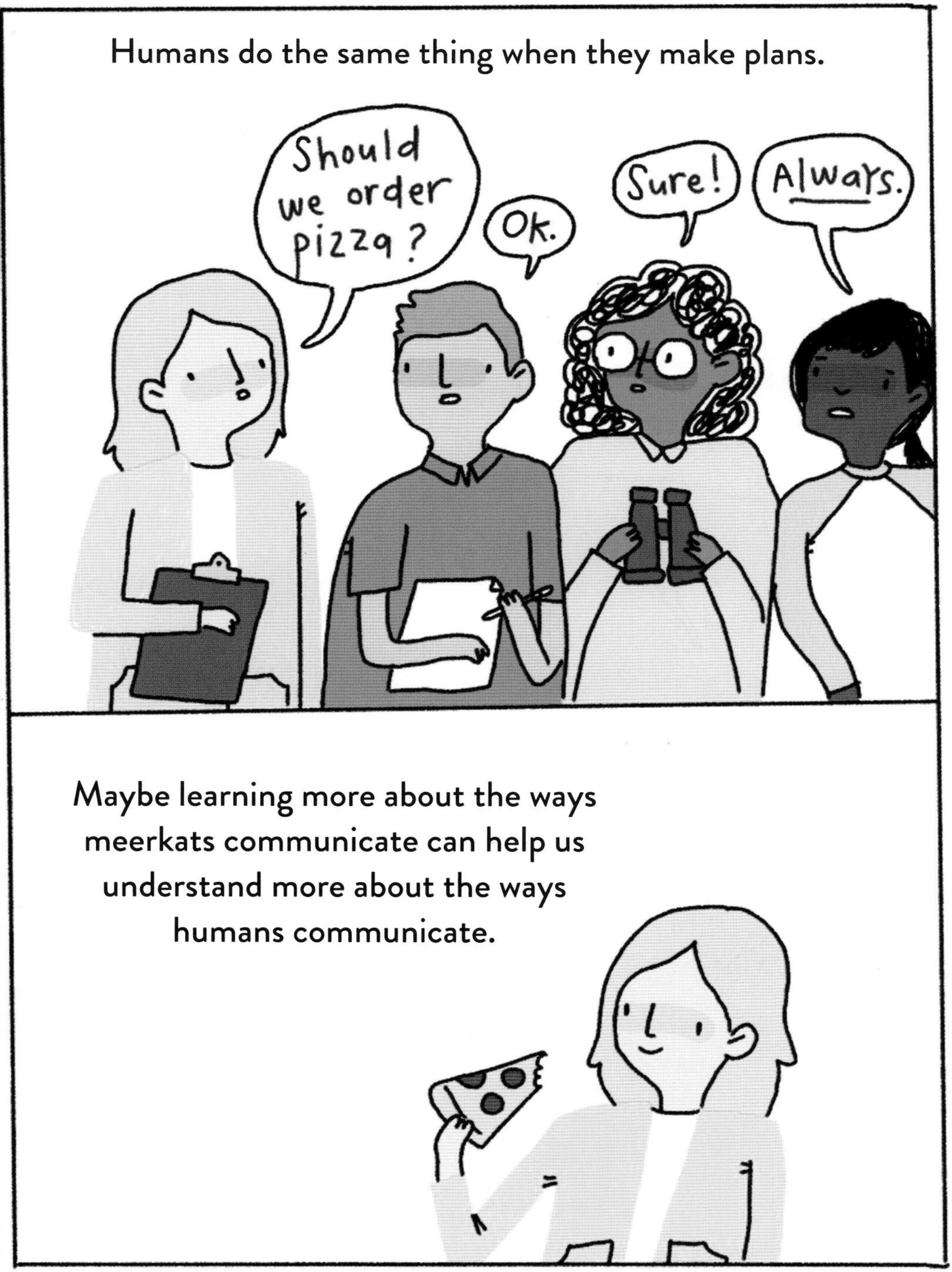
Humans do the same thing when they make plans.
Should we order pizza?
Ok.
Sure!
Always.
Maybe learning more about the ways meerkats communicate can help us understand more about the ways humans communicate.

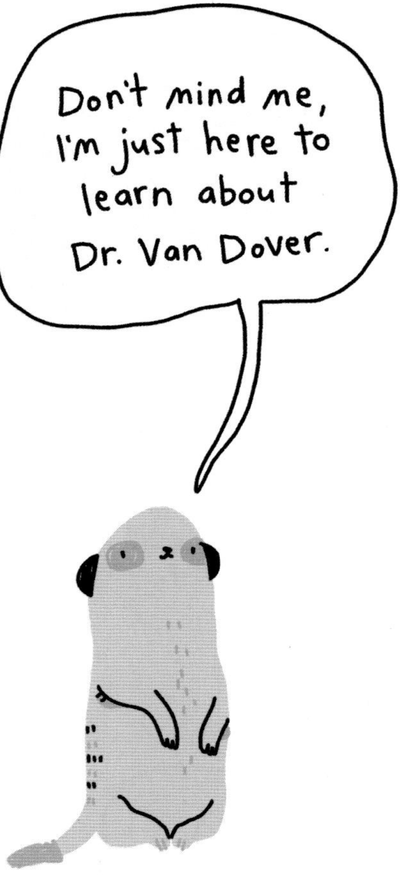
Don't mind me, I'm just here to learn about Dr. Van Dover.

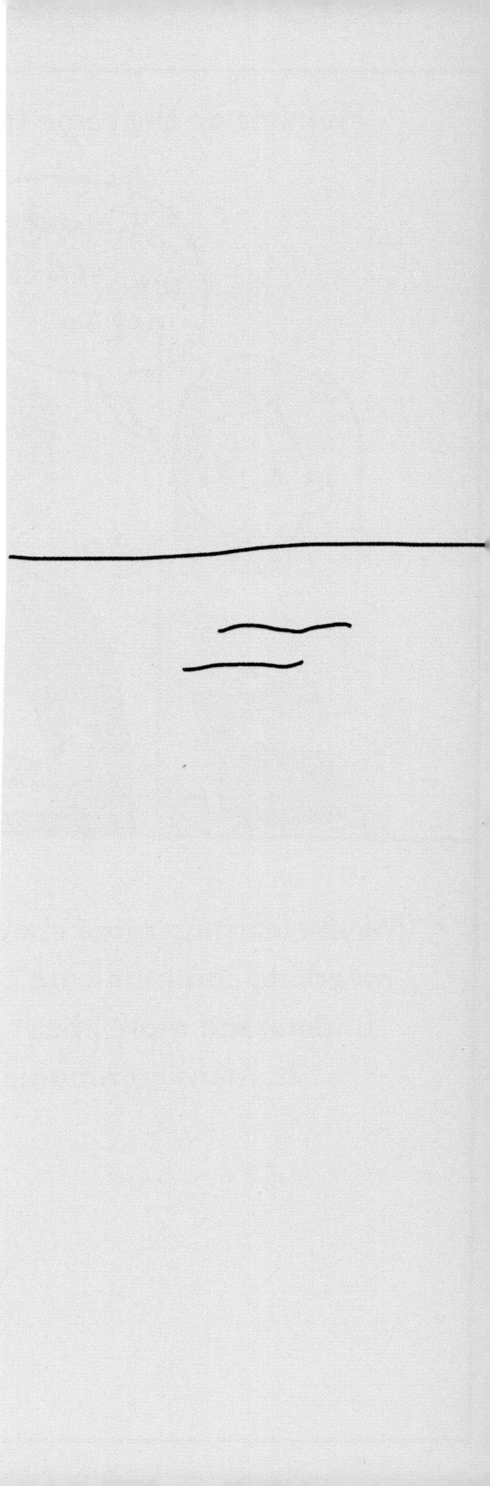

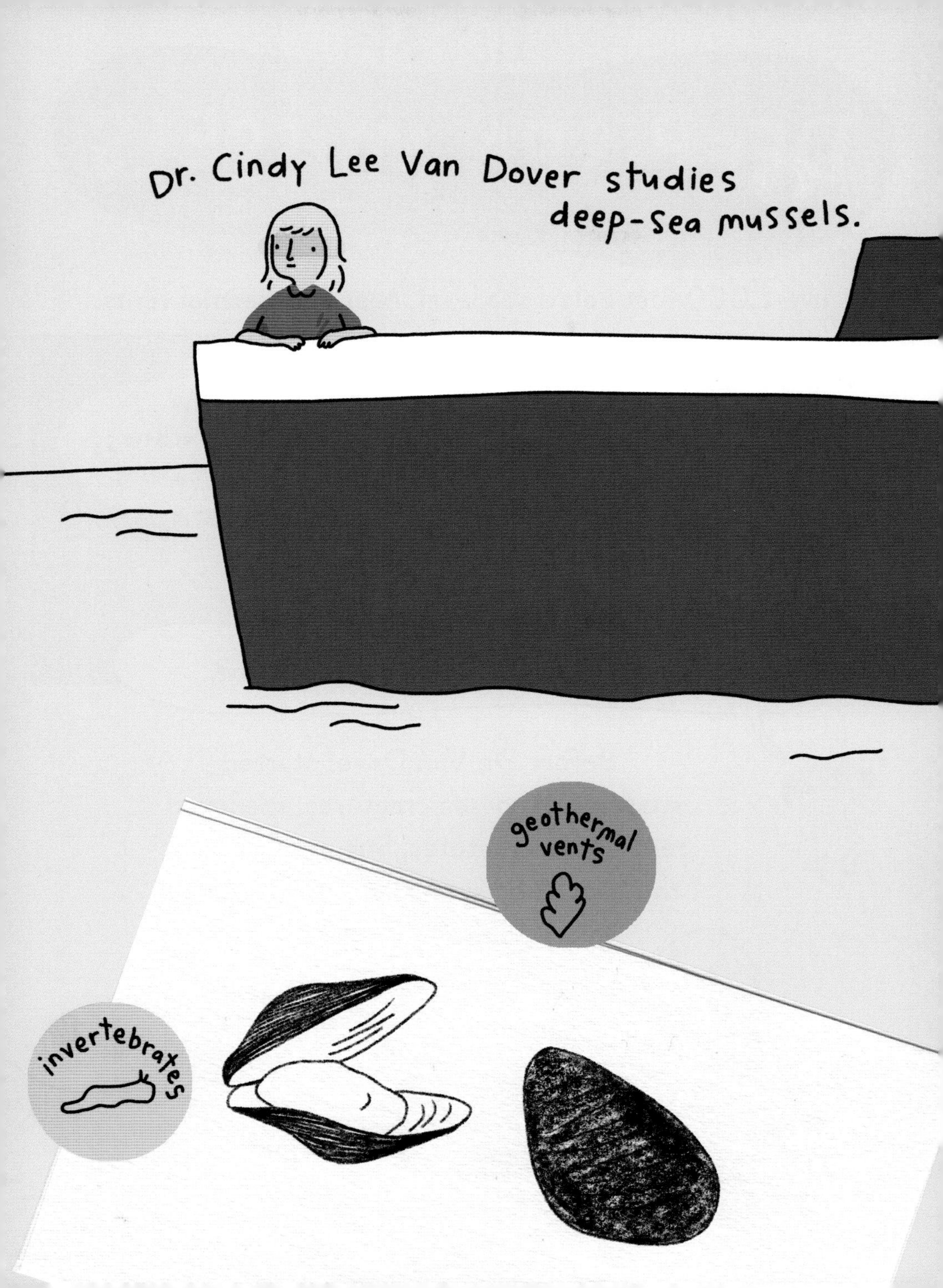
Dr. Cindy Lee Van Dover studies deep-sea mussels.
geothermal vents
invertebrates

DEEP-SEA MUSSELS

live 2,000 feet below sea level, near geothermal vents.

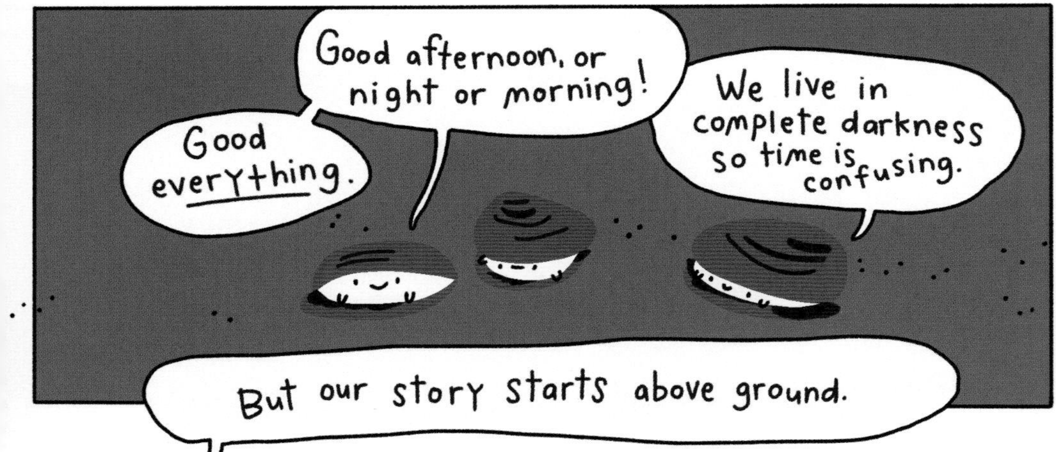
Good everything.
Good afternoon, or night or morning!
We live in complete darkness so time is confusing.
But our story starts above ground.

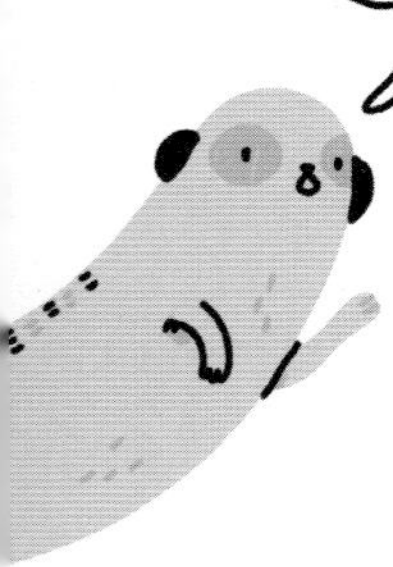

Before Dr. Van Dover started studying deep-sea creatures, she loved regular sea creatures. She grew up near the beach and spent her days studying everything she found there.

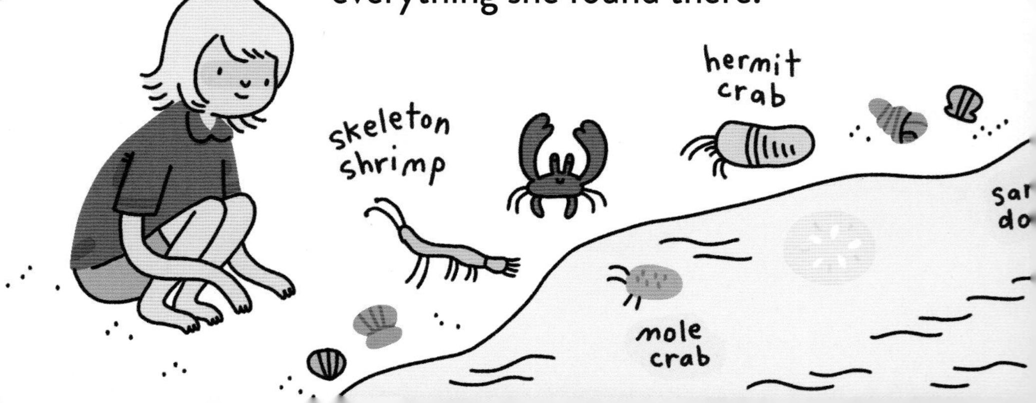
skeleton shrimp
hermit crab
mole crab

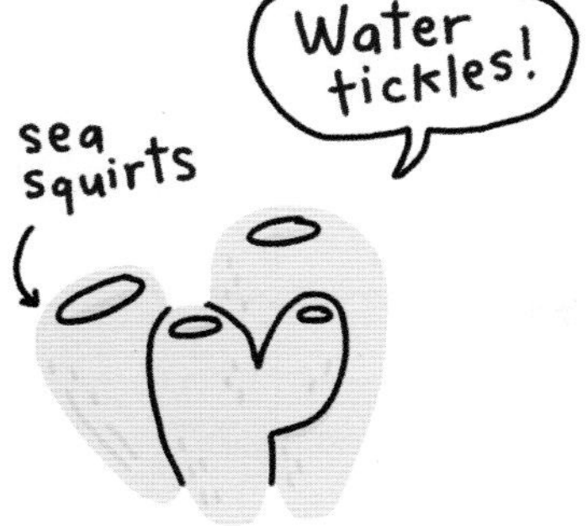
Water tickles!
sea squirts

Her favorite animal was the horseshoe crab.

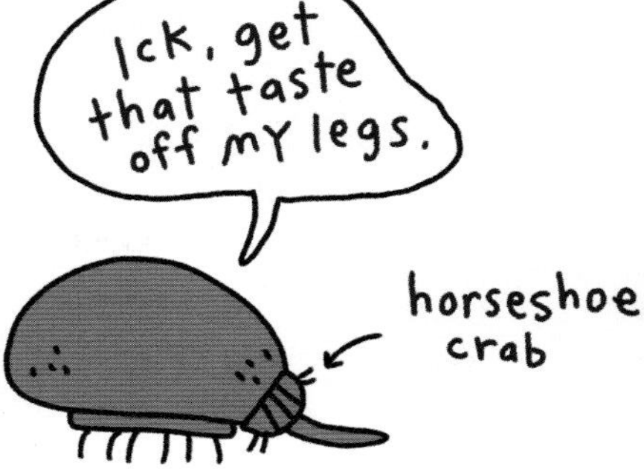
Ick, get that taste off my legs.
horseshoe crab

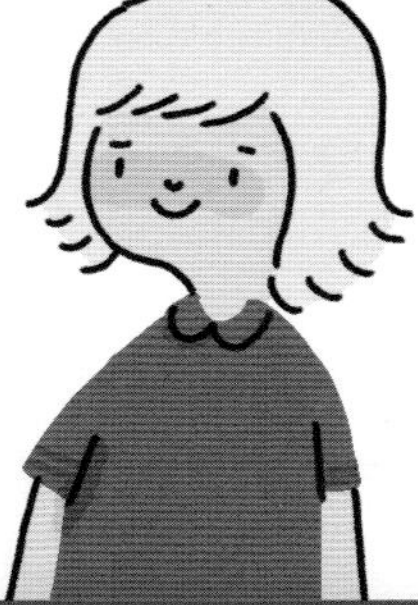

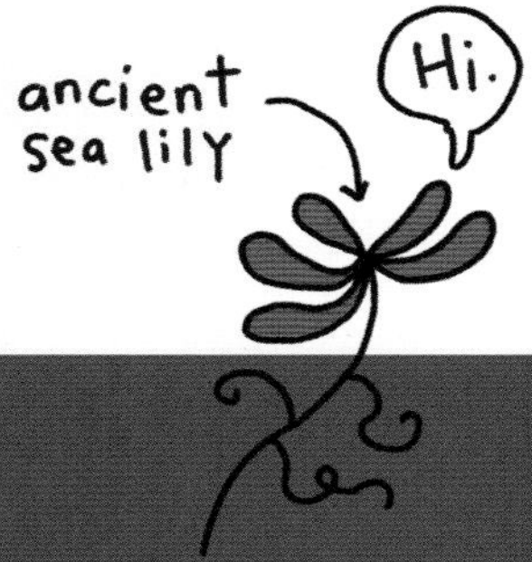
ancient sea lily
Hi.

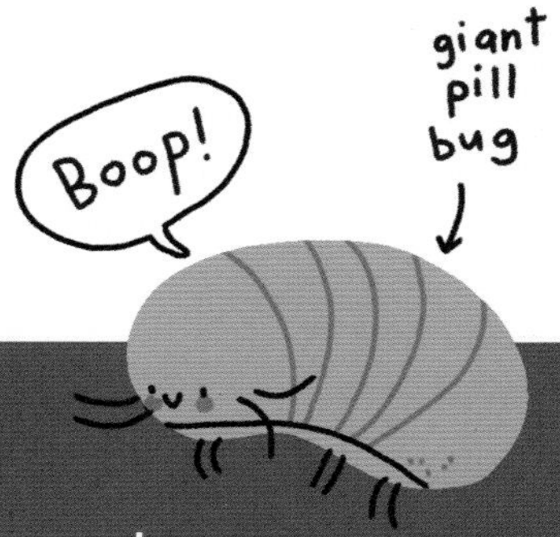
giant pill bug
Boop!

Cindy wanted to be an astronaut, but when she discovered marine biology, she realized she could travel to another world without leaving Earth.

Now she is a submarine pilot.

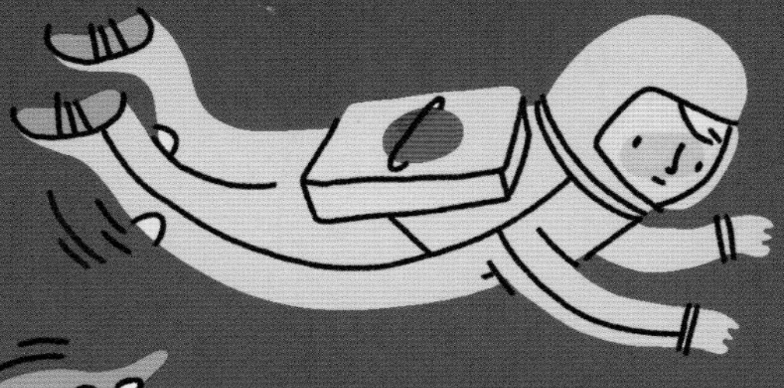

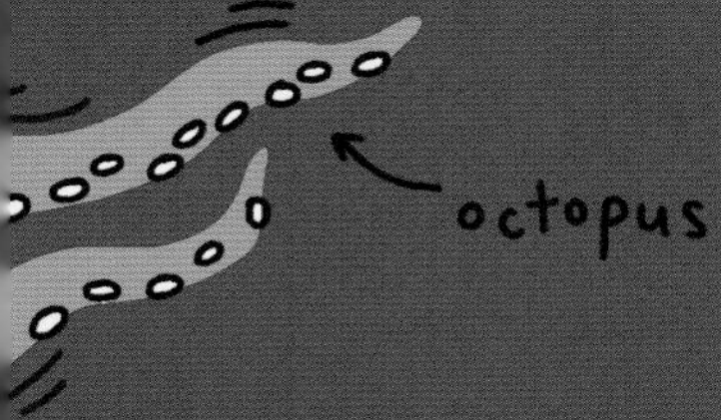
octopus

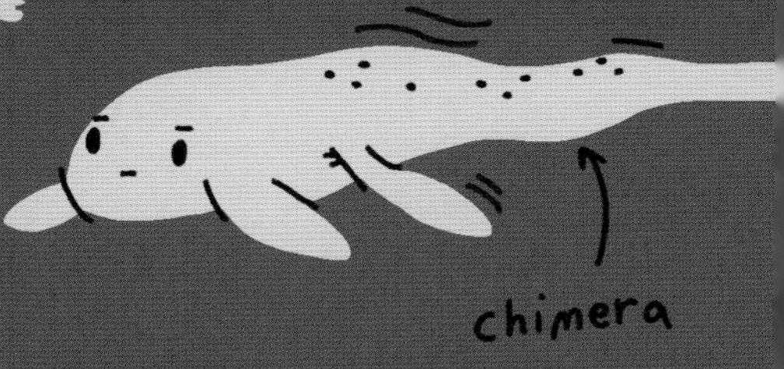
chimera

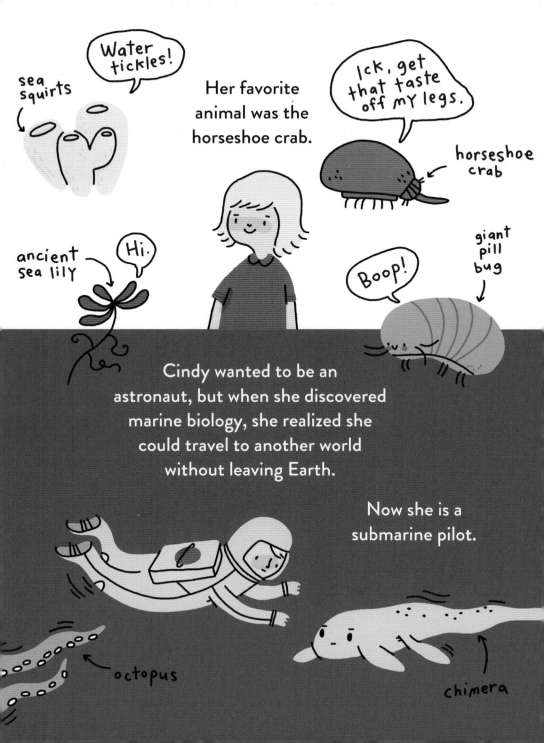

A group of scientists spends a month at sea, far enough away from the coast that the water is thousands of feet deep.

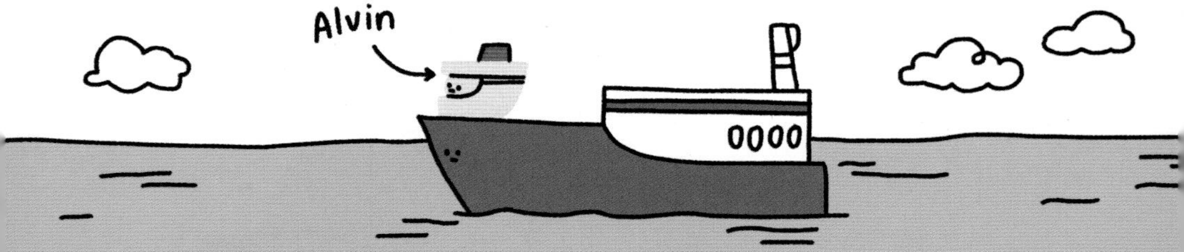
Alvin
0000

During the day, scientists make trips in Alvin.

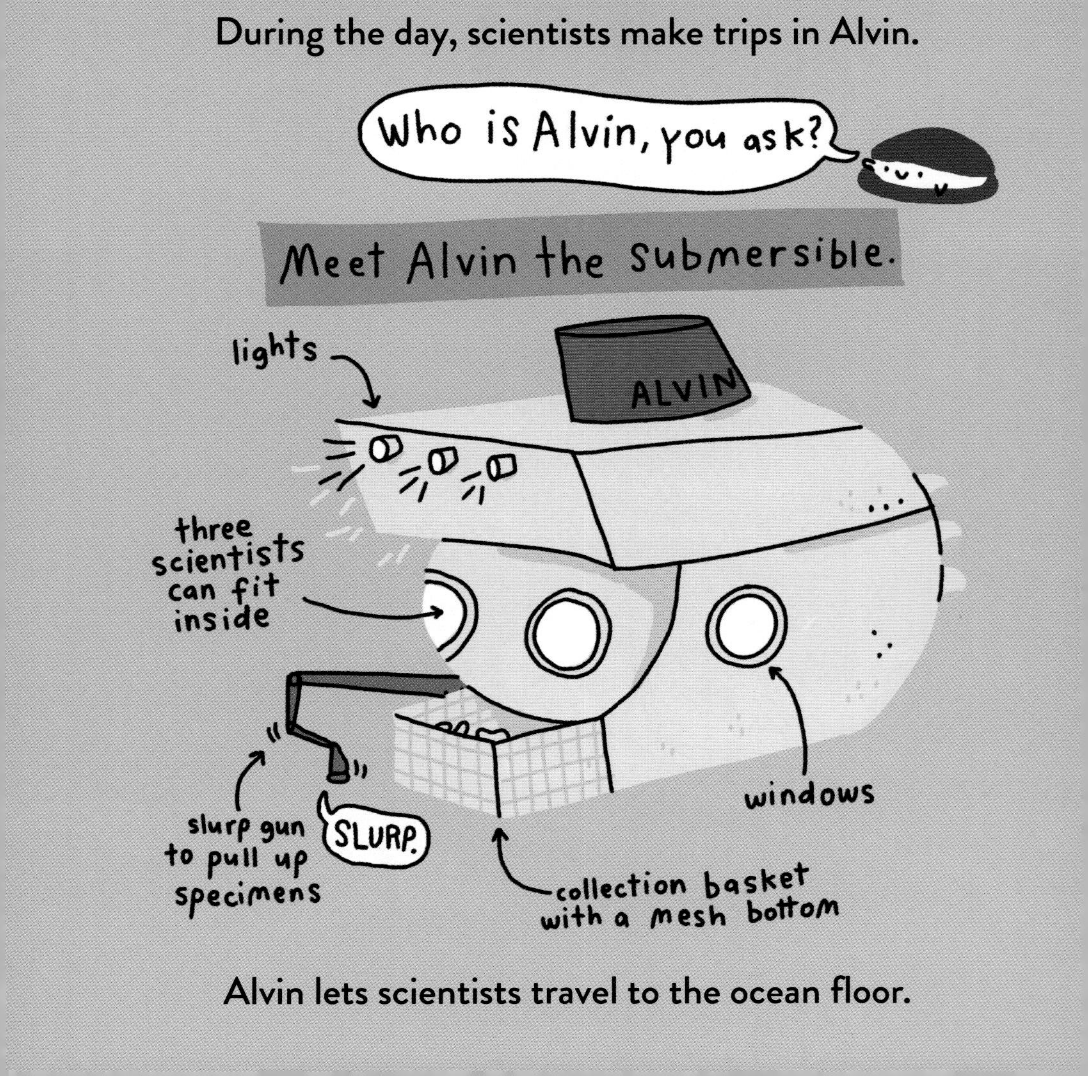
Who is Alvin, you ask?
Meet Alvin the submersible.
lights
ALVIN
three scientists can fit inside
windows
slurp gun to pull up specimens
SLURP.
collection basket with a mesh bottom

Alvin lets scientists travel to the ocean floor.

Dr. Van Dover and two other scientists climb into Alvin at 8 a.m. They leave their shoes on the ship. It can take two hours to travel to the seafloor. The water out the window changes from blue to pitch black.

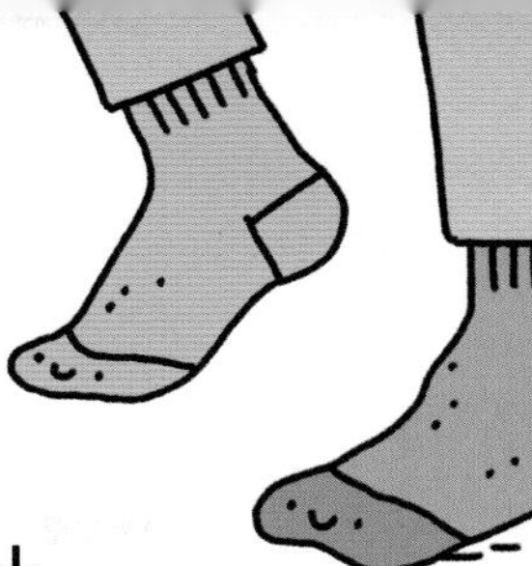

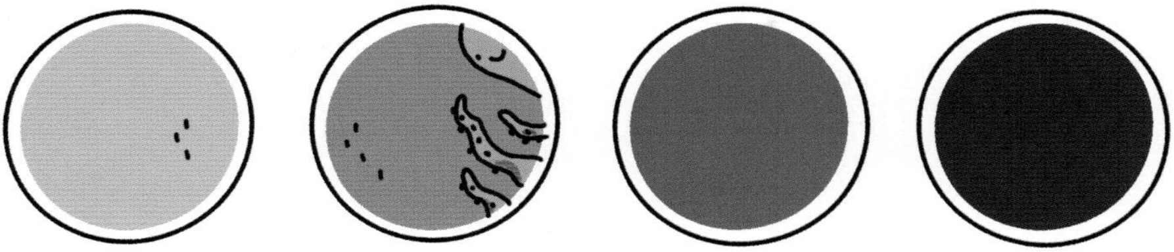

Only the pilot can see out the front window, so the other two scientists watch on a screen.

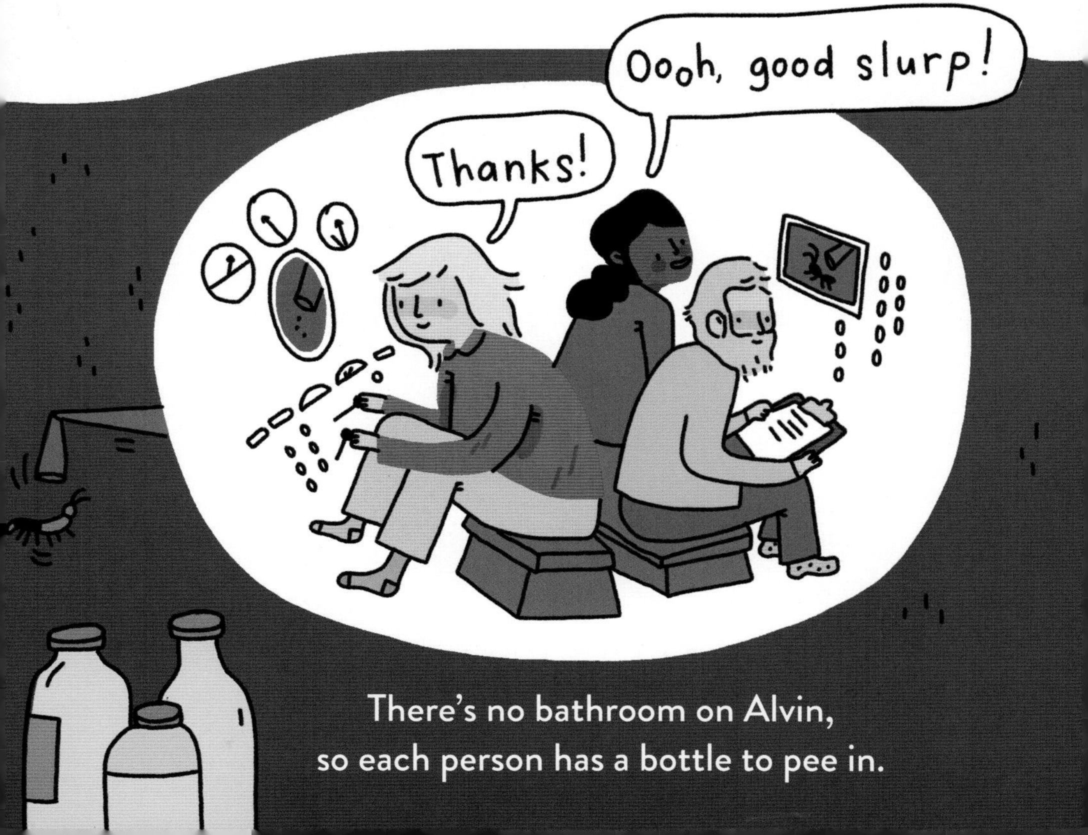
Oooh, good slurp!
Thanks!

There's no bathroom on Alvin, so each person has a bottle to pee in.

OK, it's time to talk about GEOTHERMAL VENTS

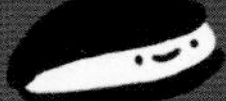

Geothermal vents are tiny cracks in the seafloor where heated water shoots out.

The vents are found along the floor in the ocean, where the water is rich in minerals, which helps bacteria to grow.

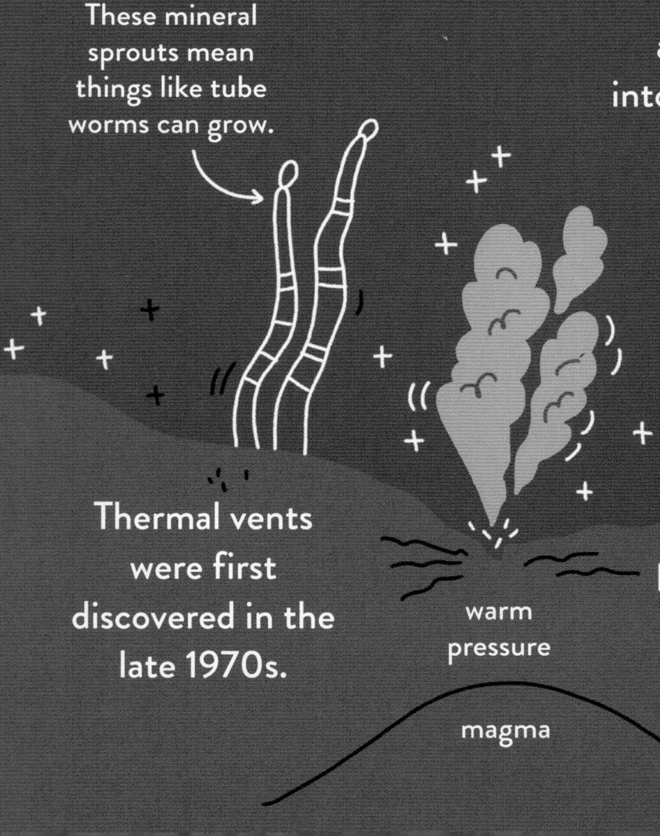
These mineral sprouts mean things like tube worms can grow.
warm pressure
magma

With no sunlight, animals turn the bacteria into energy. And creatures lik crabs, eels, shrimp,

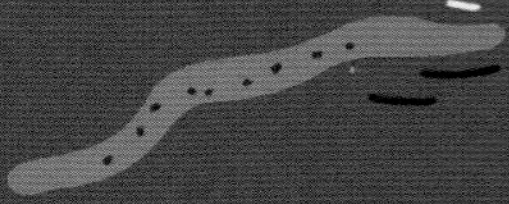

and octopus make their home here.

Thermal vents were first discovered in the late 1970s.

Now scientists think they also exist on Jupiter and Saturn's moons.

Even though Dr. Van Dover has made more than a hundred dives, it's still amazing every time.

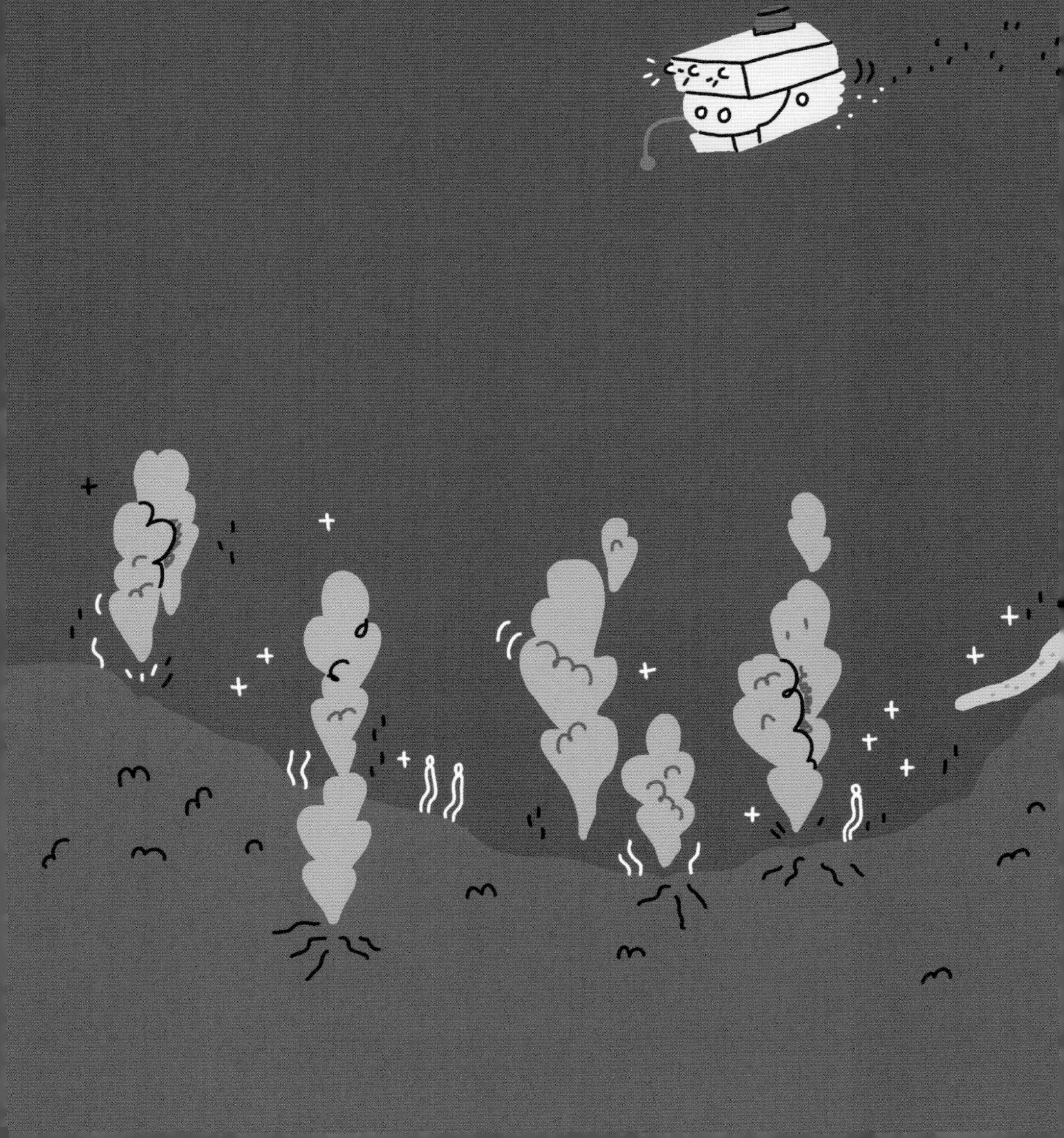

Dr. Van Dover's team is studying mussels and the other creatures that live with them, to understand how they survive at such depths.

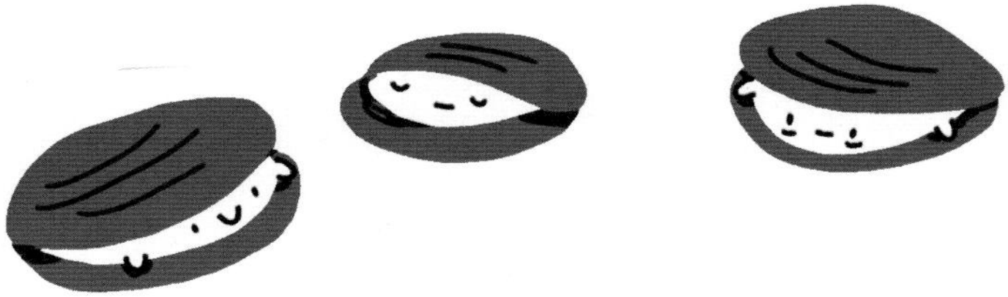

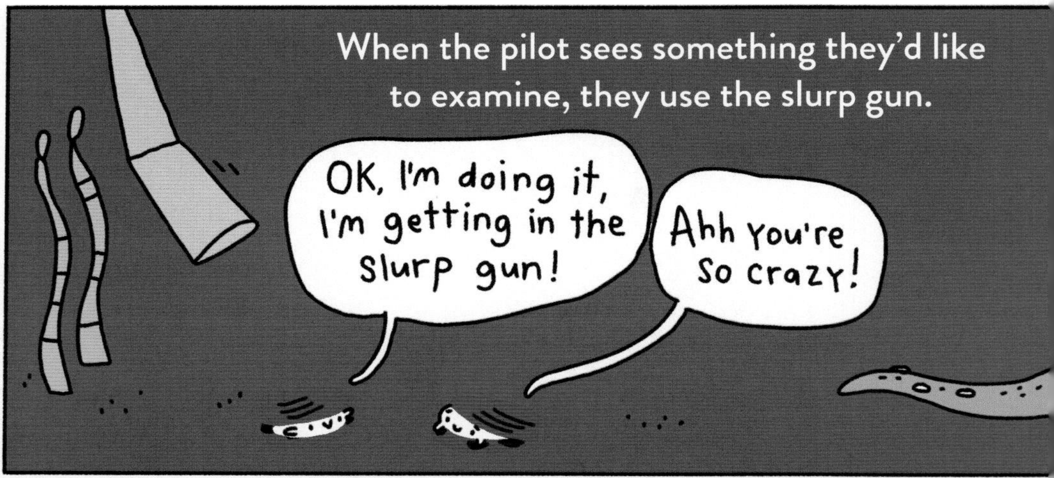
When the pilot sees something they'd like to examine, they use the slurp gun.
OK, I'm doing it, I'm getting in the slurp gun!
Ahh you're so crazy!

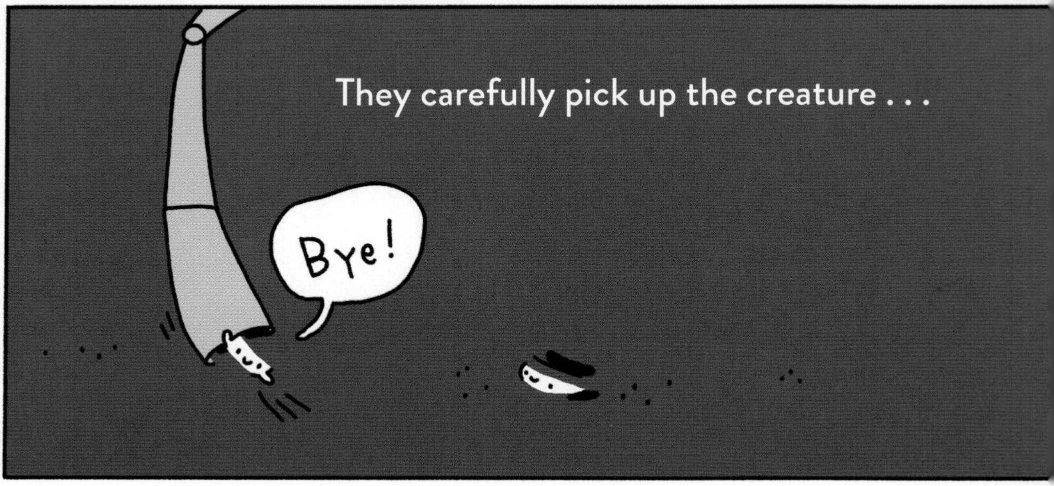
They carefully pick up the creature . . .
Bye!

and place it in Alvin's specimen basket.

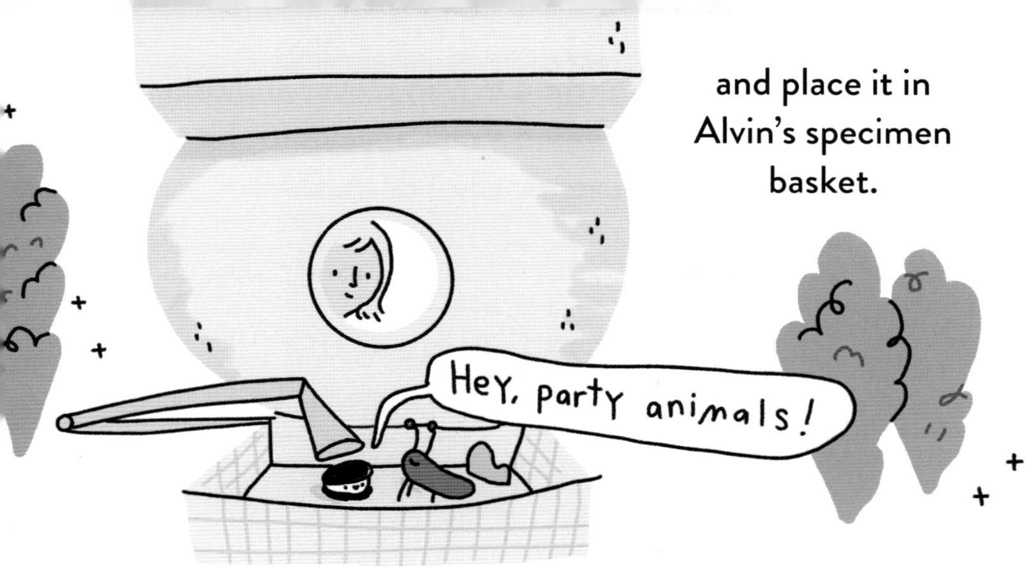
Hey, party animals!

Back on the ship, Dr. Van Dover's team sorts and stores the specimens, so they can be researched at the lab on land.

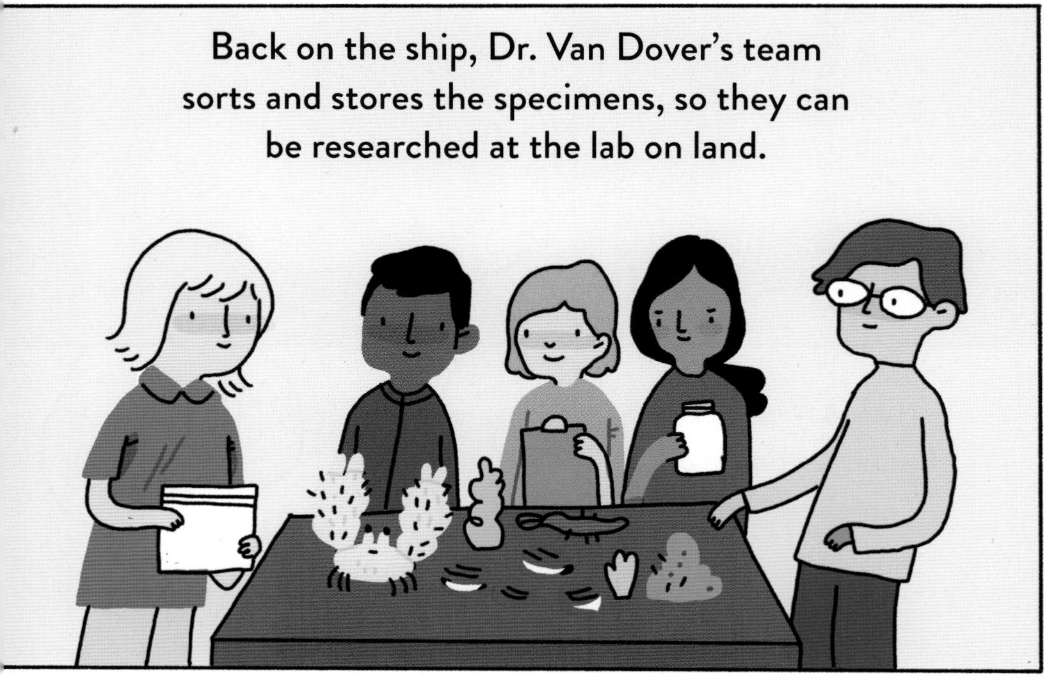

There are still huge parts of the ocean that humans have never explored.

Once, on an Alvin trip, Dr. Van Dover and other scientists discovered a new species in the geothermal vents: the YETI CRAB.

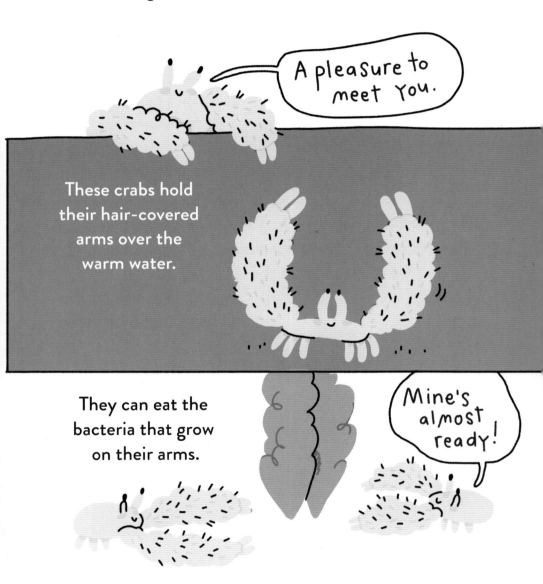

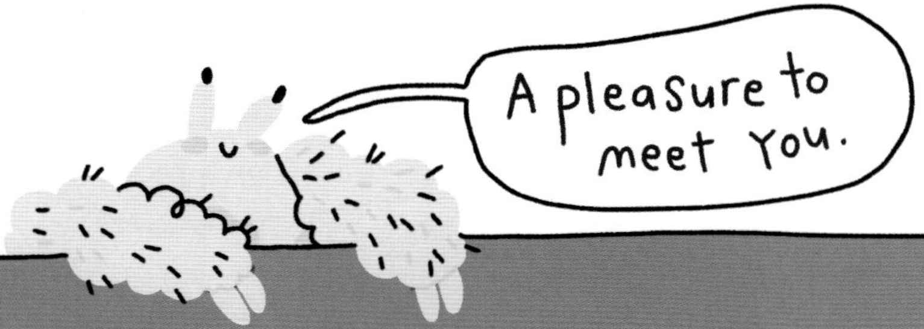
A pleasure to meet You.

These crabs hold their hair-covered arms over the warm water.

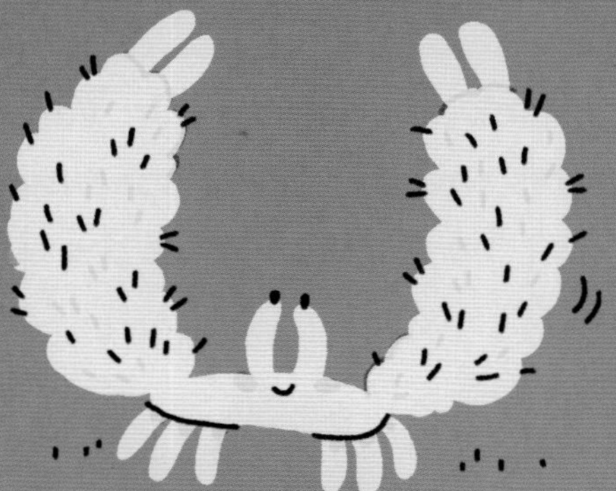

They can eat the bacteria that grow on their arms.

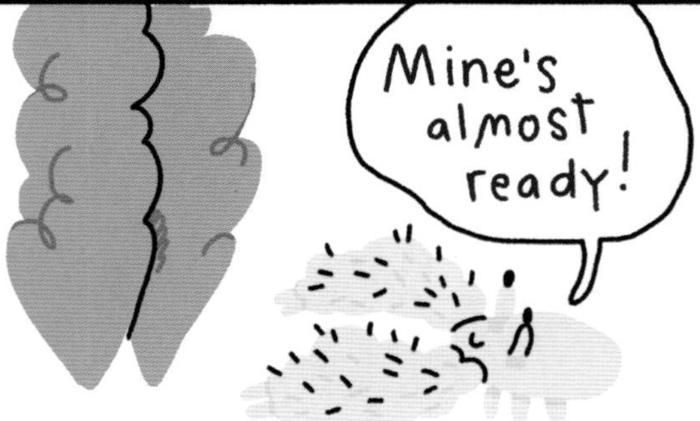
Mine's almost ready!

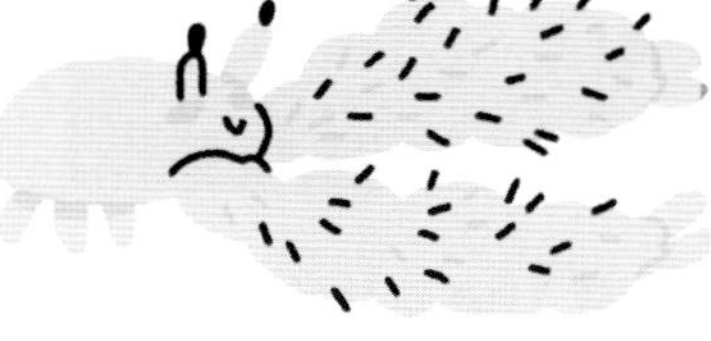

Every dive is a little different.

After nine hours underwater, the scientists head back up to the surface, eating a snack on the way.

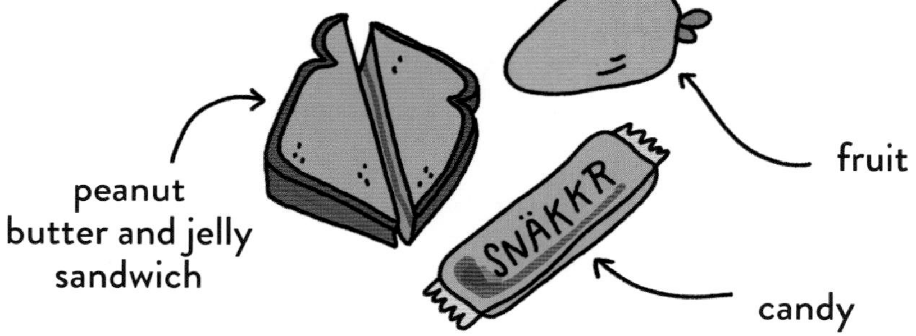
peanut butter and jelly sandwich
fruit
SNÄKKR
candy

And Dr. Van Dover goes back to her lab to study all the mysterious things she's found on her trip.

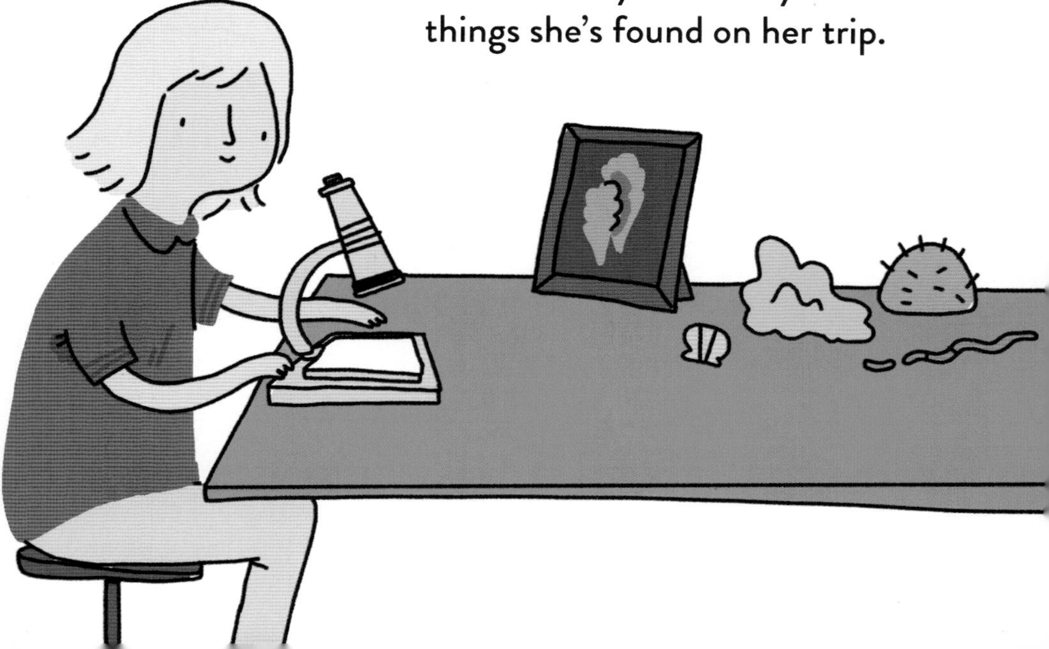

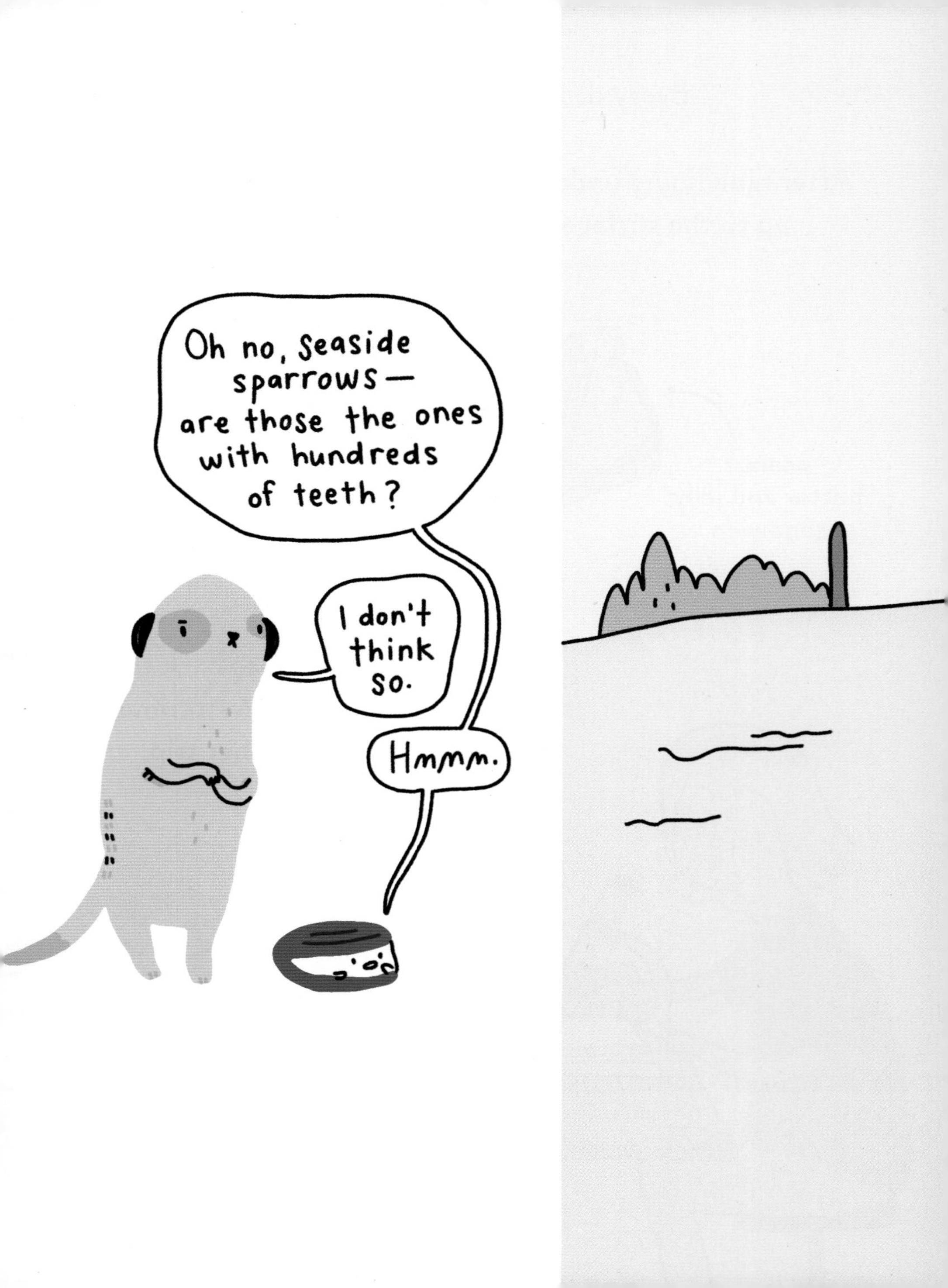
Oh no, seaside sparrows— are those the ones with hundreds of teeth?
I don't think so.
Hmmm.

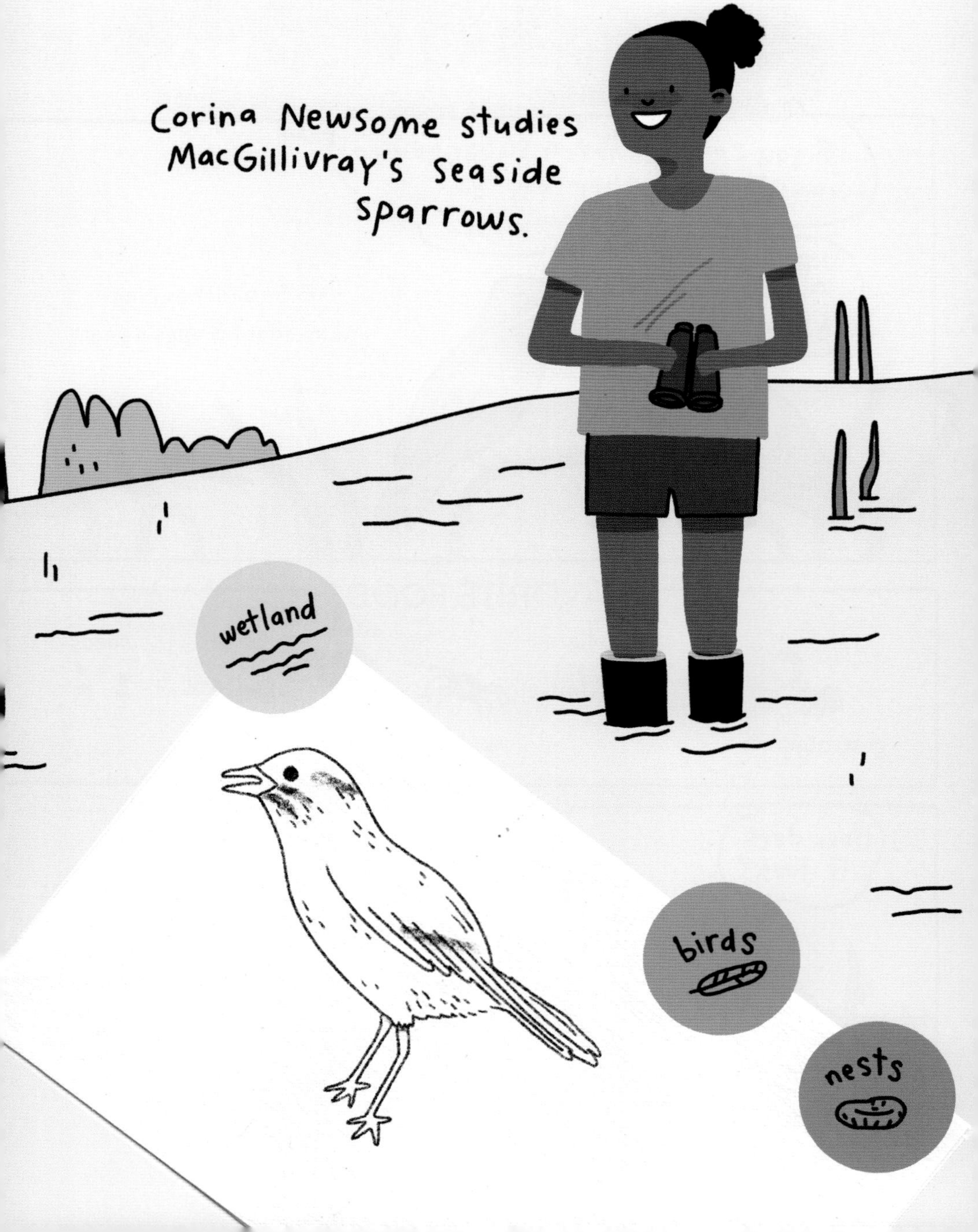
Corina Newsome studies MacGillivray's Seaside sparrows.
wetland
birds
nests

MACGILLIVRAY'S SEASIDE SPARROWS

If you could have a superpower, would you rather fly or be invisible?

Um—we can already fly.

- 5.5–6 inches long
- Lay about 3 eggs a year

FAVORITE FOODS

grasshoppers

caterpillars

spiders

snails

worms

seeds

How does it look?

The sparrows live in salt marshes in Georgia, Florida, and the Carolinas. They build their nests on the coasts, where the tide comes in and out.

But climate change has made sea levels rise lately, which makes the tides unpredictable for the sparrows.

If they build their nests too high up, predators like larger birds, raccoons, and snakes can see them.

But if they build their nests too low, they'll be underwater when the tide comes in.

Hey, look, sparrow eggs!
Oh no.
Oh no.

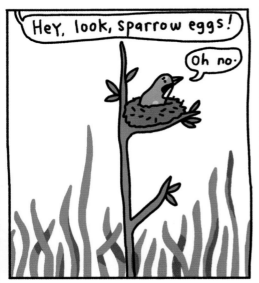

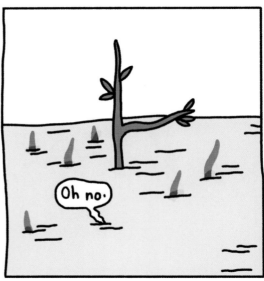

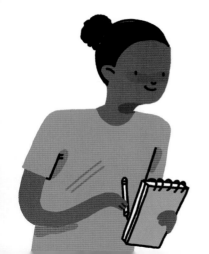

Corina is studying how often the MacGillivray's seaside sparrow nests are attacked by predators, to understand what effect the changing planet is having on these birds.

To study the sparrows, Corina spends the day out in the marsh, where it can be muddy, hot, and slippery.

When she sees male sparrows doing tricks in the air, she knows she's close to a sparrow nest.

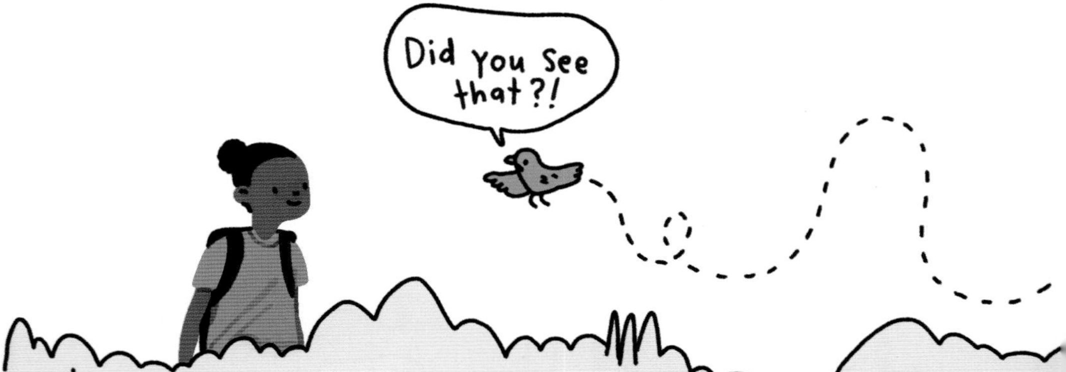
Did you see that?!

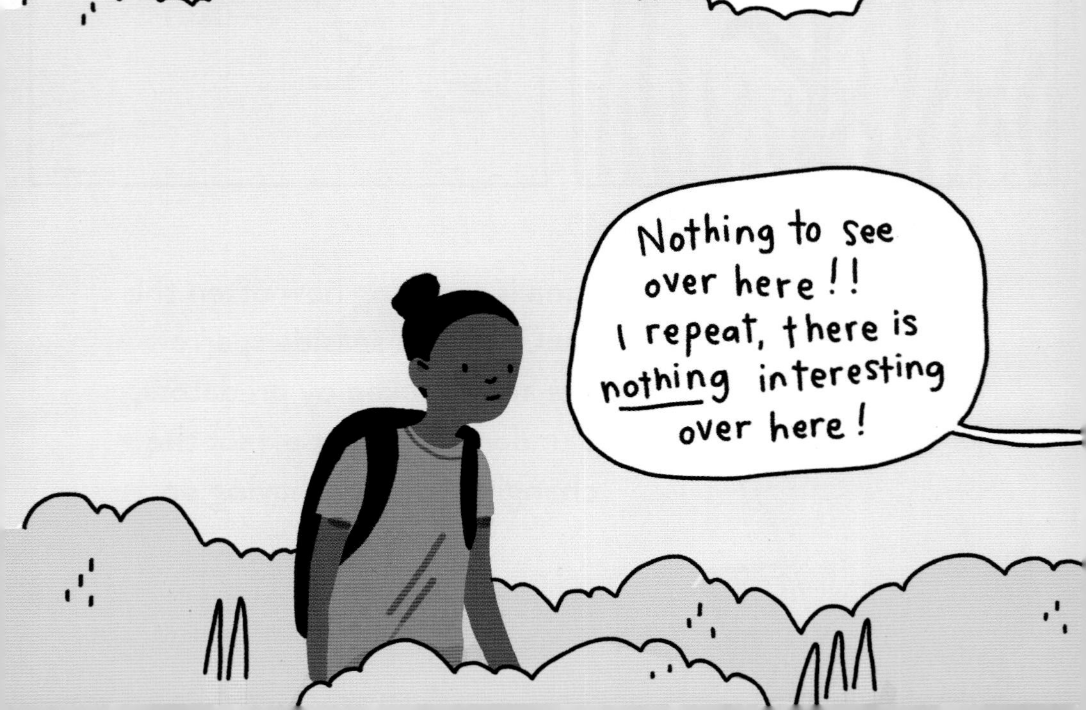
Nothing to see over here!! I repeat, there is nothing interesting over here!

When she finds a nest with eggs inside, she either leaves a camera near it, or comes back to visit every four days.

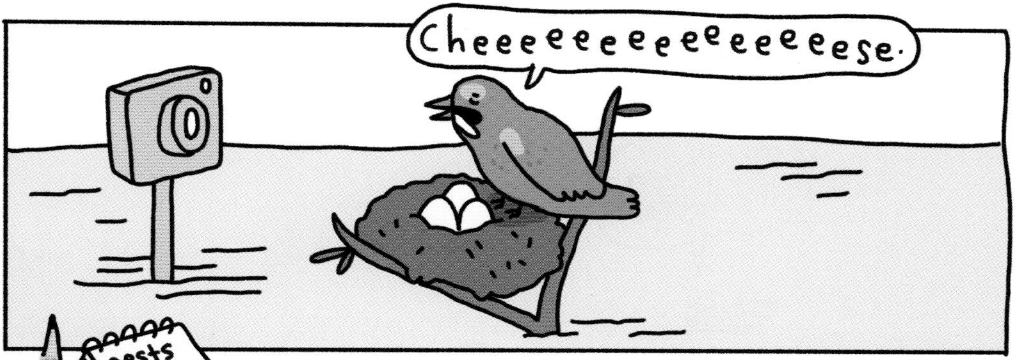
Cheeeeeeeeeeeeeeese.

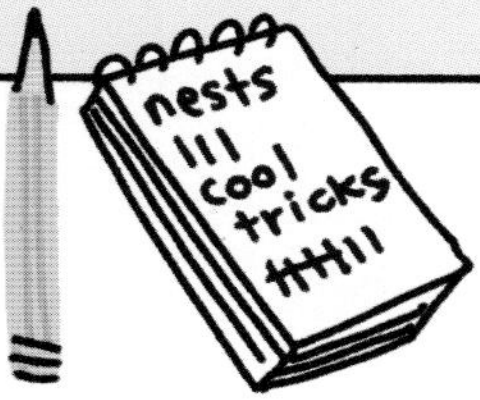
nests
cool tricks

When Corina sees that a nest has been attacked by predators, she takes notes.

With her research, she'll create a map that can be used to help protect the MacGillivray's seaside sparrows.

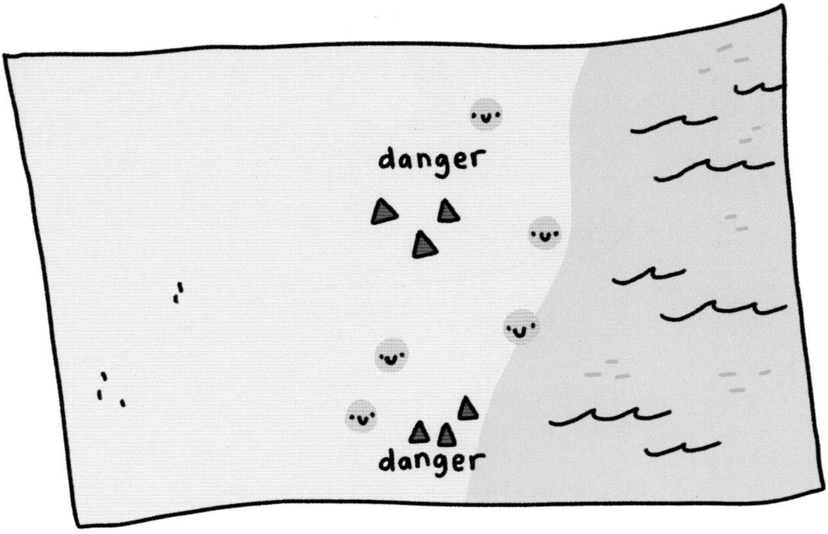
danger
danger

Her map will show where the birds need help.

The tide is only out for four hours each day, so Corina has to make sure to leave before the water comes back and turns the marsh into deep mud.

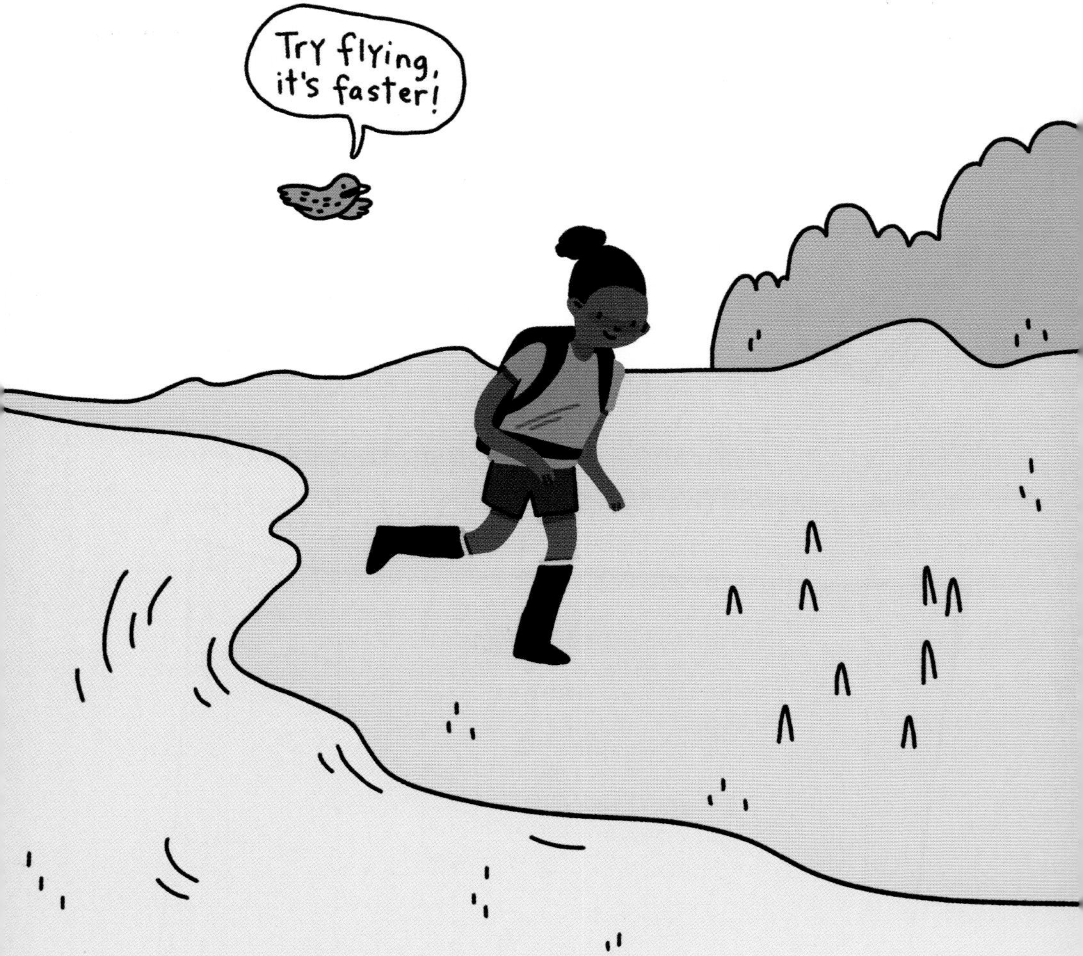
Try flying, it's faster!

She's gotten stuck a few times.

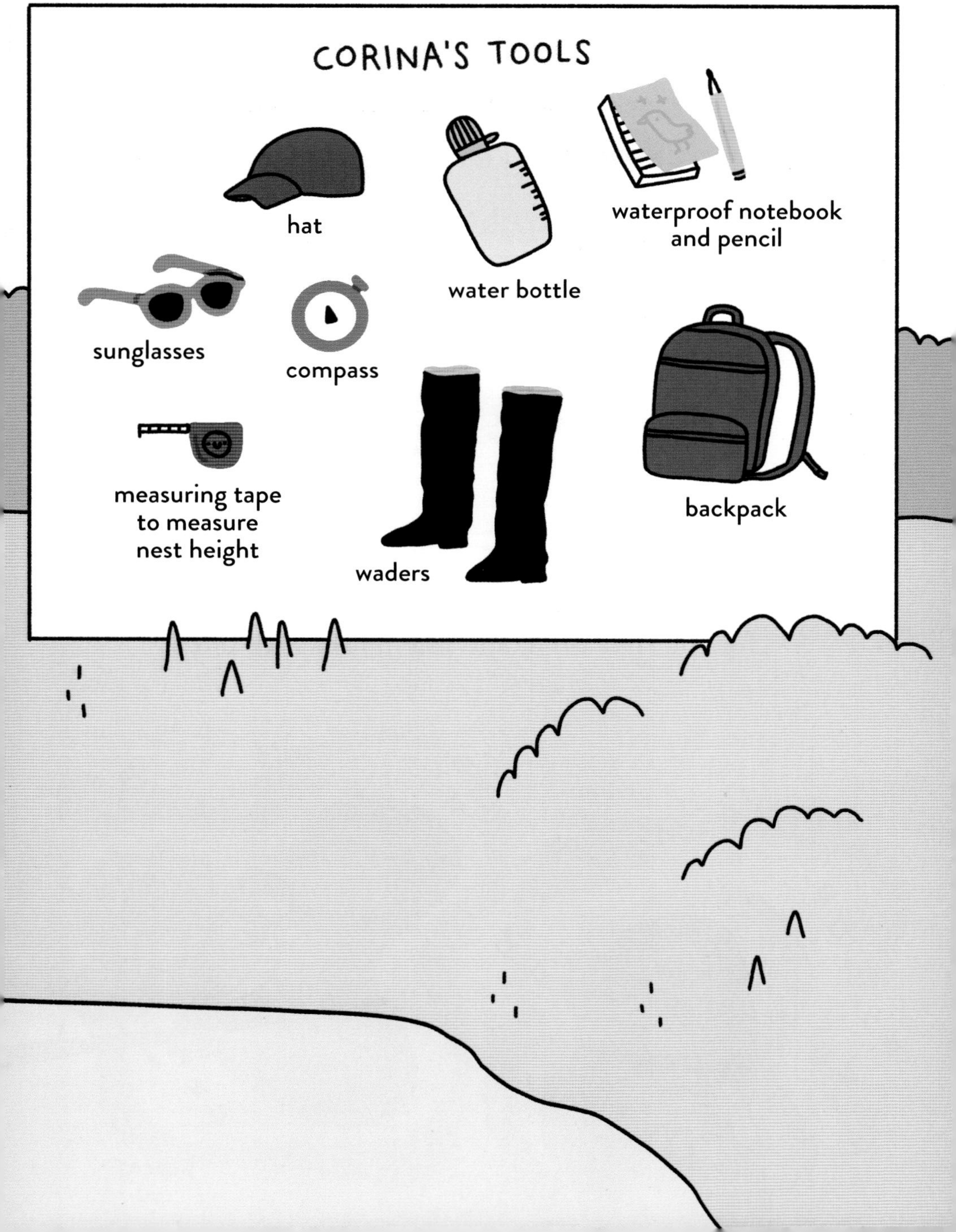
CORINA'S TOOLS
hat
water bottle
waterproof notebook and pencil
sunglasses
compass
backpack
measuring tape to measure nest height
waders

Corina has always loved animals. When she was growing up, her favorite animal was the giant otter.

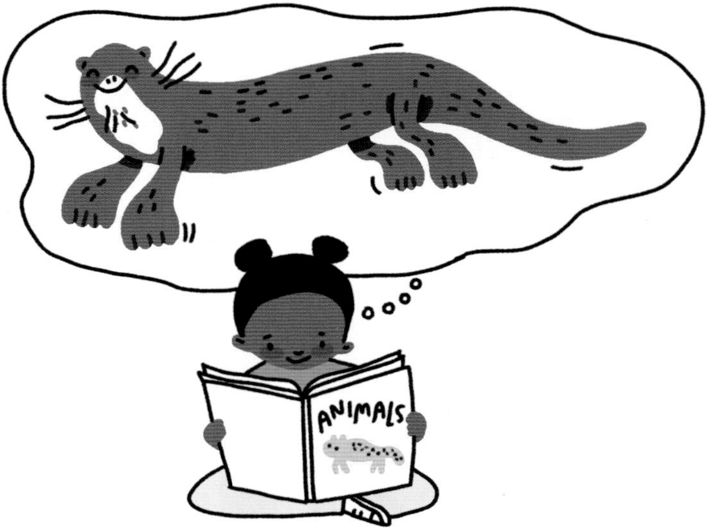
ANIMALS

On a bird-watching trip in college, she saw a blue jay for the first time, and fell in love with birds.

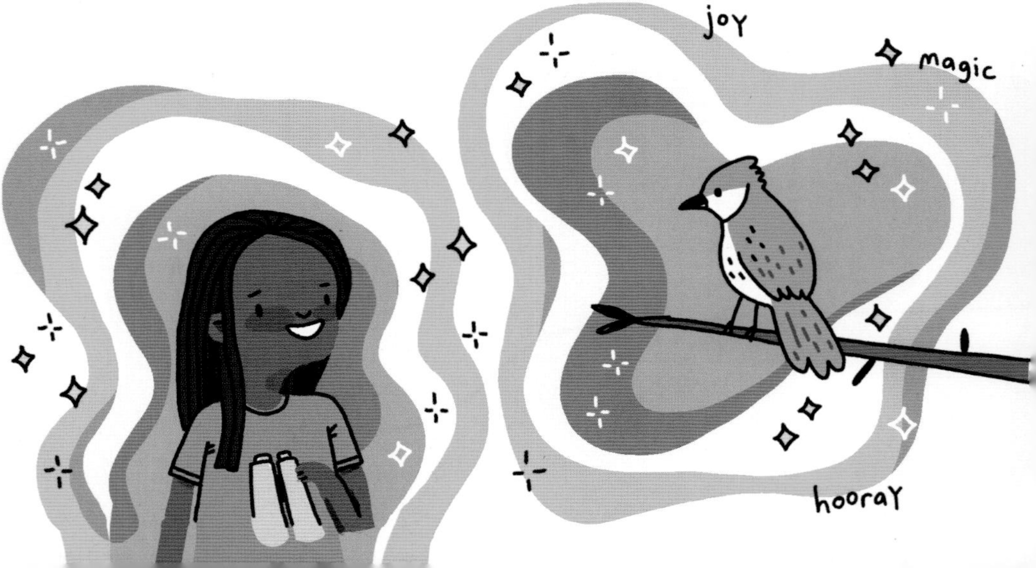
joy
magic
hooray

When she's not doing her sparrow research, Corina works to make the outdoors a more inclusive place. She wants all kids to learn about birds.

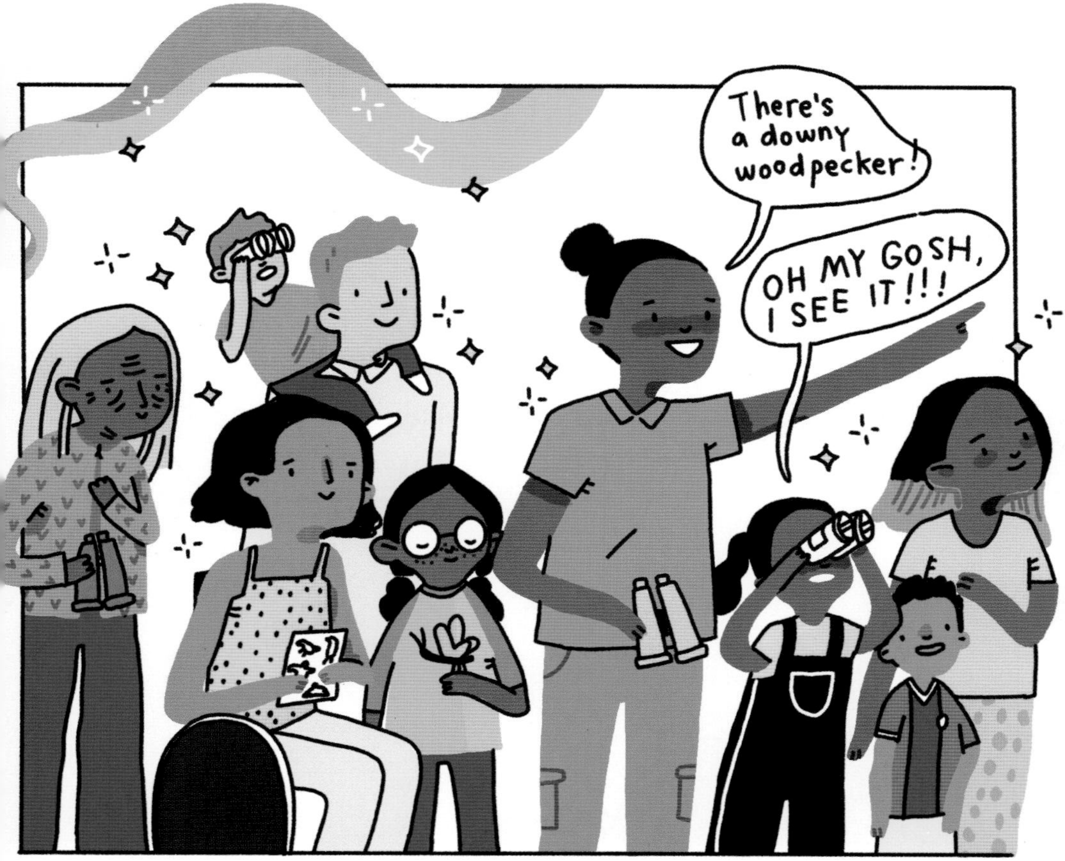
There's a downy woodpecker!
OH MY GOSH, I SEE IT!!!

One way she does this is by working with Georgia Audubon, a group that protects birds and their habitats.

Even though Corina sees birds every day, they bring her joy every time, and she loves sharing what she knows about them.

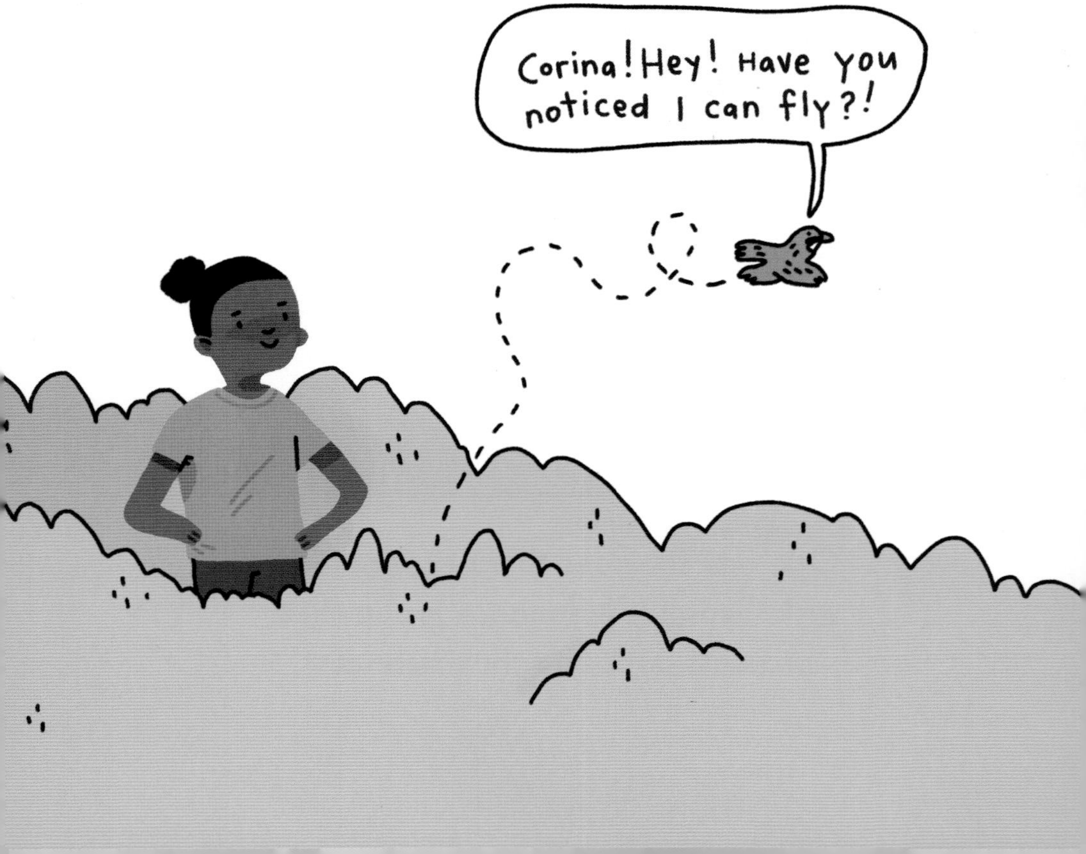
Corina! Hey! Have you noticed I can fly?!

And her favorite bird is still the blue jay.

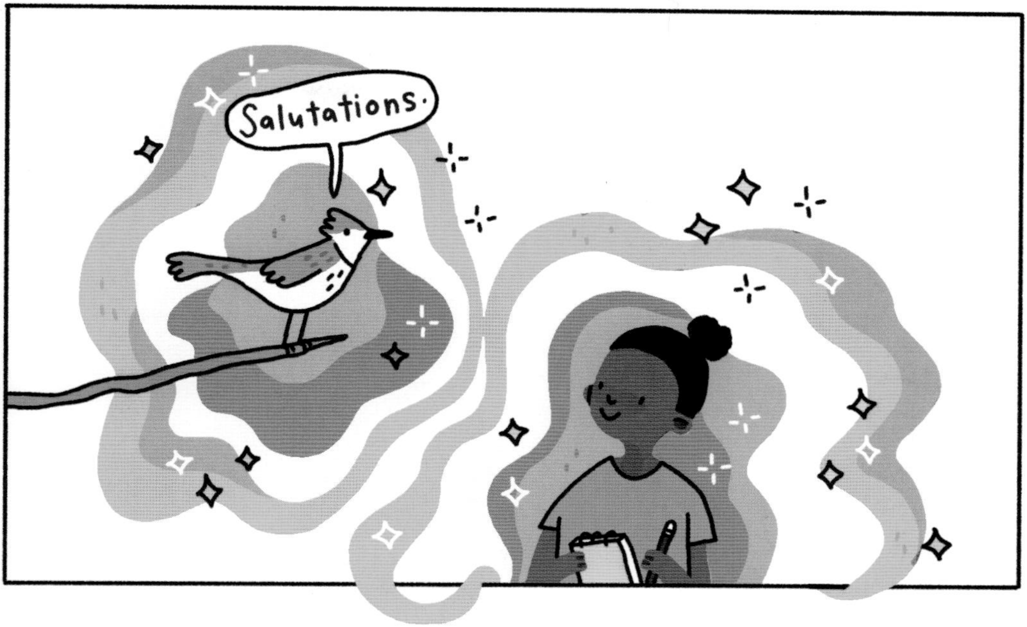
Salutations.

Next time you spot a bird, see if you can feel the joy she's talking about.

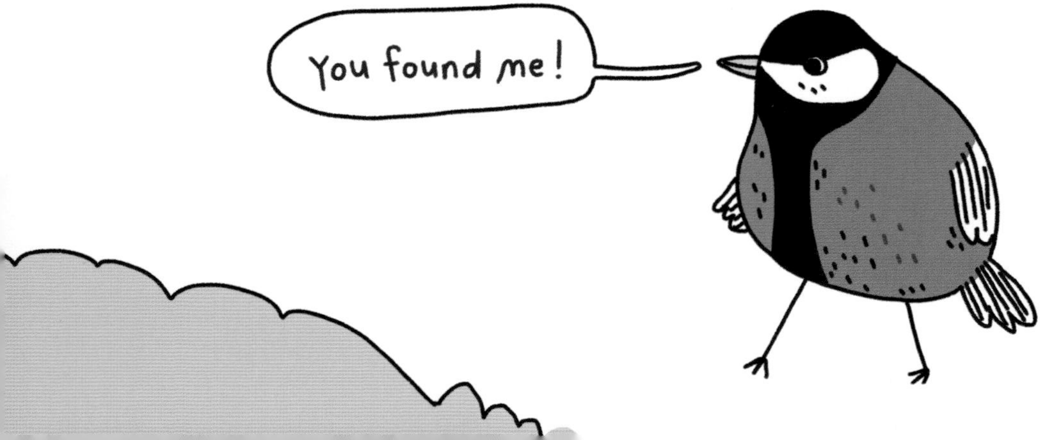
You found me!

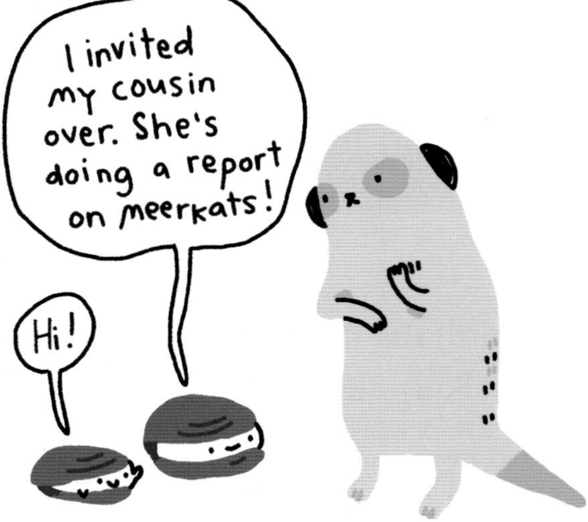
I invited my cousin over. She's doing a report on meerkats!
Hi!

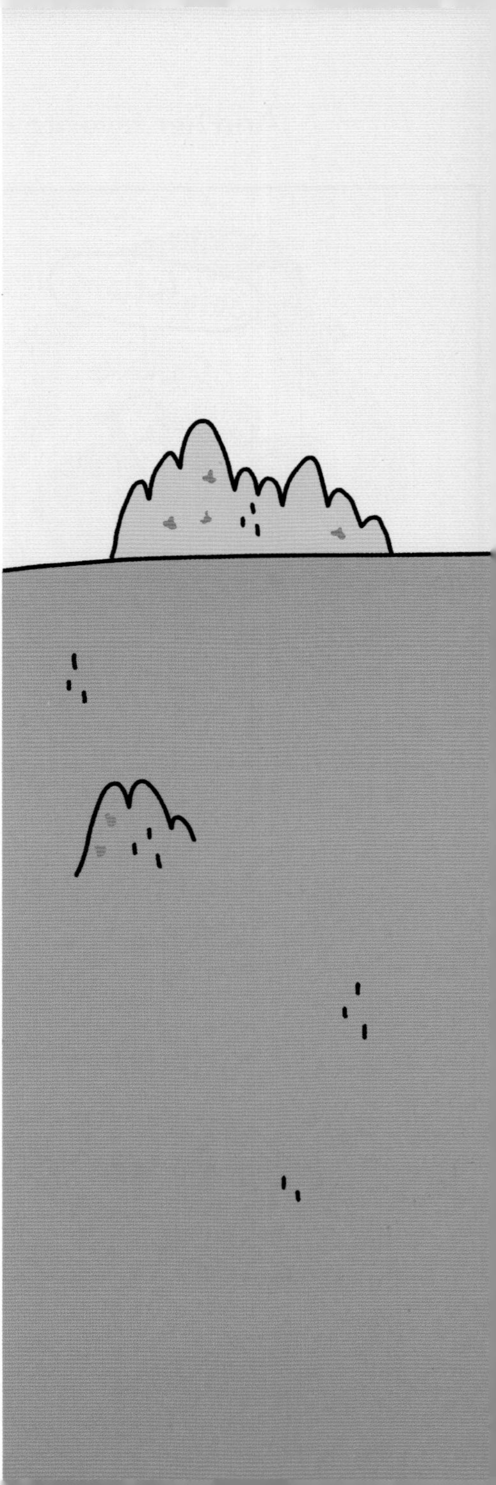

Dr. Shalene Jha studies bees.

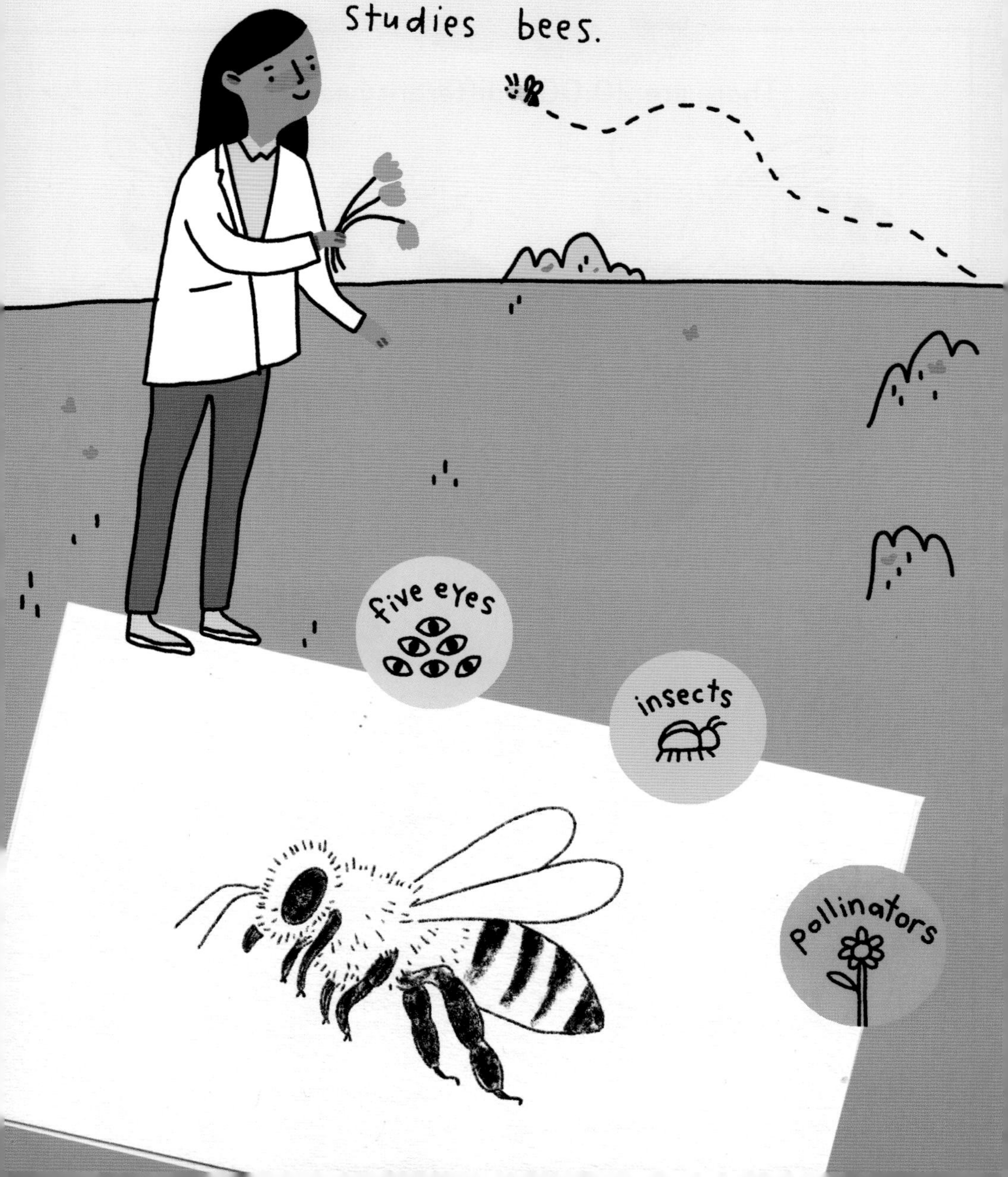
five eyes
insects
pollinators

BEES

There are 20,000 different bee species.

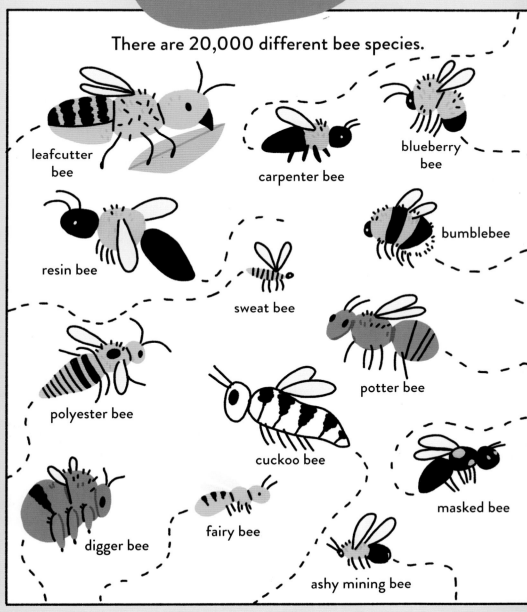

leafcutter bee

carpenter bee

blueberry bee

resin bee

sweat bee

bumblebee

polyester bee

cuckoo bee

potter bee

digger bee

fairy bee

masked bee

ashy mining bee

A few facts about bees that might surprise you:

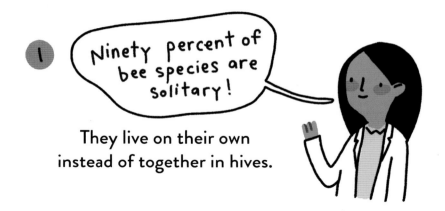

1

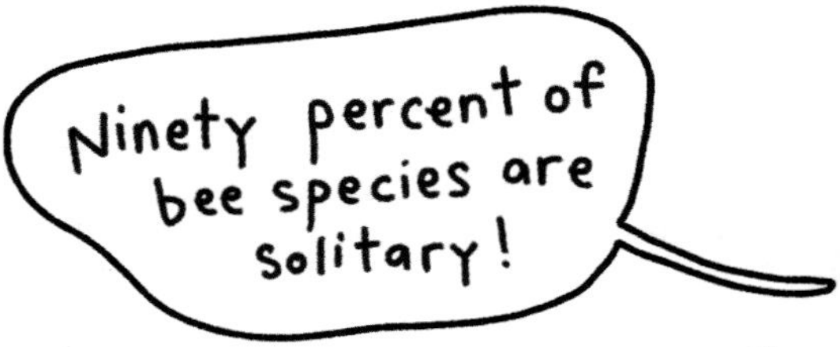
Ninety percent of bee species are solitary!

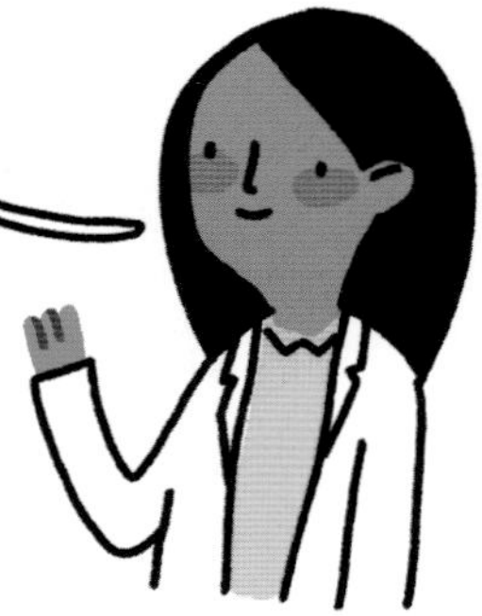

They live on their own instead of together in hives.

2 Unless you spend a lot of time inside beehives, most honeybees you see are female.

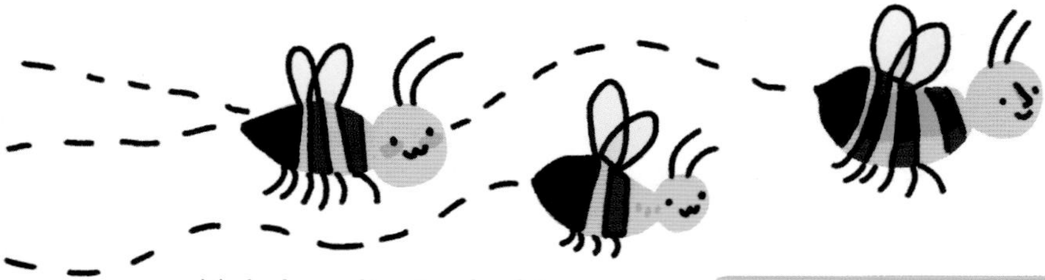

Male bees live in the hive.

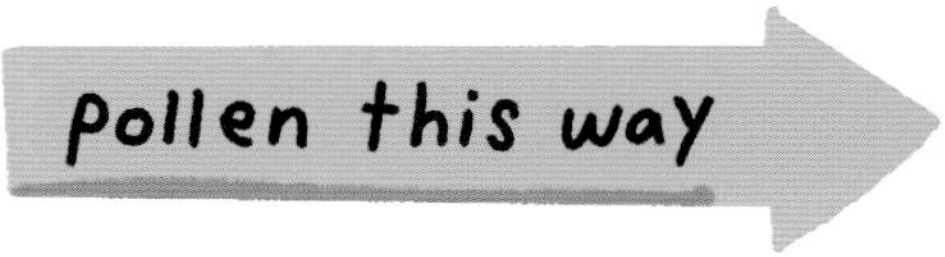
pollen this way

3 Not all bees are black and yellow (some are even green and blue).

4 Not all bees sting! Male bees don't have stingers, and some female bees don't sting either.

Bees are amazing pollinators. As they collect pollen from some flowers, pollen from *other* flowers gets dusted onto the plants. This pollen mixing (or pollination) is something plants need to grow.

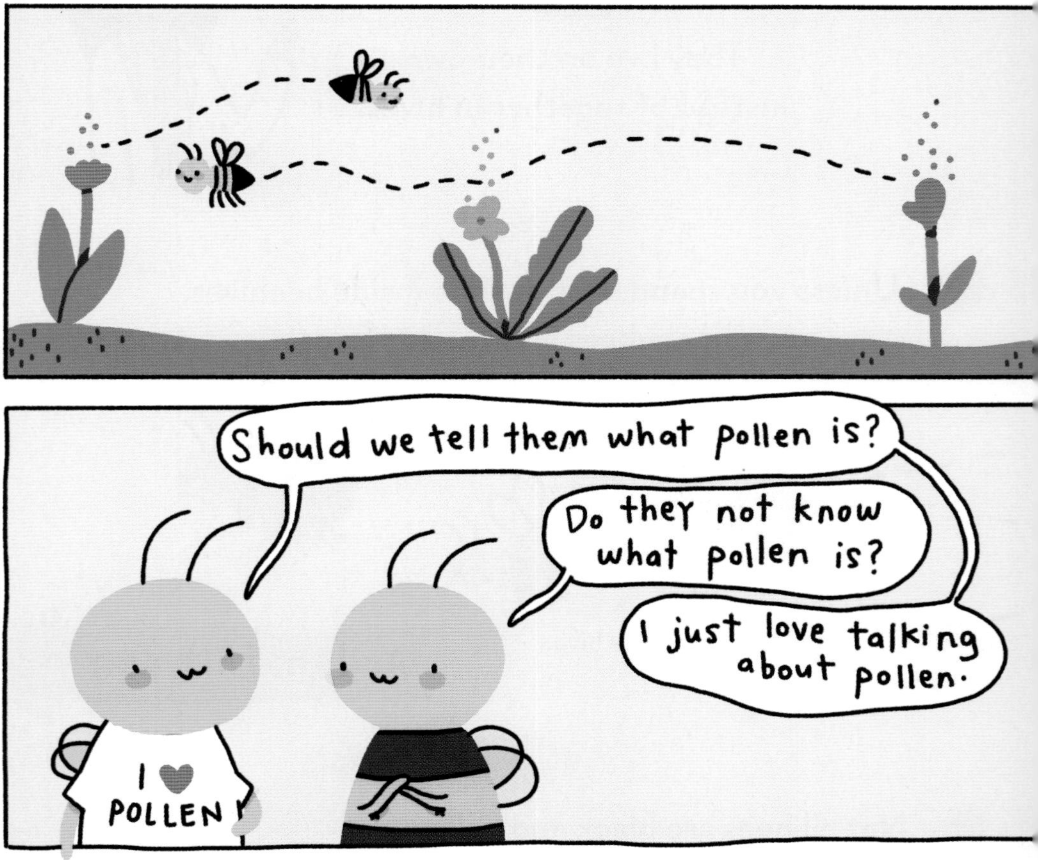
Should we tell them what pollen is?
Do they not know what pollen is?
I just love talking about pollen.
I ♥ POLLEN

Pollen is a powder made by some plants.
(Also, sad pollen fact:
some humans are allergic to it.)

And bees are *made* for collecting pollen.

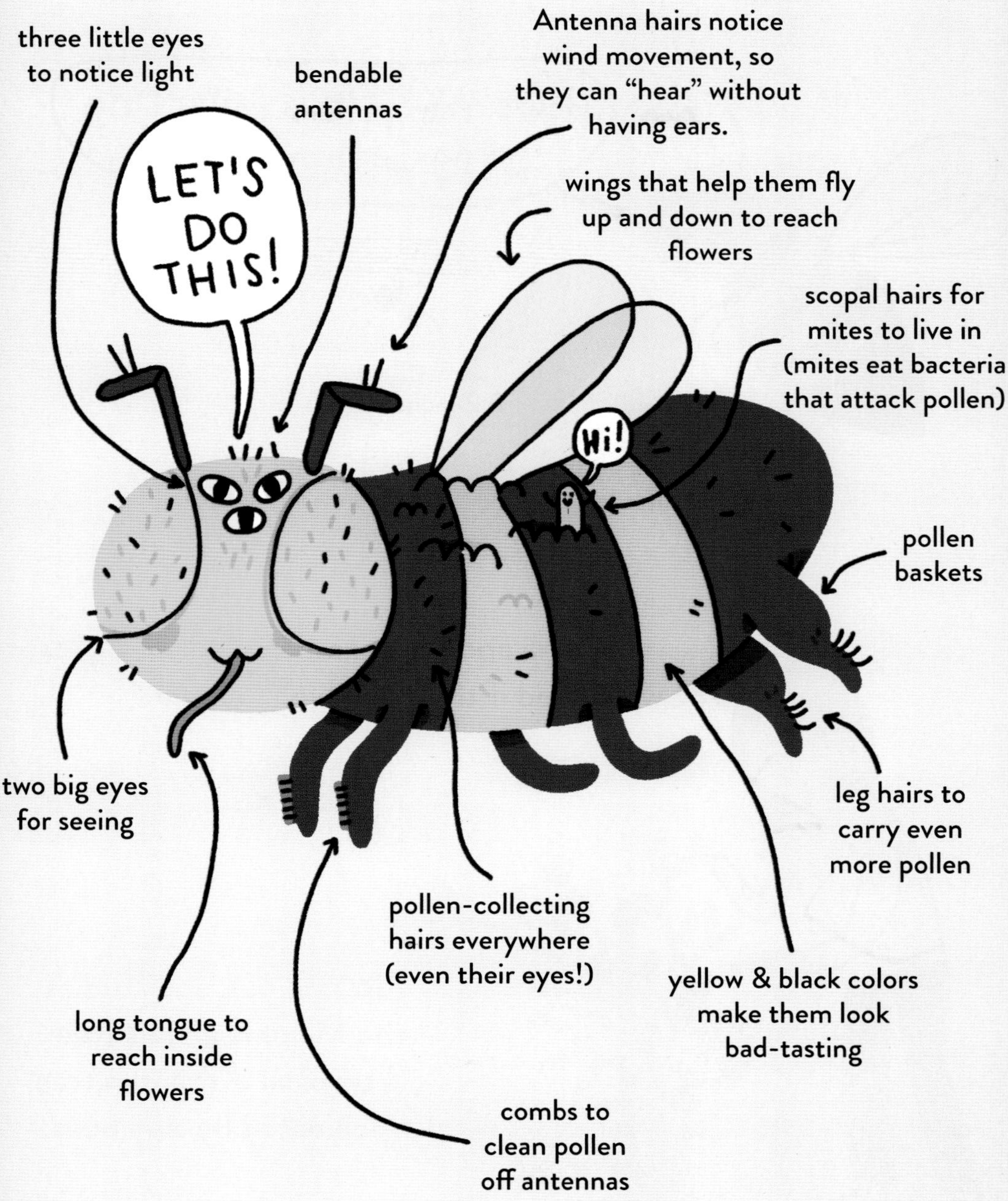
three little eyes to notice light
bendable antennas
Antenna hairs notice wind movement, so they can "hear" without having ears.
LET'S DO THIS!
wings that help them fly up and down to reach flowers
scopal hairs for mites to live in (mites eat bacteria that attack pollen)
Hi!
pollen baskets
two big eyes for seeing
leg hairs to carry even more pollen
pollen-collecting hairs everywhere (even their eyes!)
yellow & black colors make them look bad-tasting
long tongue to reach inside flowers
combs to clean pollen off antennas

Since bees come in so many sizes, some people assumed that larger bees were the most important pollinators.

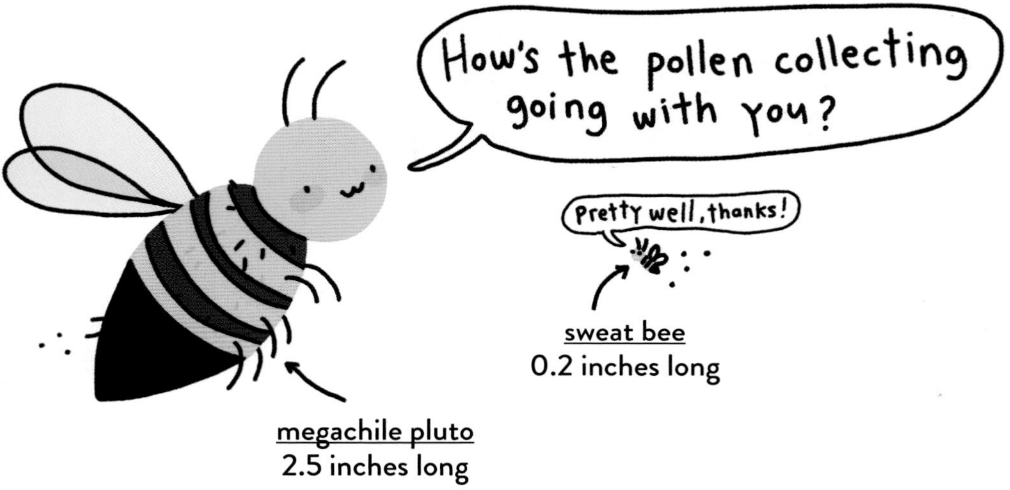
How's the pollen collecting going with you?
Pretty well, thanks!
sweat bee
0.2 inches long
megachile pluto
2.5 inches long

Dr. Jha and her team wondered if this was true.

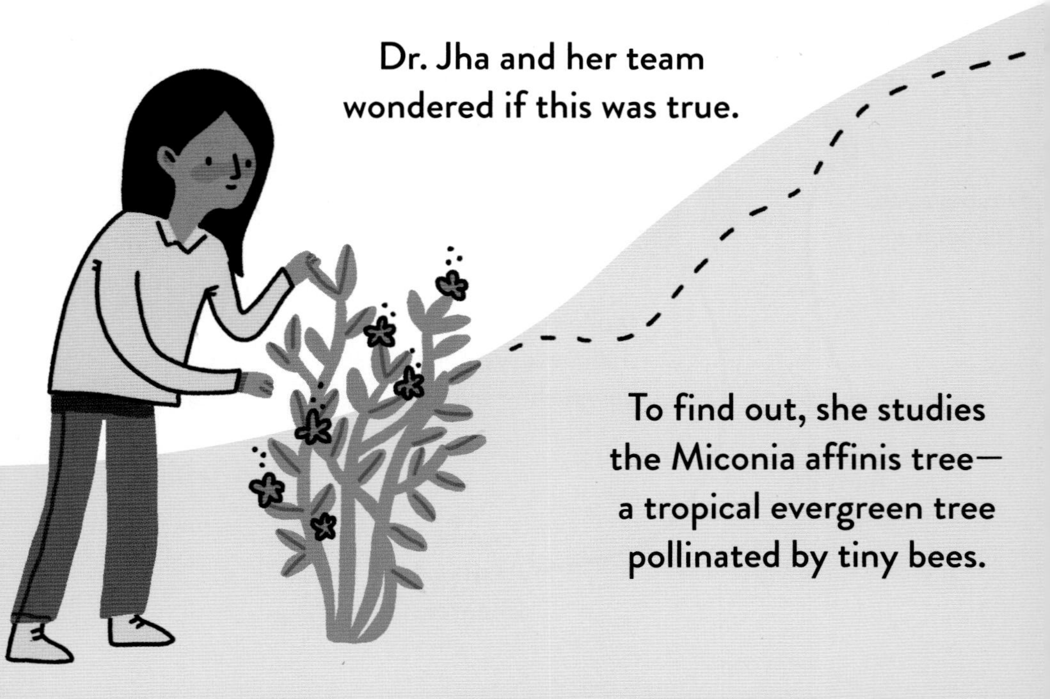

To find out, she studies the Miconia affinis tree—a tropical evergreen tree pollinated by tiny bees.

The plants only have flowers for two days, so bees don't have much time to pollinate them.

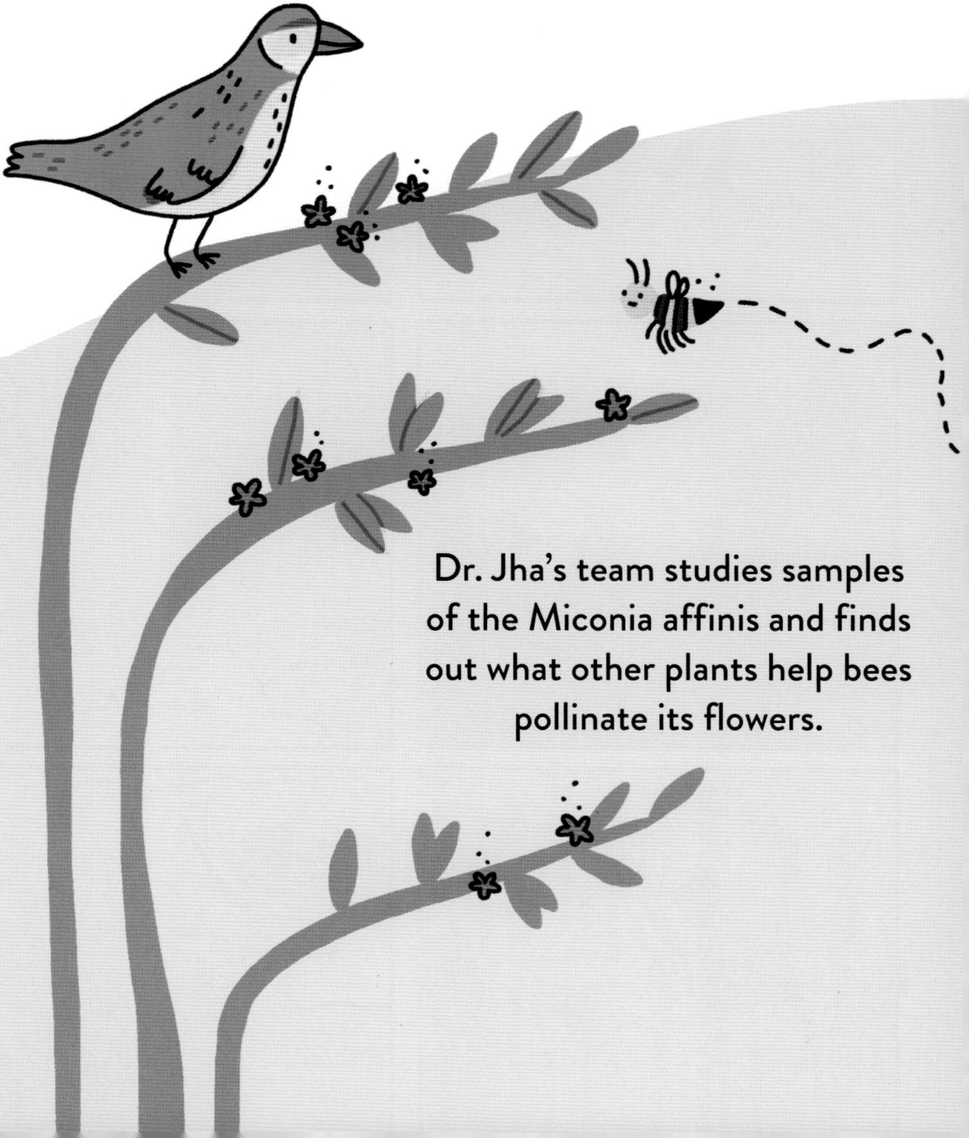

Dr. Jha's team studies samples of the Miconia affinis and finds out what other plants help bees pollinate its flowers.

Dr. Jha discovered that these bees can travel a mile in less than two days. That's like a human running from Los Angeles to Chicago in less than two days.

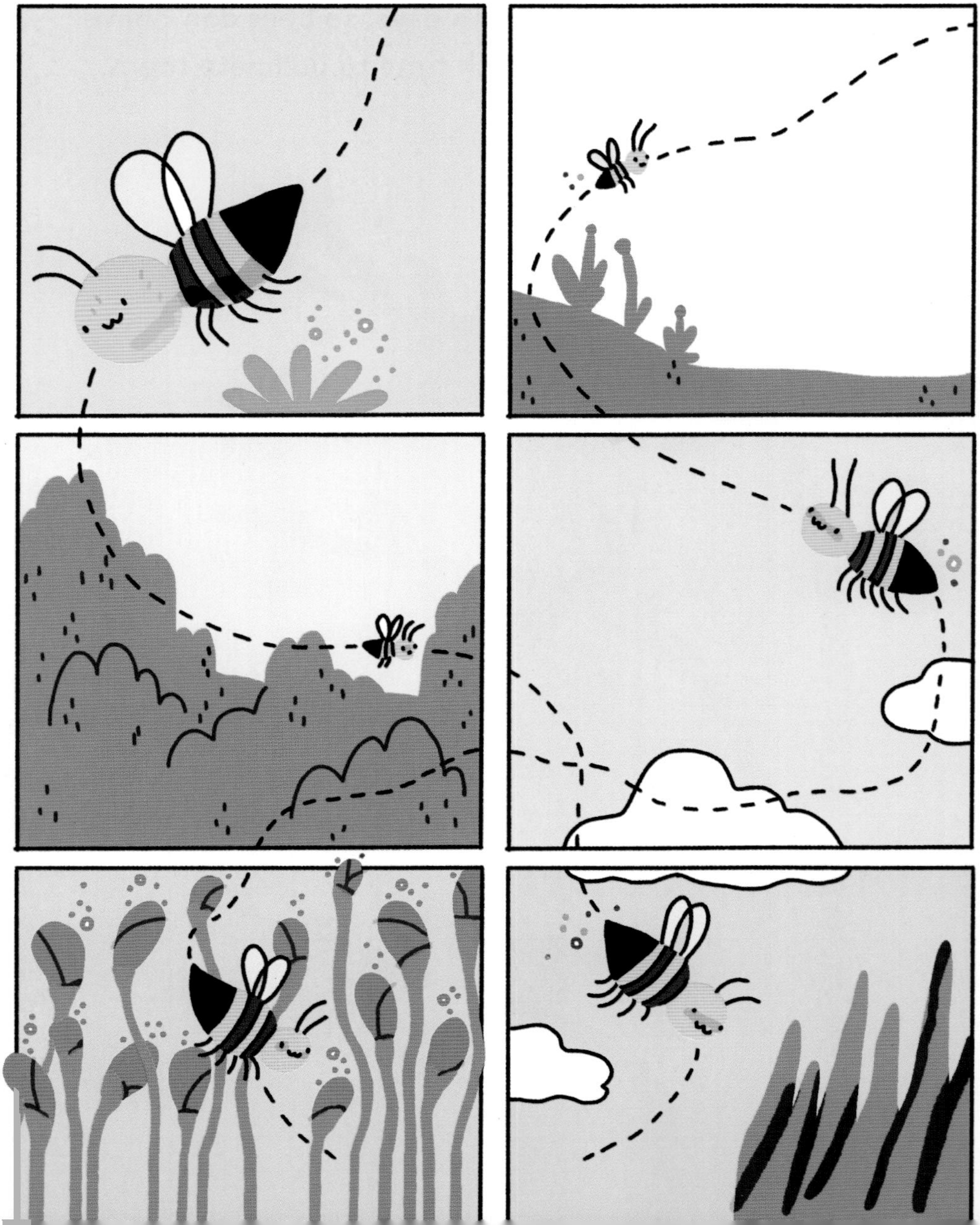

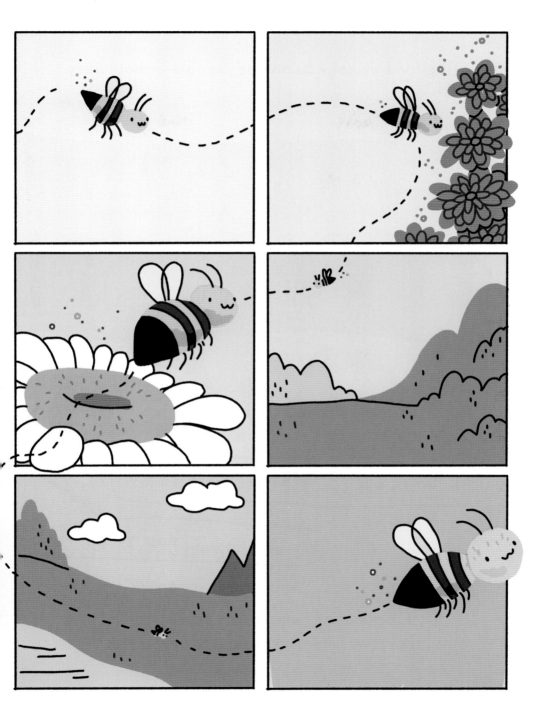

The food we eat wouldn't be possible without bees.

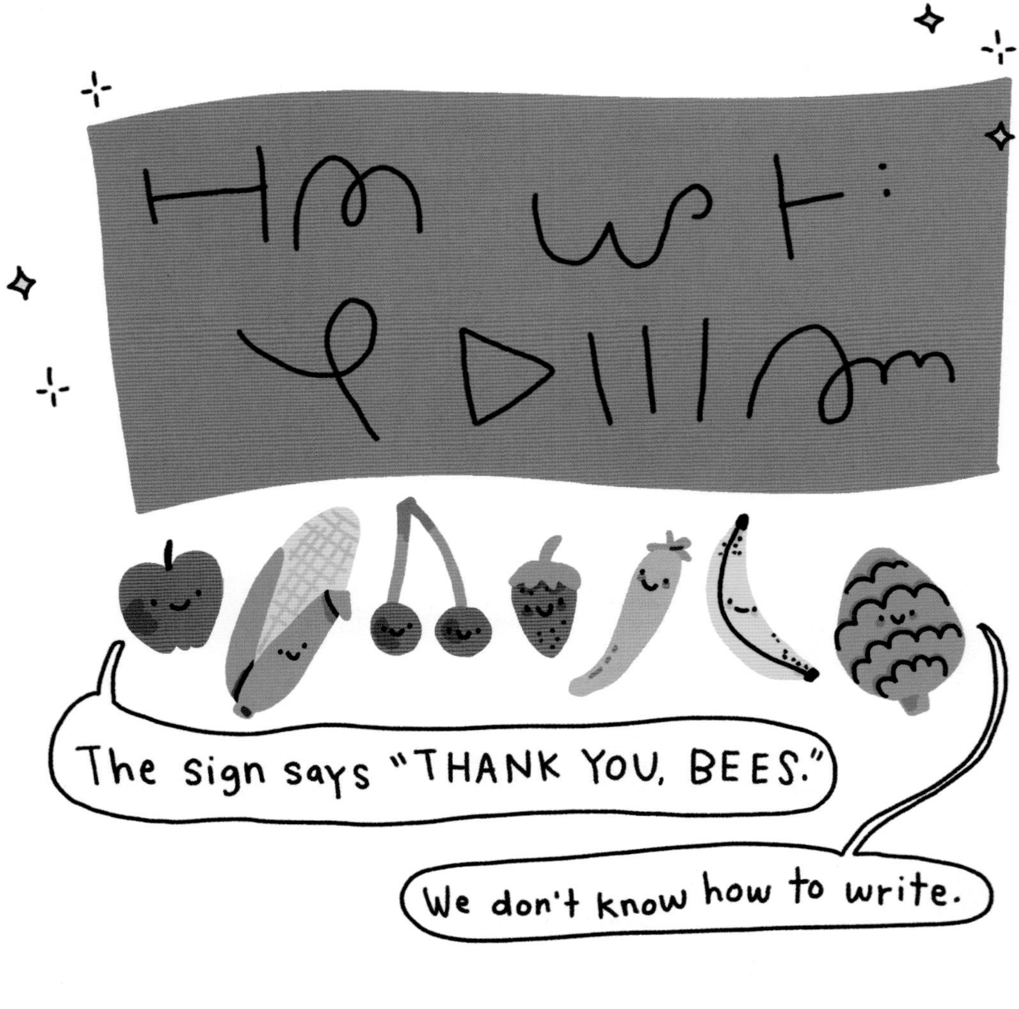
The sign says "THANK YOU, BEES."
We don't know how to write.

Their pollinating helps plants produce seeds so that they can make fruits and vegetables.

Dr. Jha's work helps
humans understand bees
and everything they do.

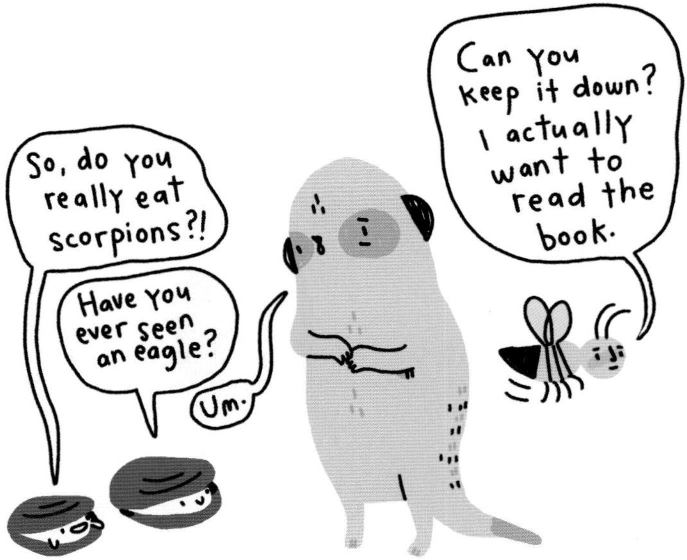
So, do you really eat scorpions?!
Have you ever seen an eagle?
Um.
Can you keep it down? I actually want to read the book.

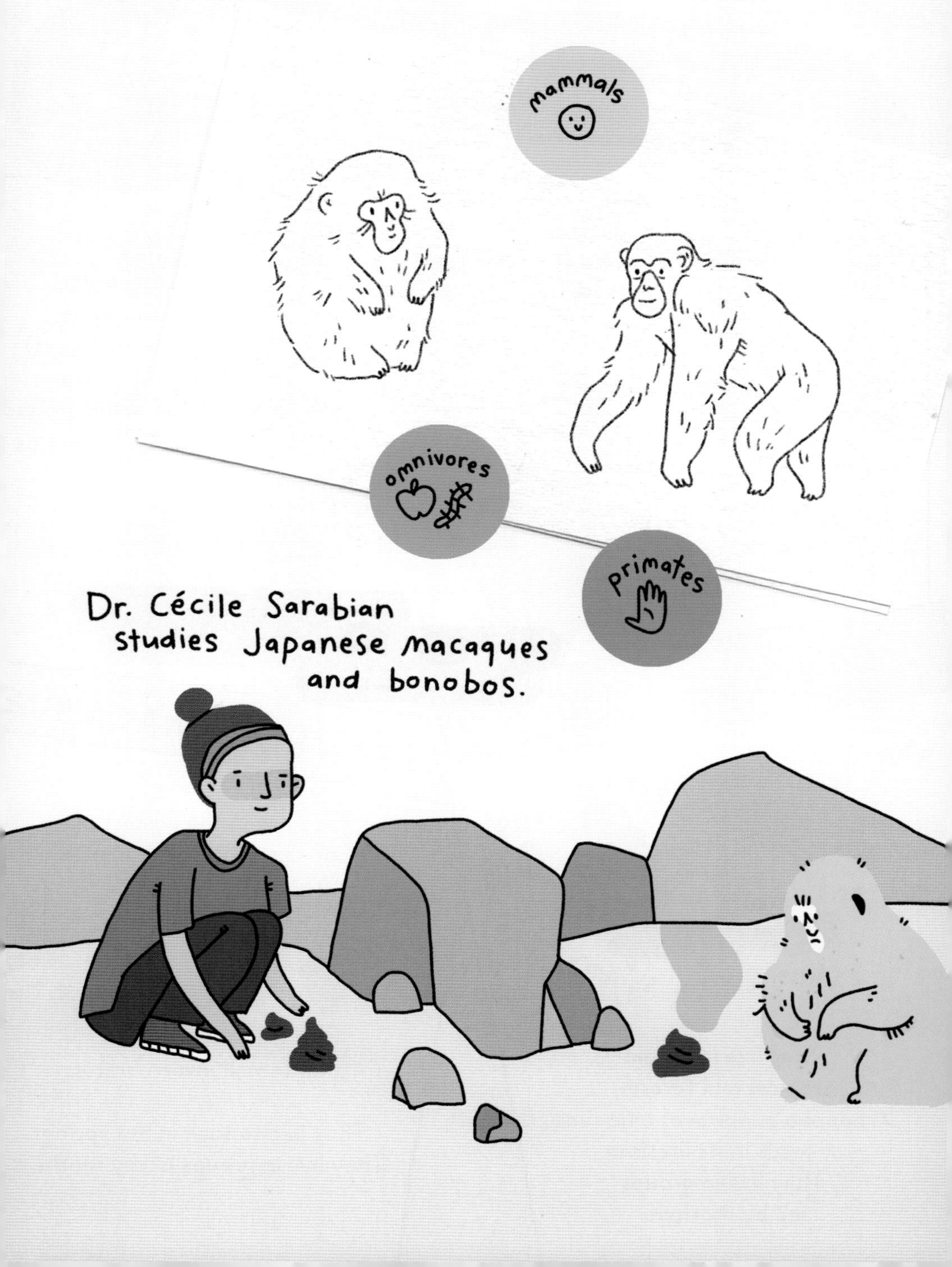
mammals
omnivores
primates
Dr. Cécile Sarabian
studies Japanese macaques
and bonobos.

BONOBOS & JAPANESE MACAQUES

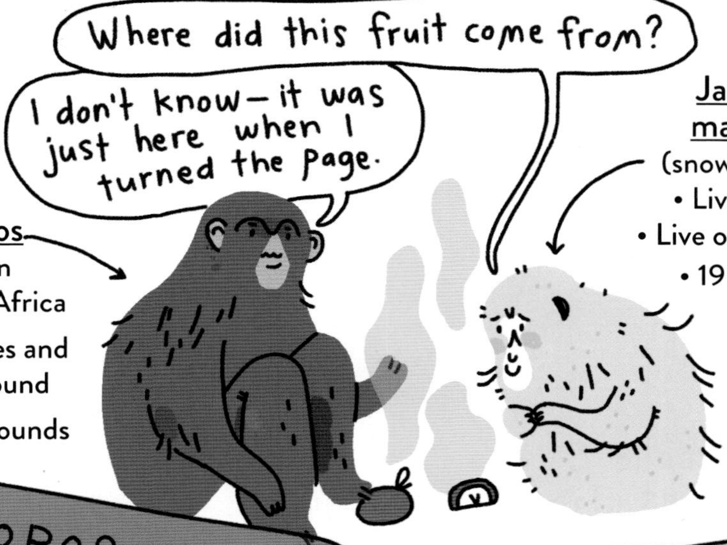

Where did this fruit come from?
I don't know—it was just here when I turned the page.

<u>bonobos</u>
- live in equatorial Africa
- live in trees and on the ground
- 66–130 pounds

<u>Japanese macaques</u>
(snow <u>monkeys</u>)
- Live in Japan
- Live on the ground
- 19–25 pounds

BONOBOS

They eat:
fruit
honey
eggs
and small mammals
(like flying squirrels)

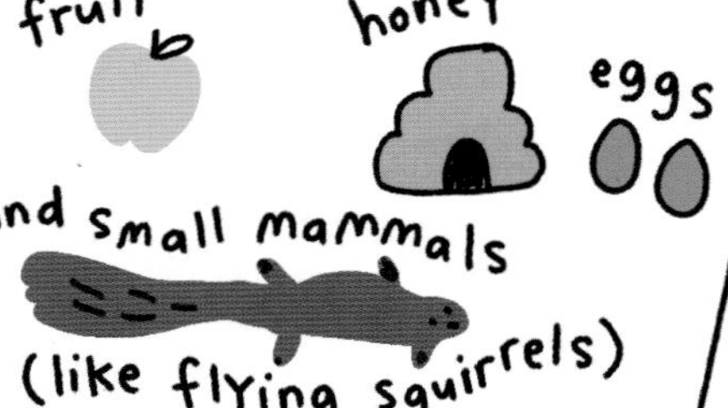

They live in humid tropical rain forests.
A bonobo poops over nine tons of seeds in its lifetime.
They live in groups led by mothers.

JAPANESE MACAQUE

They live in the coldest place of all nonhuman primates.

They eat:
fruit
fungi
plants
nuts and seec

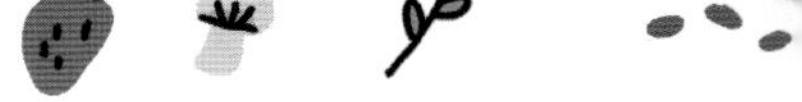

and small invertebrates.

They like to soak in hot springs.
They live in groups led by mothers.

Primates are our closest relatives.
In the wild, and in zoos and sanctuaries, their
lives involve a lot of bugs and dirt.

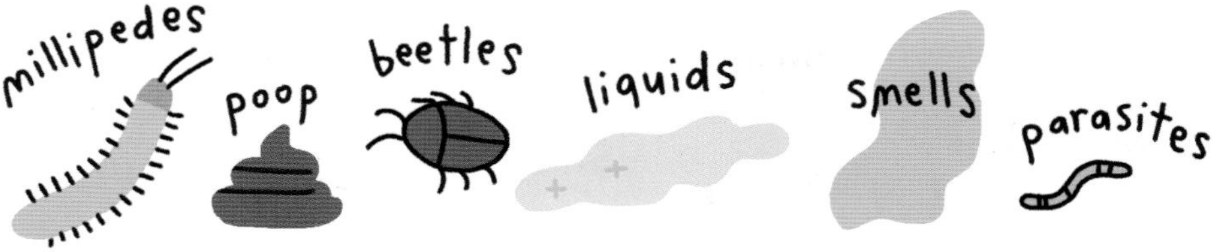
millipedes
poop
beetles
liquids
smells
parasites

Dr. Sarabian wondered:

Do primates get grossed out, like humans do?

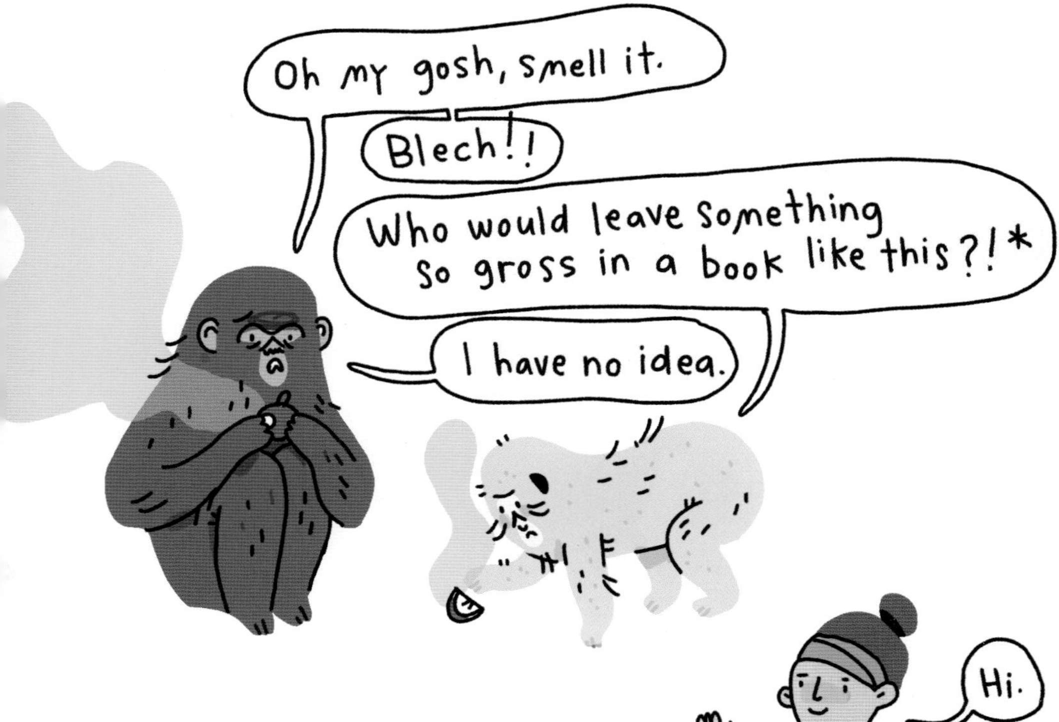
Oh my gosh, smell it.
Blech!!
Who would leave something so gross in a book like this?!*
I have no idea.

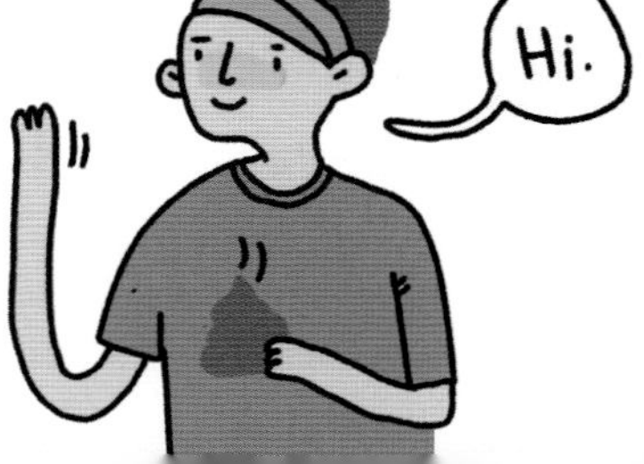
Hi.

*Dr. Sarabian would.

Dr. Sarabian wanted to learn more about what grosses out primates.

She put some fruit on piles of poop.

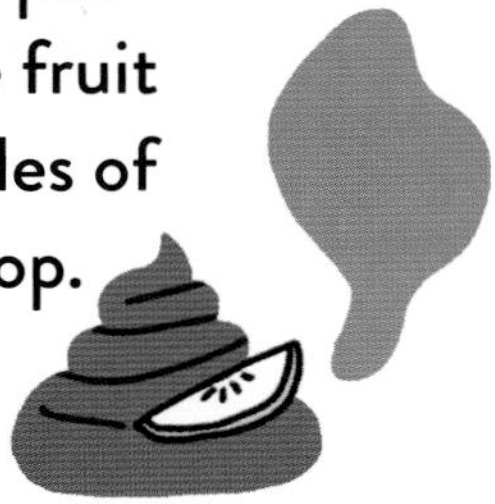

She put some on *pretend* poop.

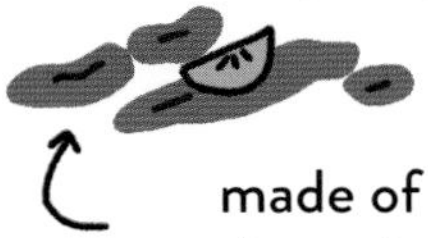

made of papier-mâché

And she put some fruit in dirt.

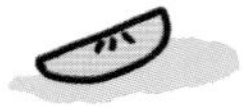

Then she took notes on what the primates did.

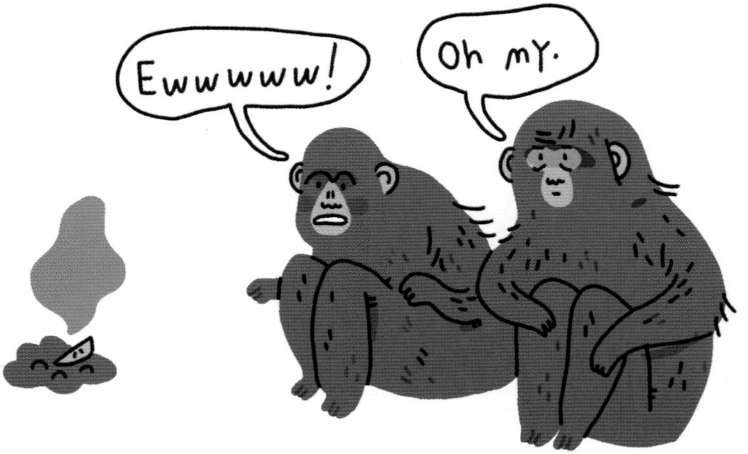
Ewwwww!
Oh my.

The primates were disgusted by the food that was near poop, and wouldn't eat it. But it depended on how realistic the poop looked and smelled. If the poop didn't smell like poop and wasn't the right color, the primates weren't grossed out.

Young bonobos and Japanese macaques
weren't as grossed out as older ones.

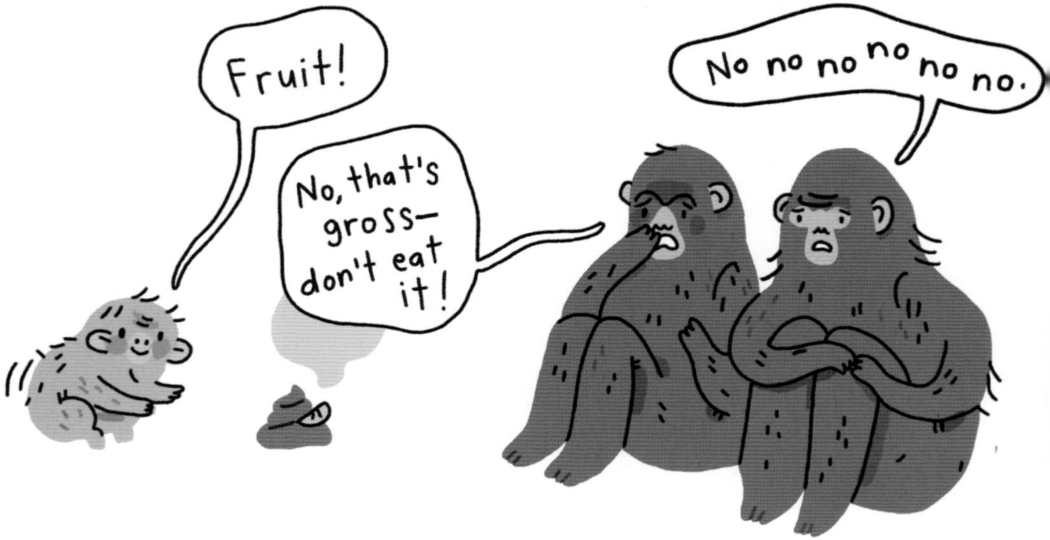
Fruit!
No, that's gross— don't eat it!
No no no no no no.

So it might be something they learn as they get older.

Being grossed out is important!
It keeps us safe from parasites and illness, and it's something
we have in common with bonobos and Japanese macaques,
even though in a lot of ways we're very different.

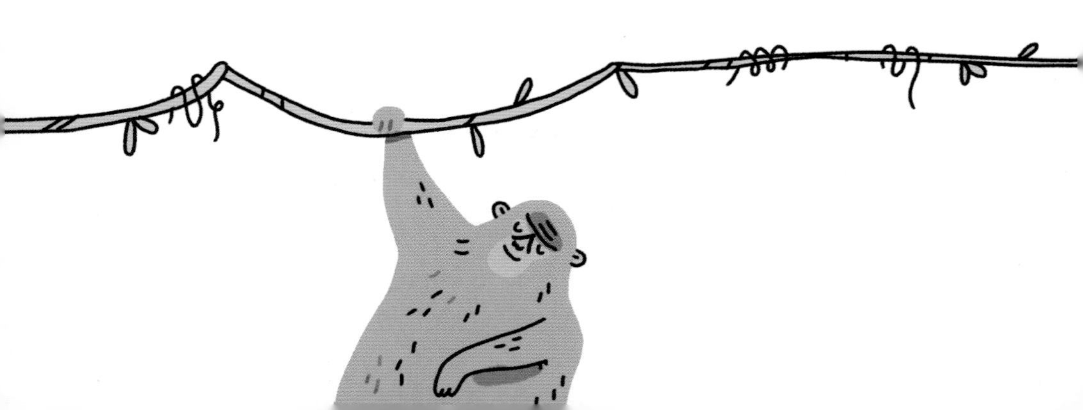

Dr. Sarabian grew up in France and loved animals. Her family didn't have any pets, but on weekends she visited her aunt in the countryside to spend time with Tigra, her aunt's dog.

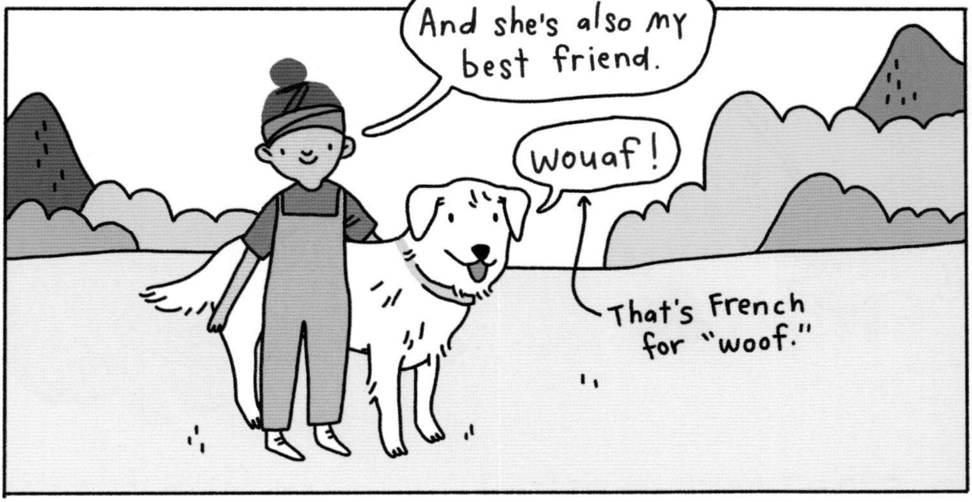
And she's also my best friend.
Wouaf!
That's French for "woof."

She also wrote Tigra letters.

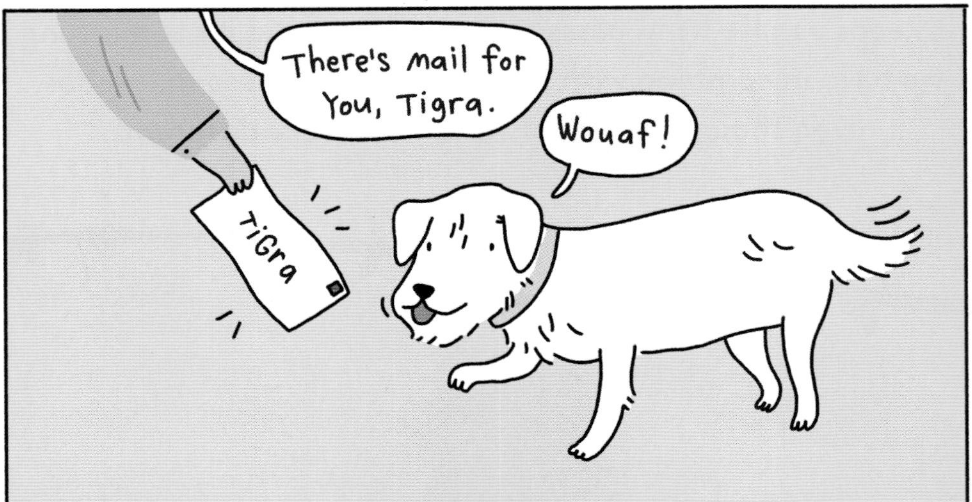
There's mail for You, Tigra.
Wouaf!
TiGra

Cécile would also visit her grandmother and study her collection of animal fact cards.

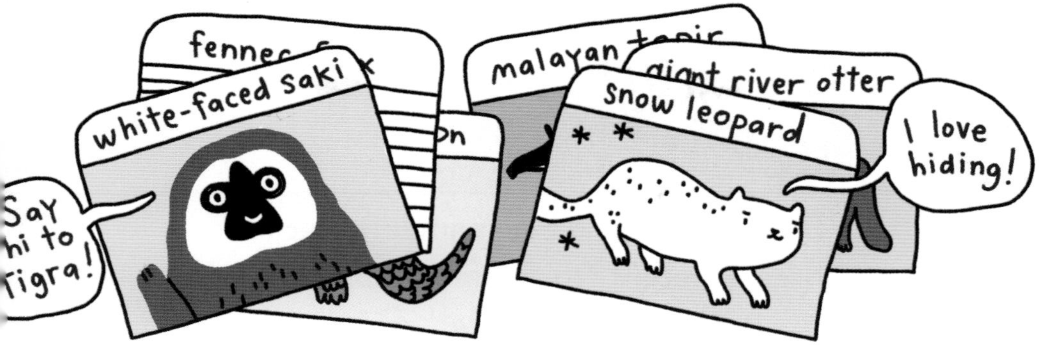
fennec
malayan
giant river otter
white-faced saki
snow leopard
Say hi to Tigra!
I love hiding!

Her favorites were the white-faced saki and the snow leopard.

The cards had a lot of information, but they didn't have all the information, so Cécile had to use her imagination until she could find out more about the animals.

For example, she imagined that white-faced sakis might be giant and walk on two legs—but they're actually pretty small.

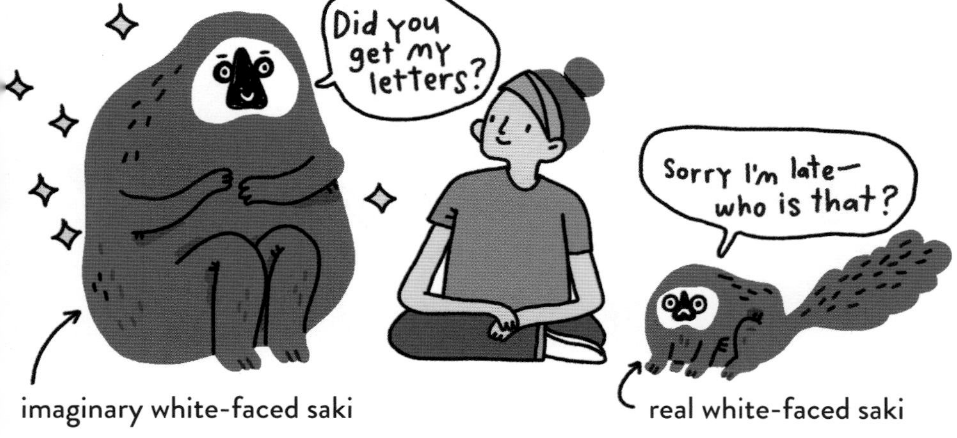
Did you get my letters?
Sorry I'm late— who is that?
imaginary white-faced saki
real white-faced saki

Some animals and humans also have food neophobia . . .

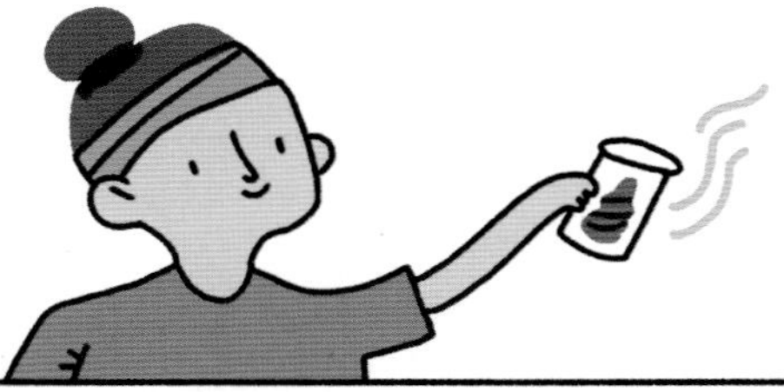

which means they don't want to eat new foods.

Dr. Sarabian and her team left pieces of three different fruits for bonobos to find:

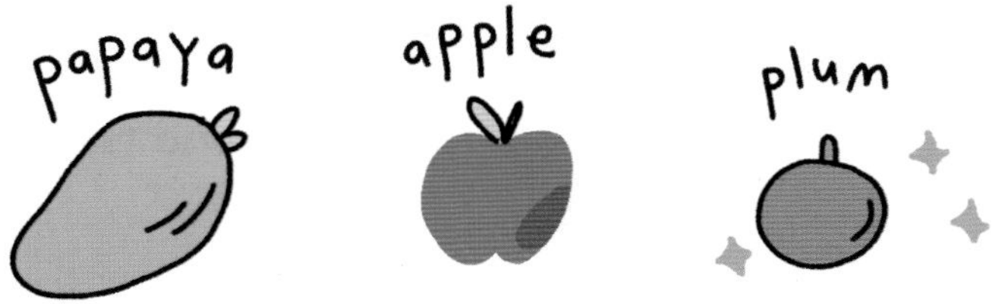
papaya
apple
plum

Bonobos eat these all the time.

They see these sometimes.

This is a *brand-new food* they've never seen.

Even though they'd never had it before, the bonobos wanted to try the plum first.

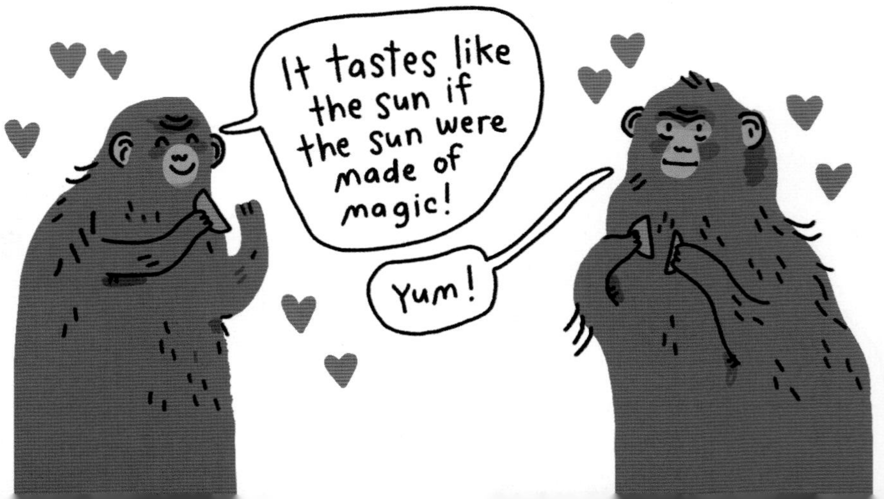
It tastes like the sun if the sun were made of magic!
Yum!

Here's what Dr. Sarabian brings with her:

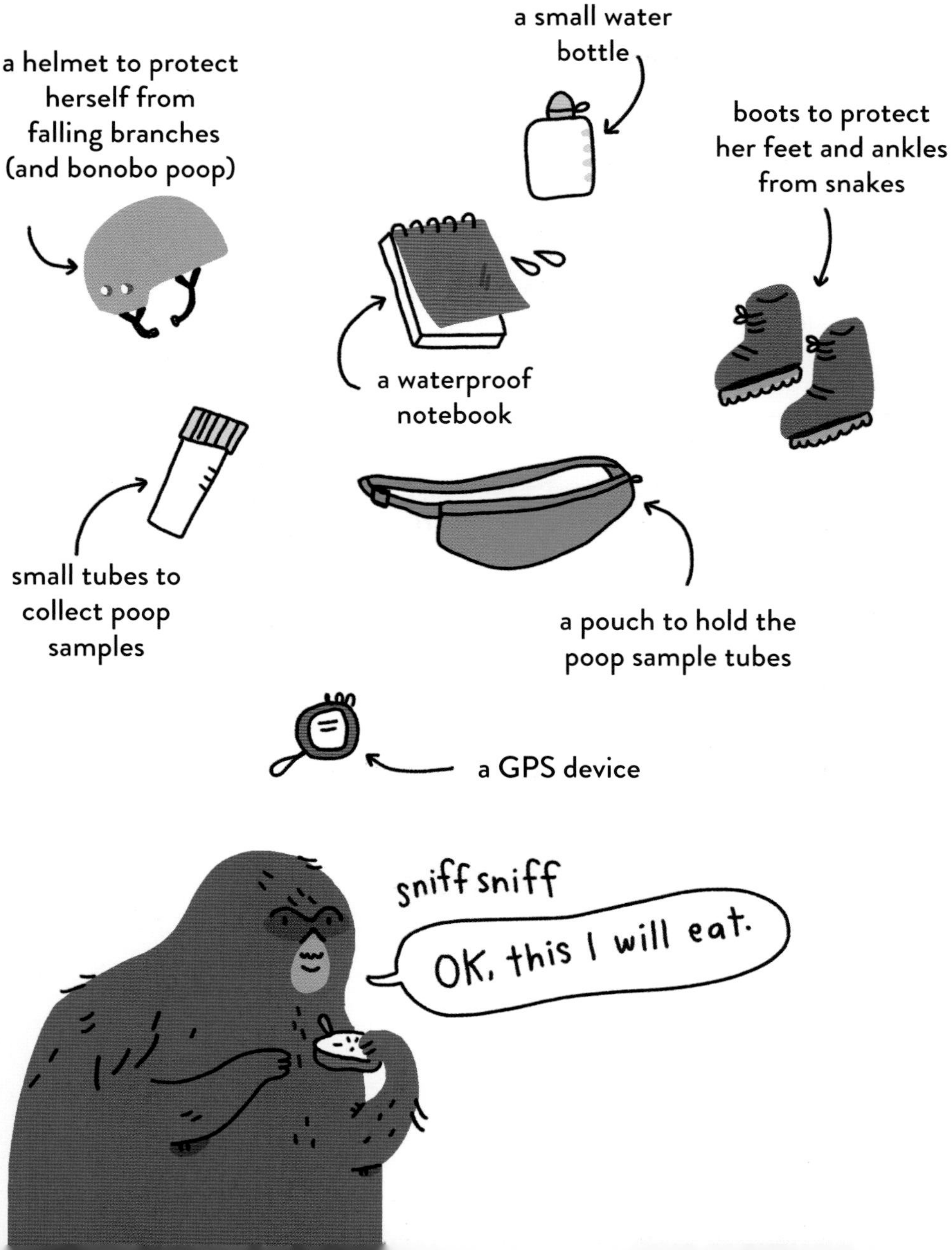
a helmet to protect herself from falling branches (and bonobo poop)
a small water bottle
boots to protect her feet and ankles from snakes
a waterproof notebook
small tubes to collect poop samples
a pouch to hold the poop sample tubes
a GPS device
sniff sniff
OK, this I will eat.

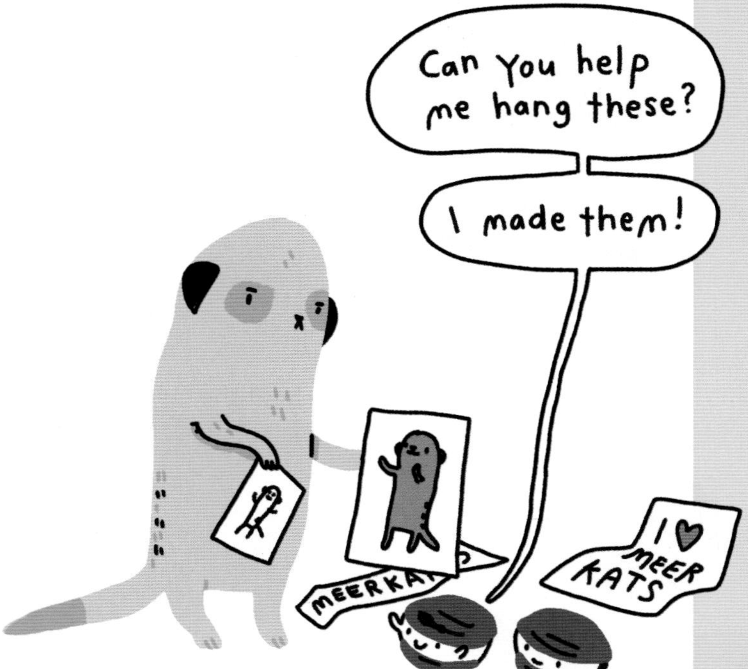
Can you help me hang these?
I made them!
MEERKA
I ♥ MEER KATS

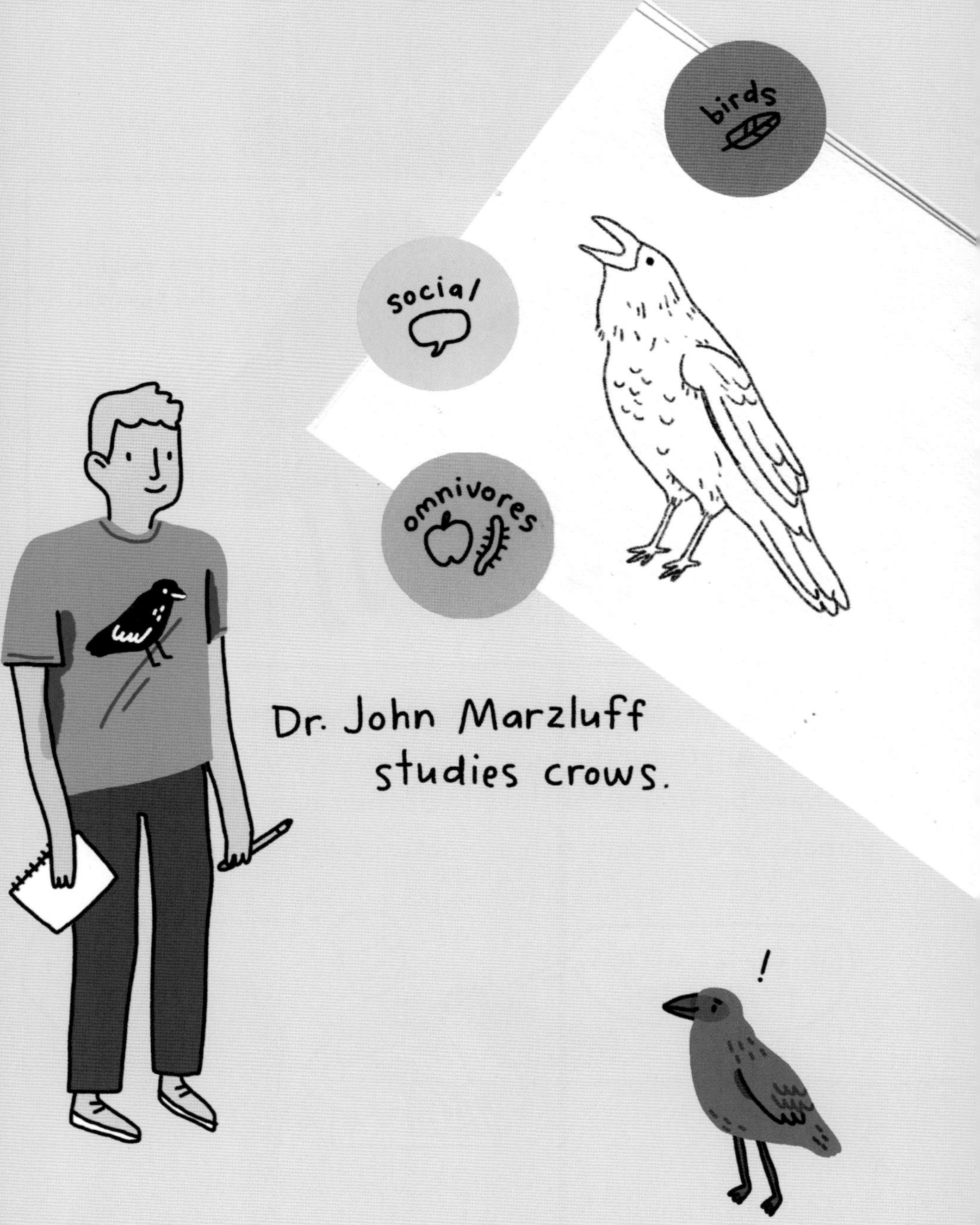
birds
social
omnivores
!

Dr. John Marzluff studies crows.

CROWS

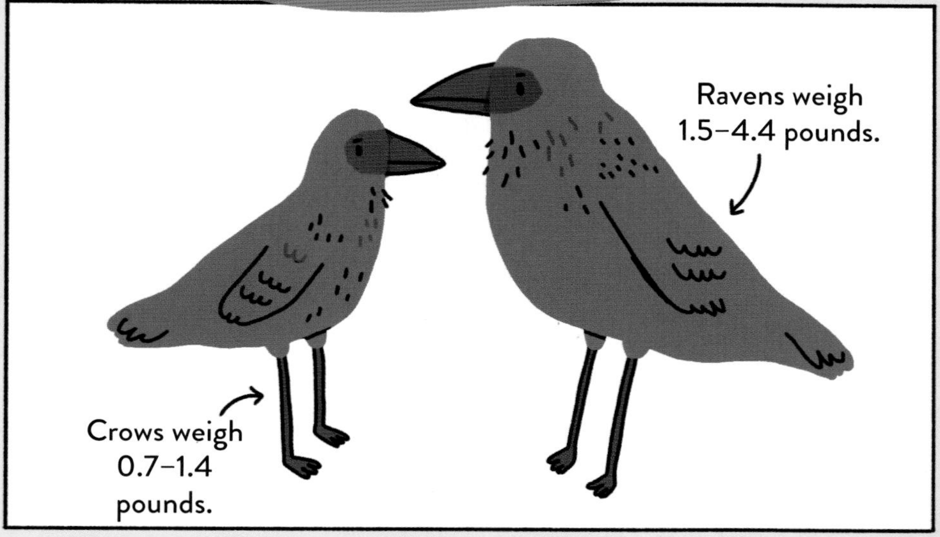
Ravens weigh 1.5–4.4 pounds.
Crows weigh 0.7–1.4 pounds.

They eat nuts, seeds, worms, eggs, frogs, mice, fruit, eggs, and really anything they can find. Crows are incredibly smart and have big brains for the size of their body.* Humans and primates are the only other creatures with brains this large.

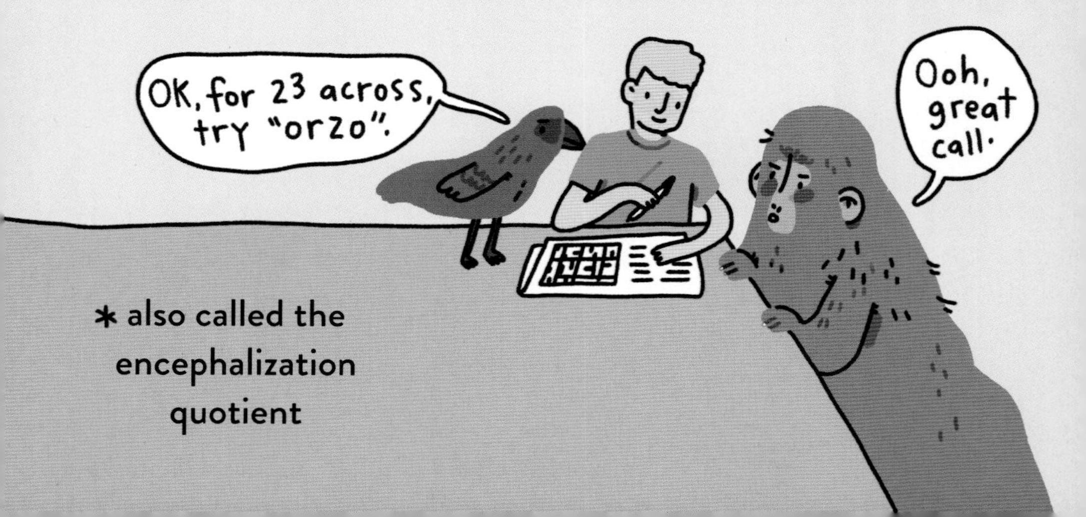
OK, for 23 across, try "orzo".
Ooh, great call.

* also called the encephalization quotient

Crows use their brains to make tools, to keep themselves from getting lost, and to remember their family members. They also—

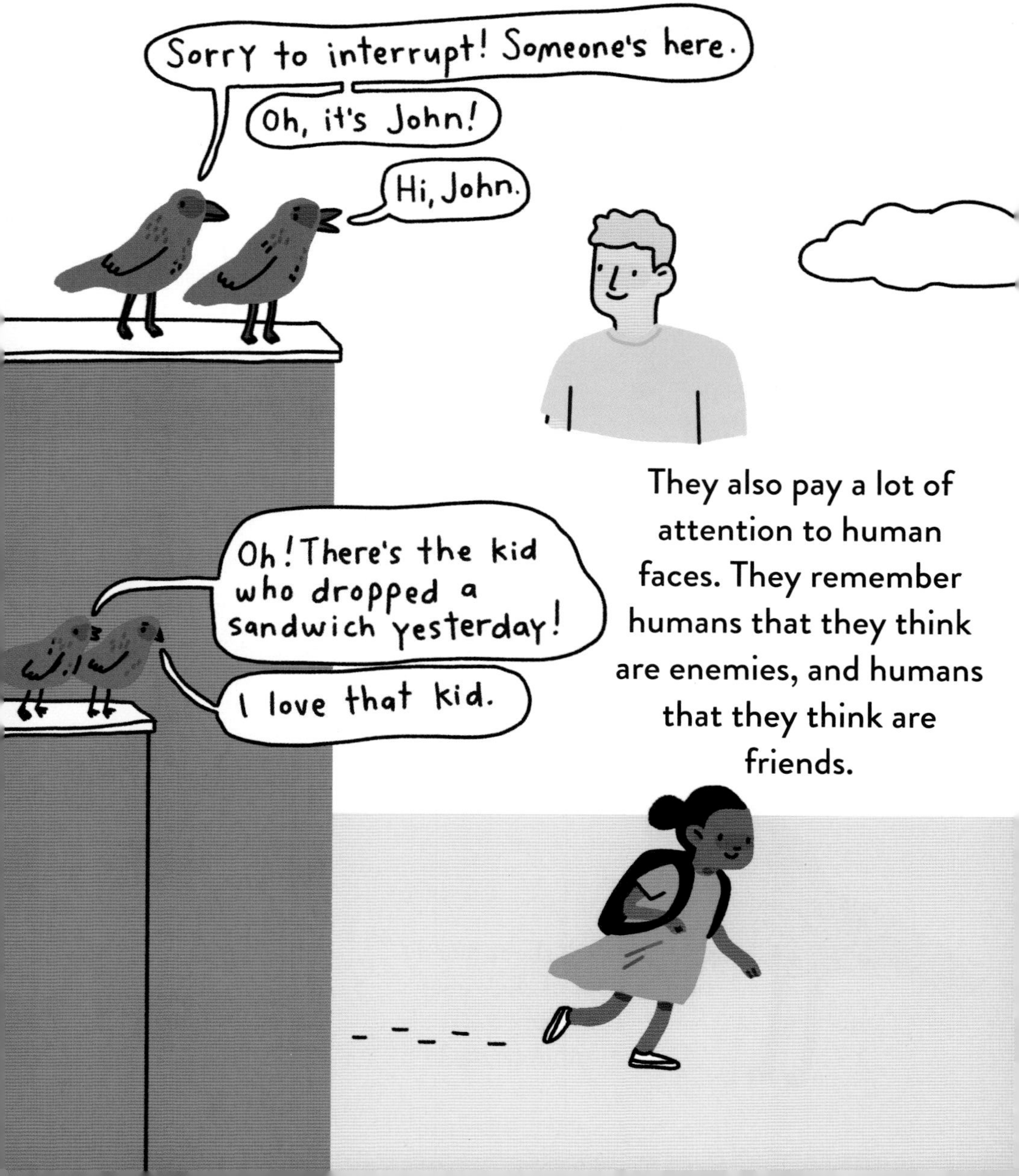

Sorry to interrupt! Someone's here.
Oh, it's John!
Hi, John.
Oh! There's the kid who dropped a sandwich yesterday!
I love that kid.

They also pay a lot of attention to human faces. They remember humans that they think are enemies, and humans that they think are friends.

When he was growing up, John's favorite animal was the horned lizard.

He saw them on the beach as a kid.

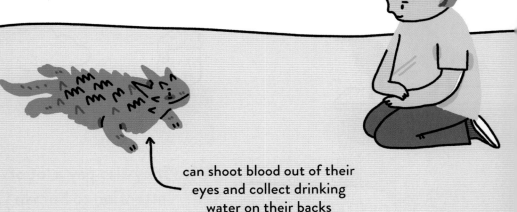

can shoot blood out of their eyes and collect drinking water on their backs

Today he loves learning more about crows and how smart they are.

can't shoot blood out of their eyes (but can do lots of other things)

Dr. Marzluff wanted to study just how well crows remember human faces, and whether they can explain faces to other crows. For his experiment, he used two masks:

a caveman mask and a Dick Cheney mask

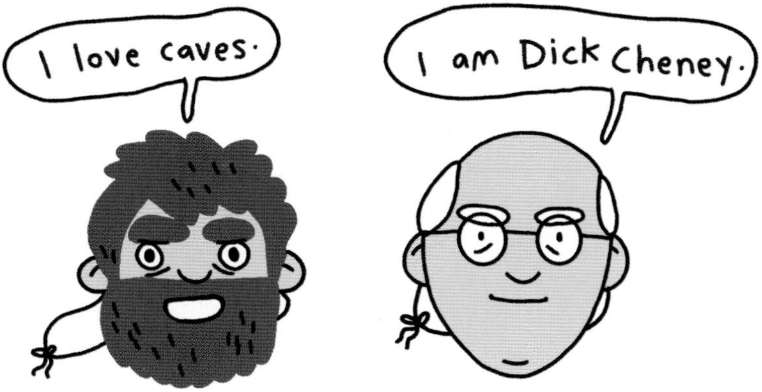
I love caves.
I am Dick Cheney.

First, a researcher put on the caveman mask, then caught and banded two crows.

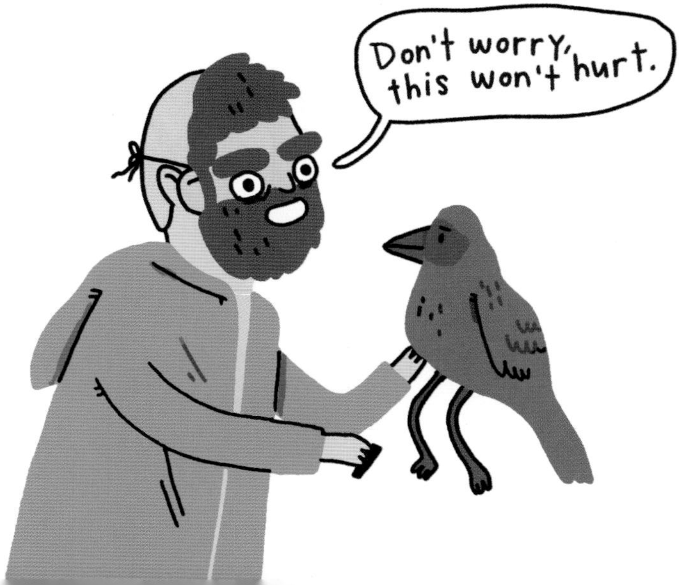
Don't worry, this won't hurt.

Banding didn't hurt the crows,
but they didn't like it.

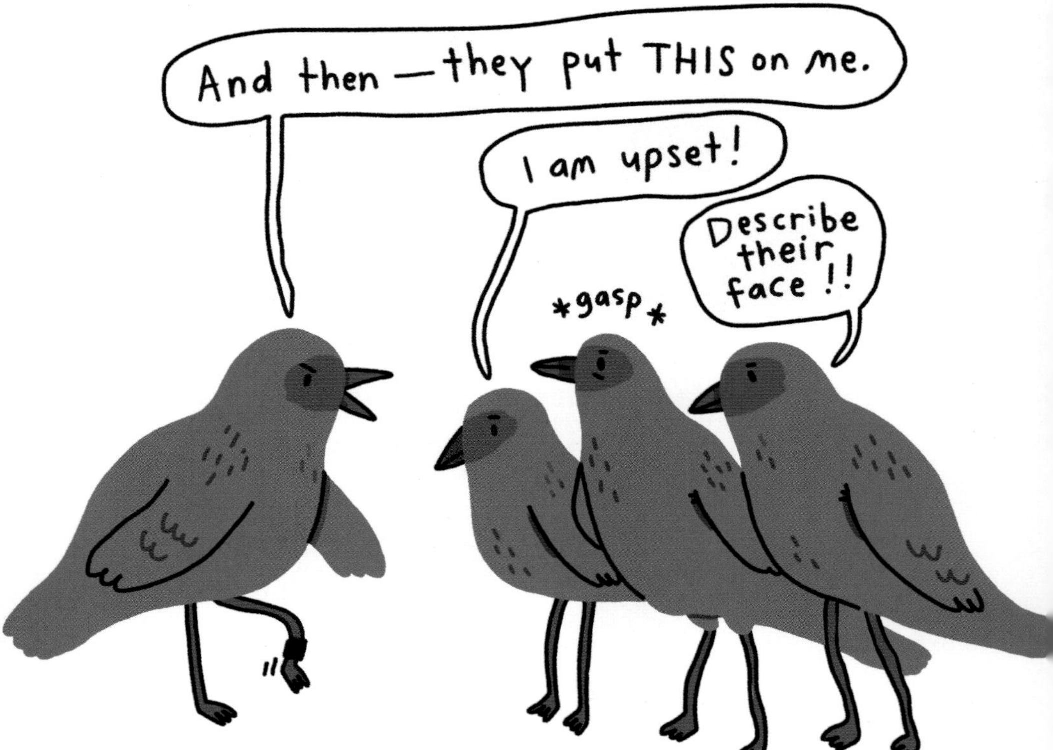
And then—they put THIS on me.
I am upset!
gasp
Describe their face!!

His team wondered if the two crows would remember the caveman mask.

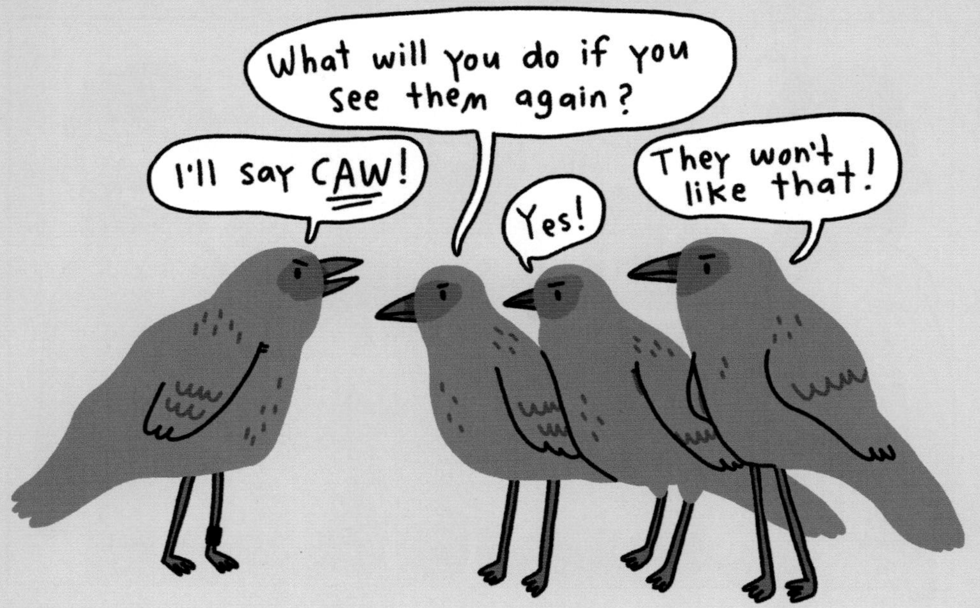
What will you do if you see them again?
I'll say CAW!
Yes!
They won't like that!

Some of the things Dr. Marzluff brings when he's researching birds:

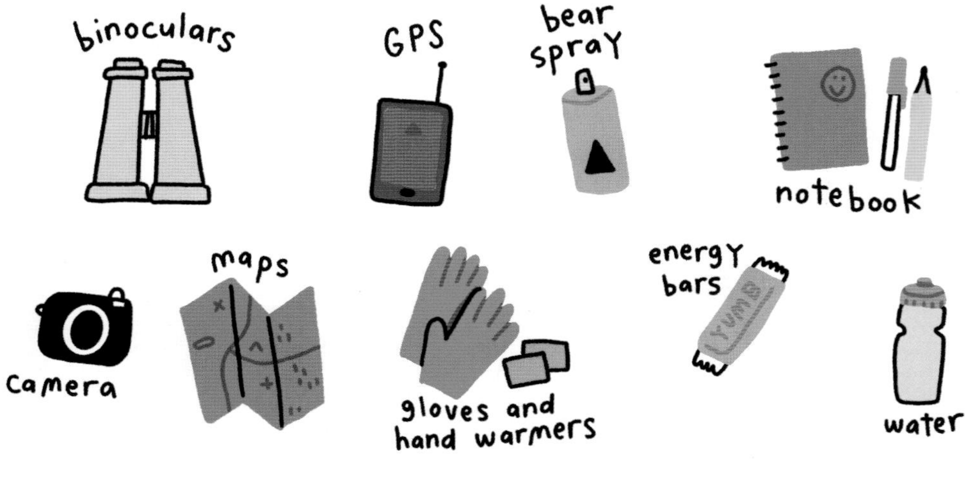
binoculars
GPS
bear spray
notebook
camera
maps
gloves and hand warmers
energy bars
YUM
water

Next, researchers wore the mask
and walked around the area.

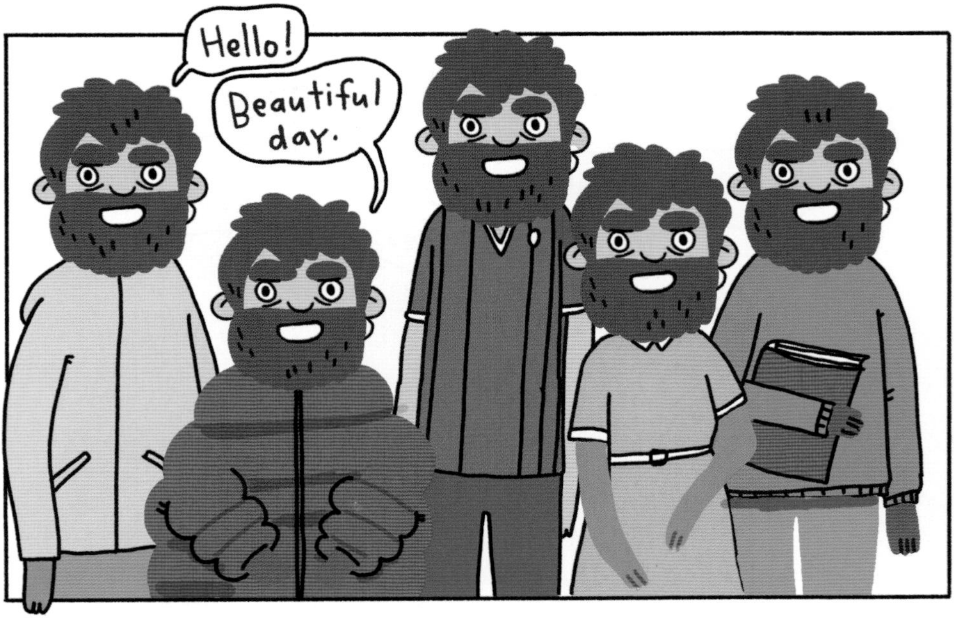
Hello!
Beautiful day.

The crows cawed anytime they saw someone wearing the mask.

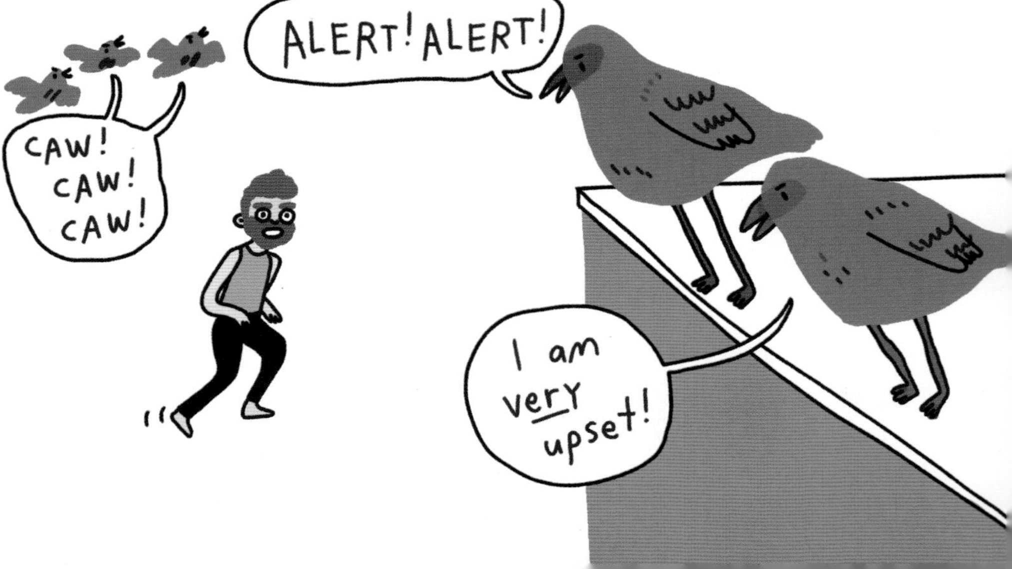
ALERT! ALERT!
CAW! CAW! CAW!
I am very upset!

But it wasn't just the two banded crows who squawked and cawed. All the crows in the area were upset by the mask.

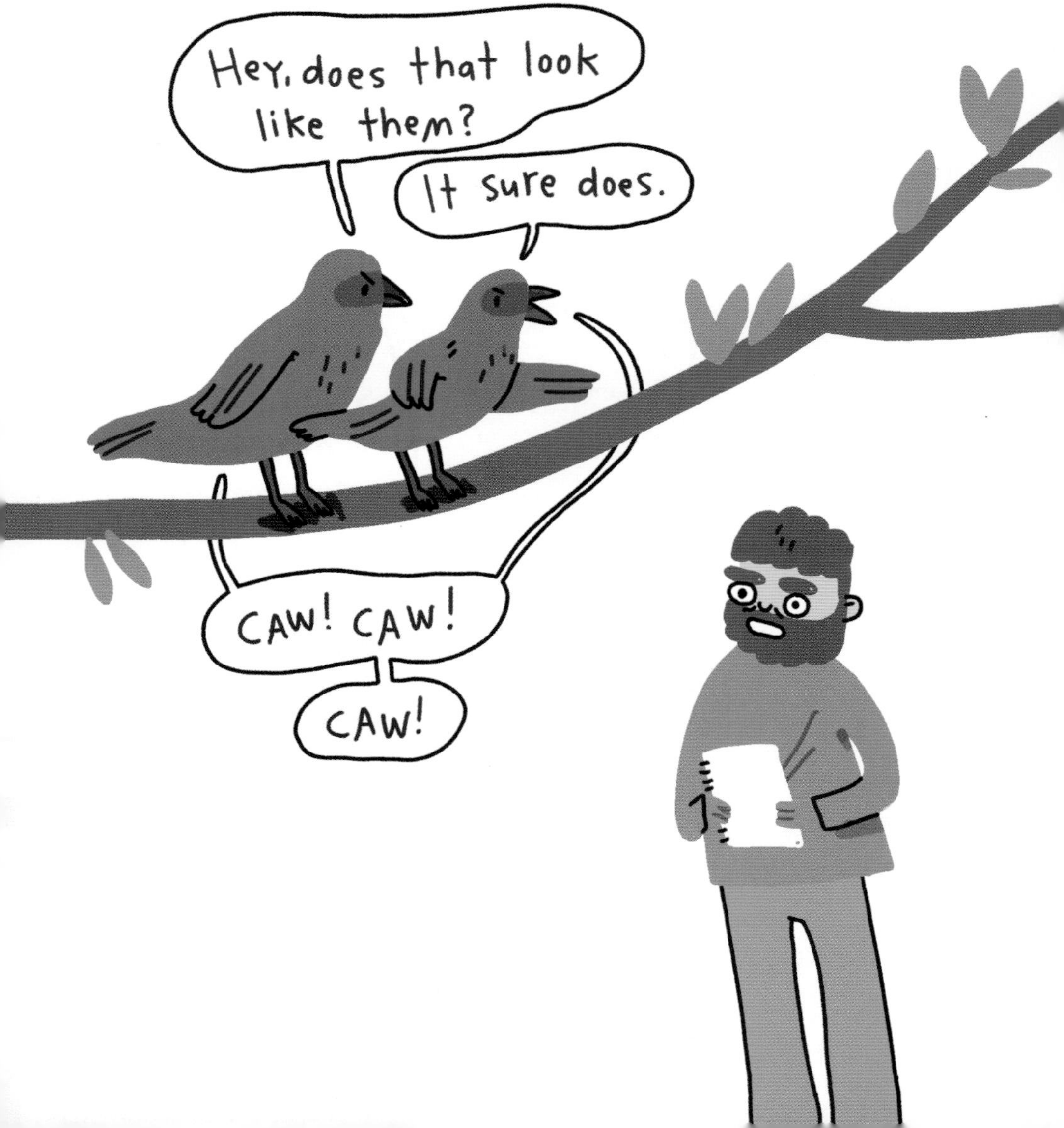
Hey, does that look like them?
It sure does.
CAW! CAW!
CAW!

Dr. Marzluff also had his team walk around wearing the Dick Cheney mask, to see if crows were just upset by masks.

But when they wore the new mask, the crows had no reaction.

Hello, birds.

Hello, stranger I have no feelings about.

This meant that the crows could remember human faces and communicate details about them to each other.

If you make friends with crows in your neighborhood, not only will they remember you, they'll tell other crows about you.

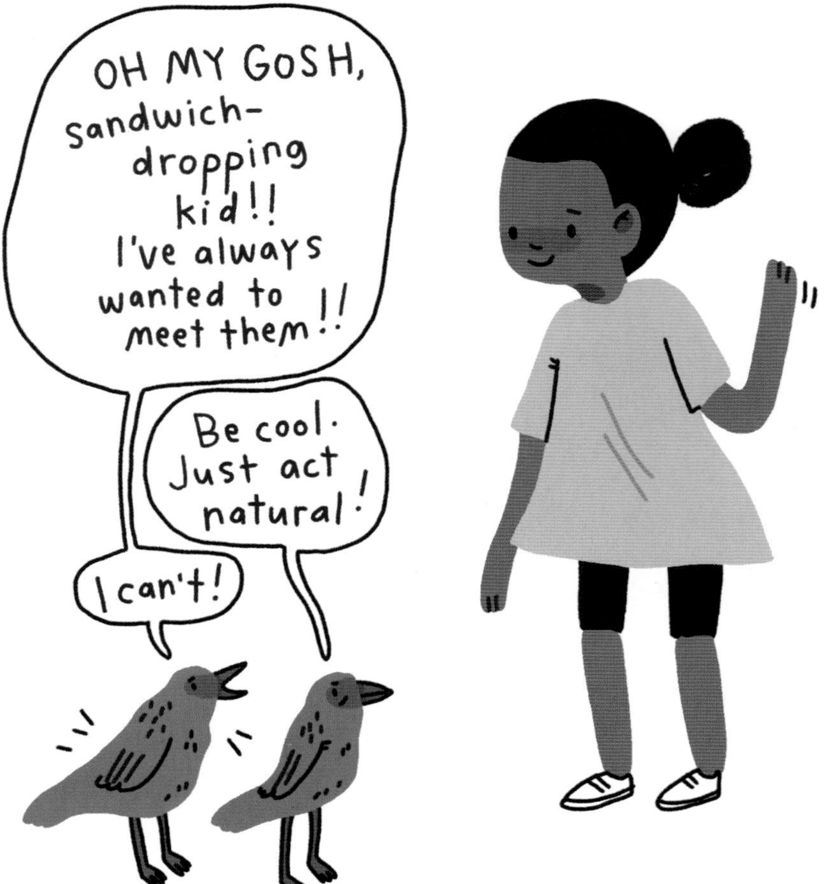
OH MY GOSH, sandwich-dropping kid!! I've always wanted to meet them!!
Be cool. Just act natural!
I can't!

Being able to describe faces, friends, and dangers is one way crows use their brains to keep the whole group safe.

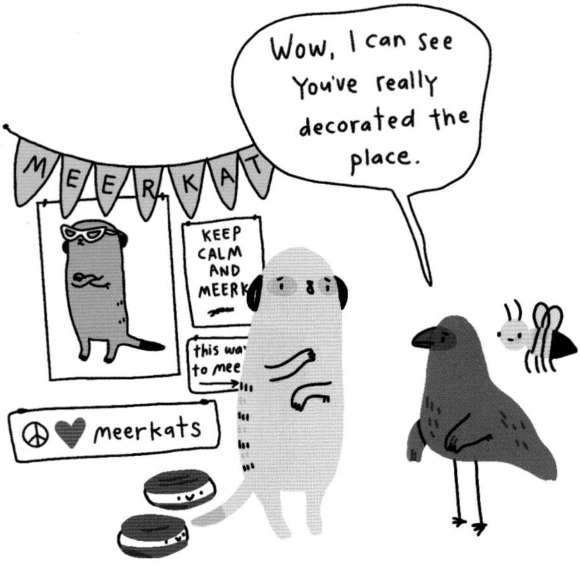
Wow, I can see You've really decorated the place.
MEERKAT
KEEP CALM AND MEERK
this wa
to mee
meerkats

Dr. Solomon David studies gars.

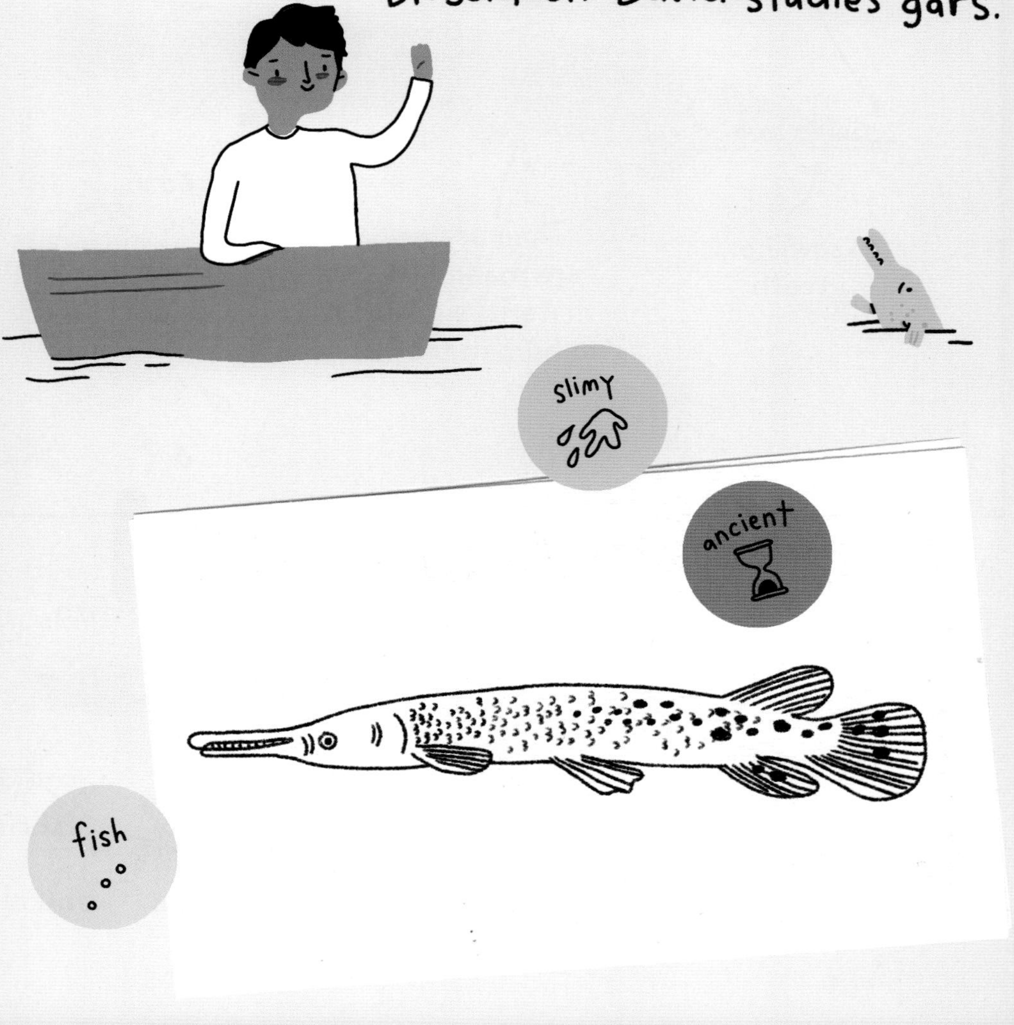
slimy
ancient
fish

GARS

aren't your average fish.

Some species can grow 7–8 feet long and weigh 300 pounds.

They can taste with the tops of their noses.

They can regrow their tails.

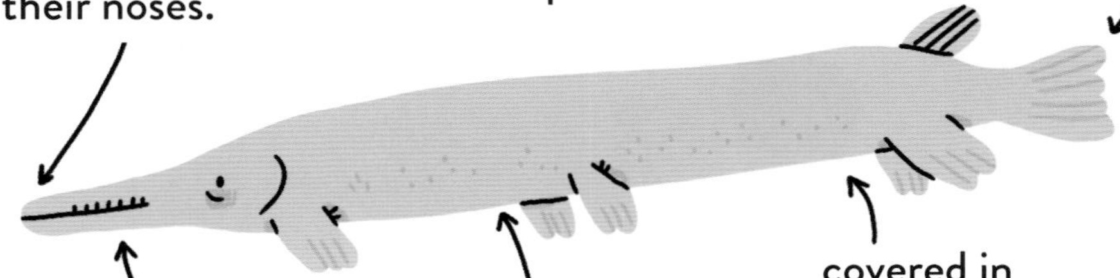

sawlike teeth

Their scales are made of a material similar to human teeth.

covered in slime

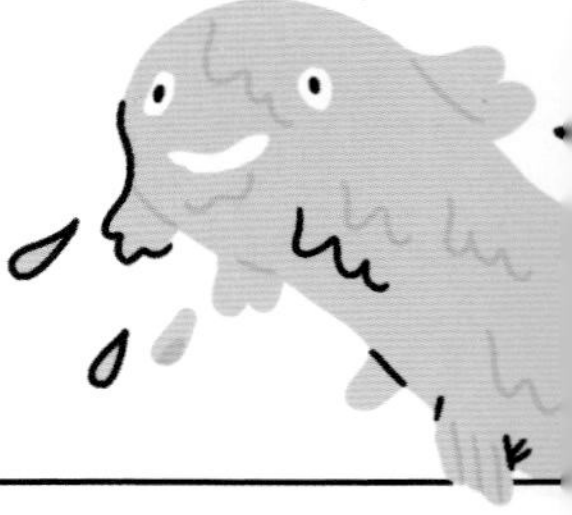

They live in warm, slow-moving water.

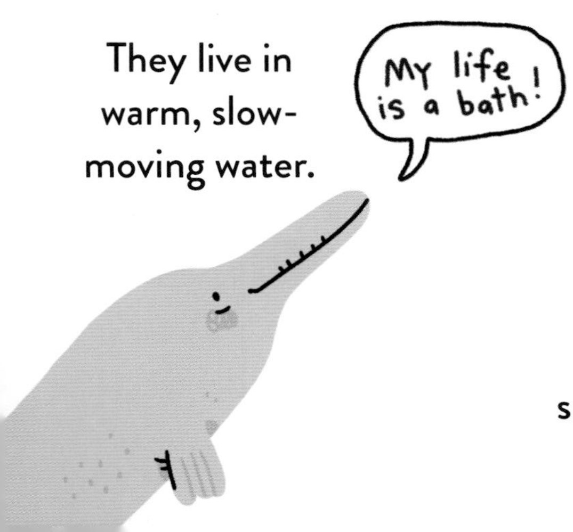
My life is a bath!

And they eat

catfish,

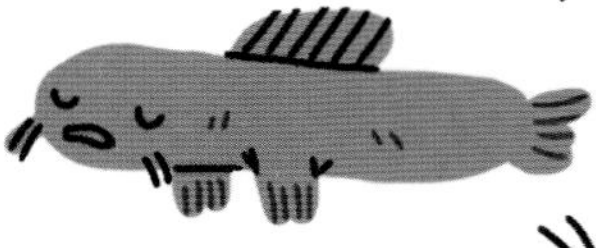

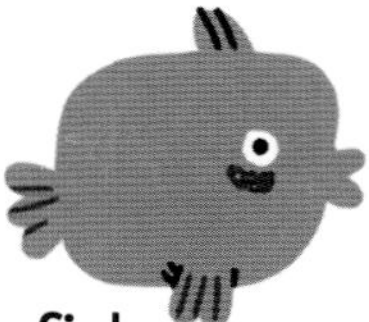

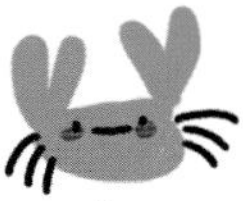

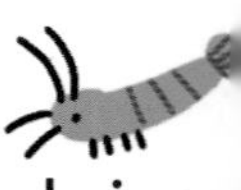

shrimp

sunfish,

crabs,

and algae

Gars are ancient fish.
They're almost identical to their ancestors from 157 million years ago.

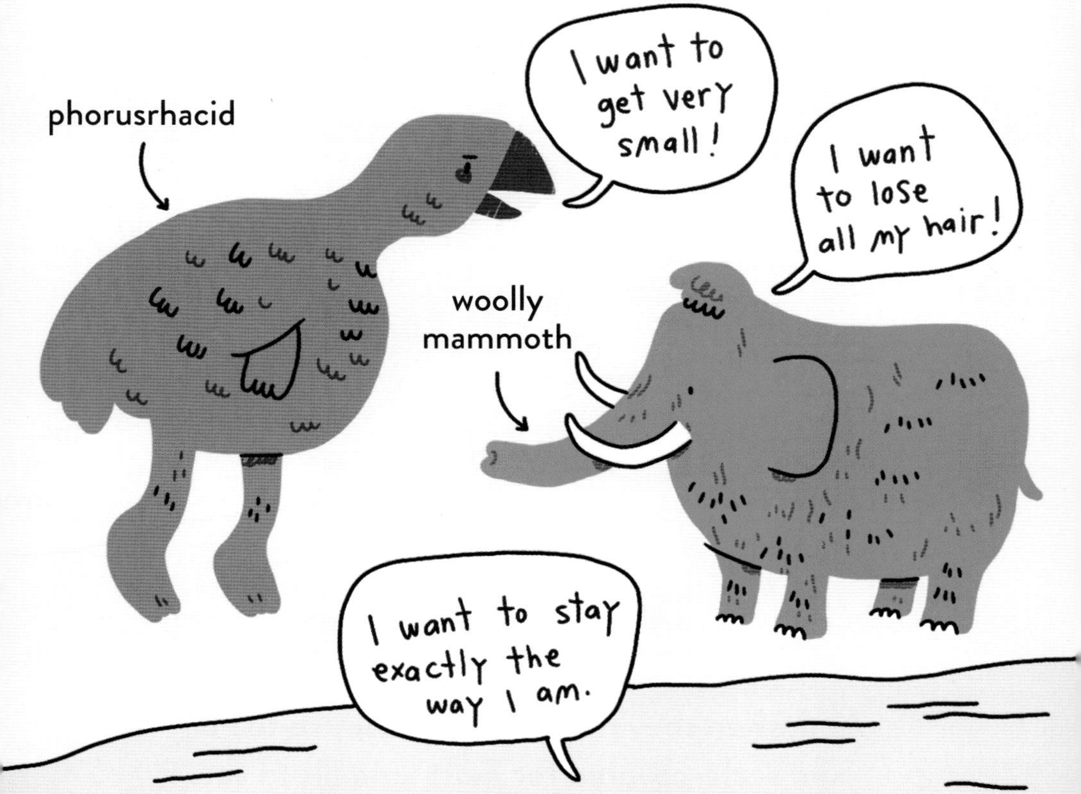
phorusrhacid
I want to get very small!
I want to lose all my hair!
woolly mammoth
I want to stay exactly the way I am.

Most other creatures have changed, but gars look the same today as they did when the *Tyrannosaurus rex* was alive.

Gars are great just how they are. Their eggs and young are toxic to reptiles, invertebrates, birds, and mammals.

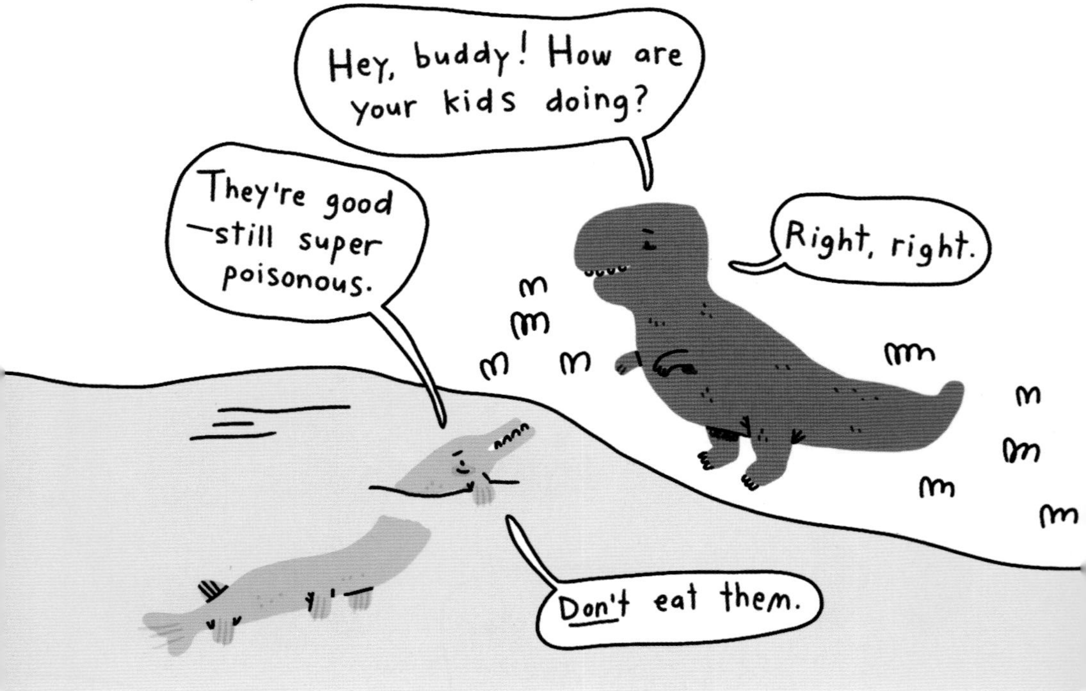
Hey, buddy! How are your kids doing?
They're good —still super poisonous.
Right, right.
Don't eat them.

And when they're full-grown, they're too big and scale-covered for most animals to eat.

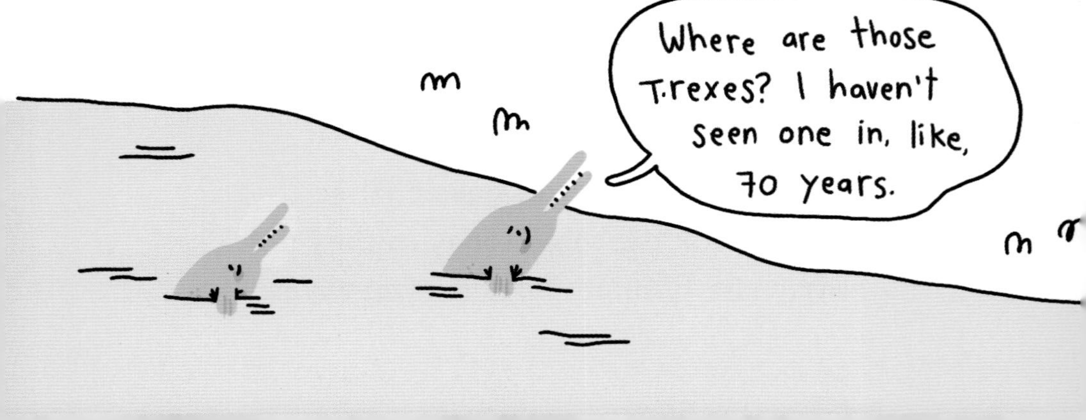
Where are those T.rexes? I haven't seen one in, like, 70 years.

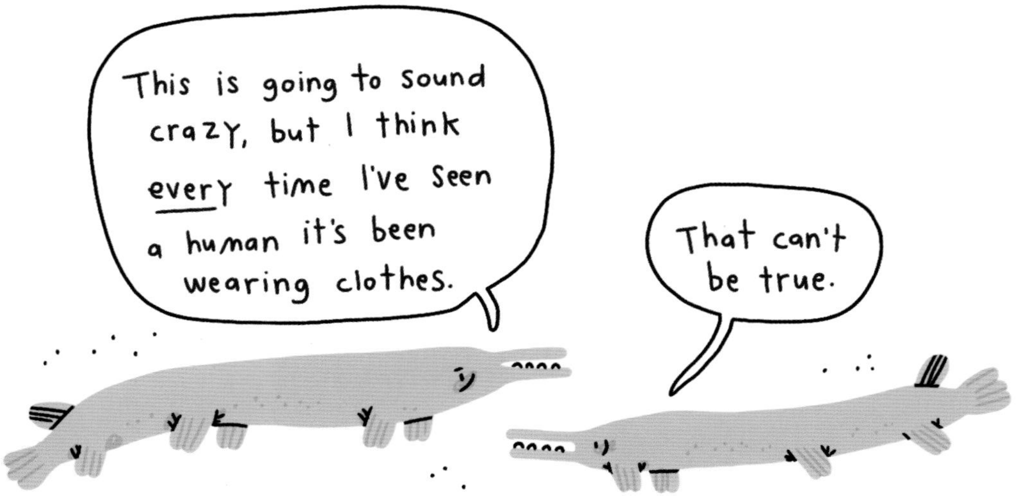
This is going to sound crazy, but I think every time I've seen a human it's been wearing clothes.
That can't be true.

Even though gars have gills, they come to the surface of the water and take gulps of air.

Usually they come up in groups when they know it's safe.

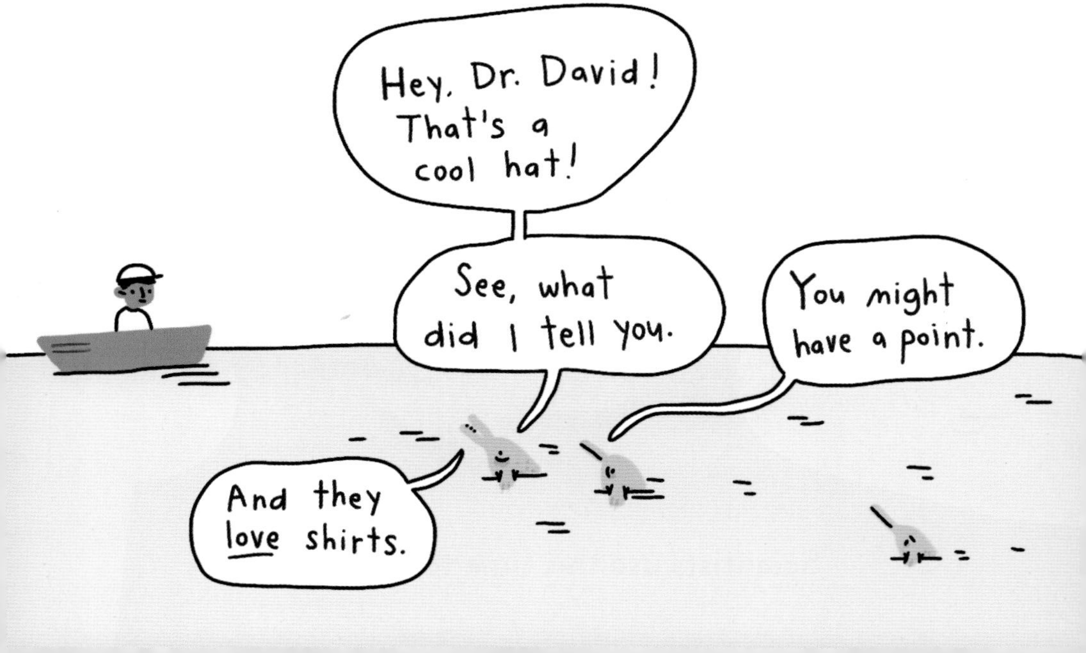
Hey, Dr. David! That's a cool hat!
See, what did I tell you.
You might have a point.
And they love shirts.

To understand gars better, Dr. David and his team need to measure, count, and study them.

His team goes out in a small boat, in shallow water in Louisiana.

There are two ways to catch and release a gar for research:

1. Put an electric current near the boat.

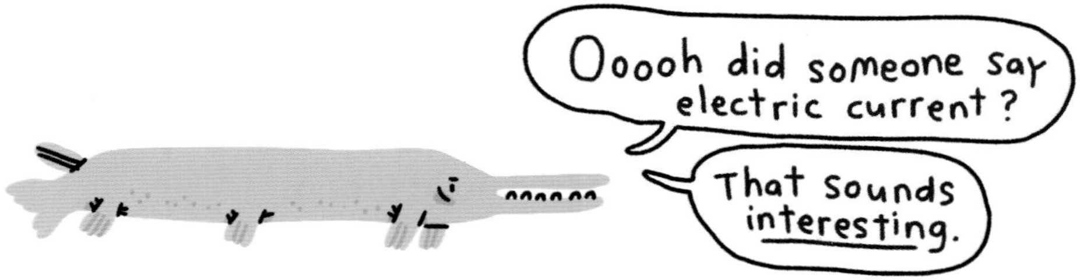
Ooooh did someone say electric current?
That sounds interesting.

Gars are attracted to the electricity, but when they come close, they're shocked for a few seconds.

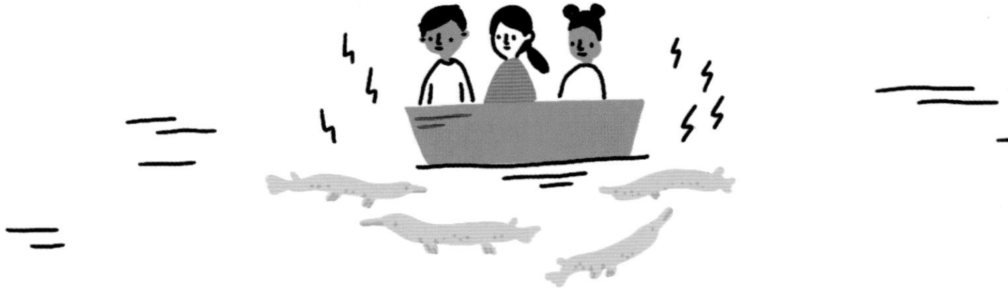

Scientists use this time to count them.

2. Put a piece of meat on the end of a fishing line and attach it to a drone. The scientists fly the drone 400 feet away from the boat and then lower it and catch a gar.

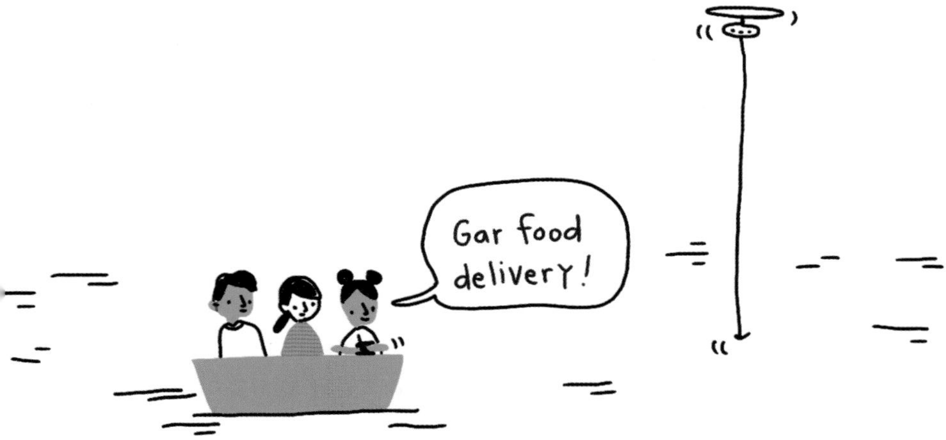
Gar food delivery!

While they measure the fish, they put a cool, wet towel over the fish's head to help calm it down.

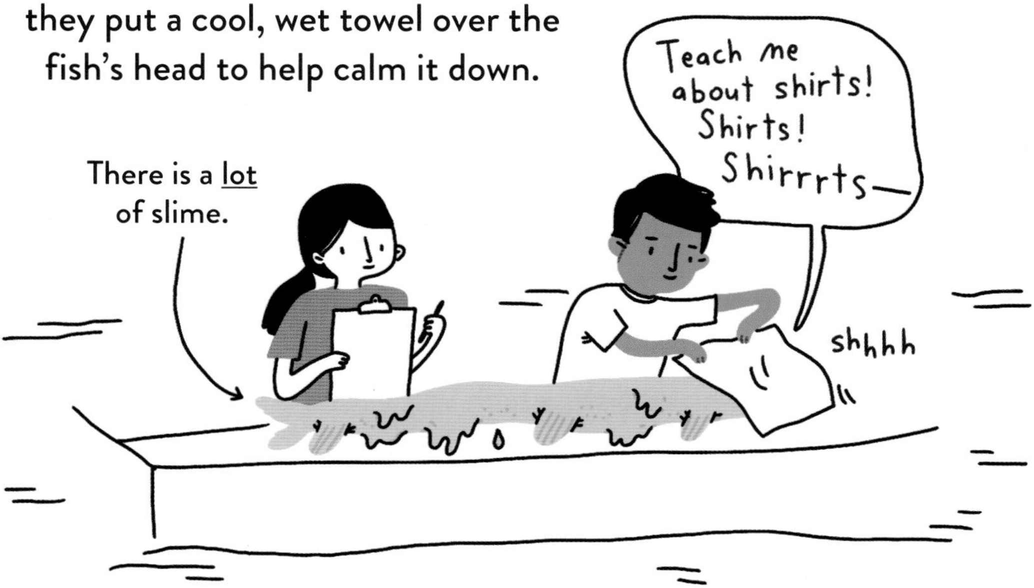
There is a lot of slime.
Teach me about shirts! Shirts! Shirrrts—
shhhh

Solomon has always loved animals,
and he's always loved gars.

He first saw one
in a *Ranger Rick*
magazine when he
was little.

He had never seen a fish like it, and he loved it
right away. Now he teaches about gars, studies
gars, and has a tank of gars in his office.

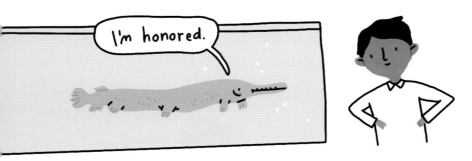

I'm honored.

Gars don't have predators, but when bogs and streams become
buildings and parks, it hurts gar populations. Fewer gars means
more medium-sized fish, which will eat all the small fish.

Dr. David wants to make sure the gars are protected.

And he wants people to love gars as much as he does.

In a way, studying gars is a bit like stepping into a time machine.

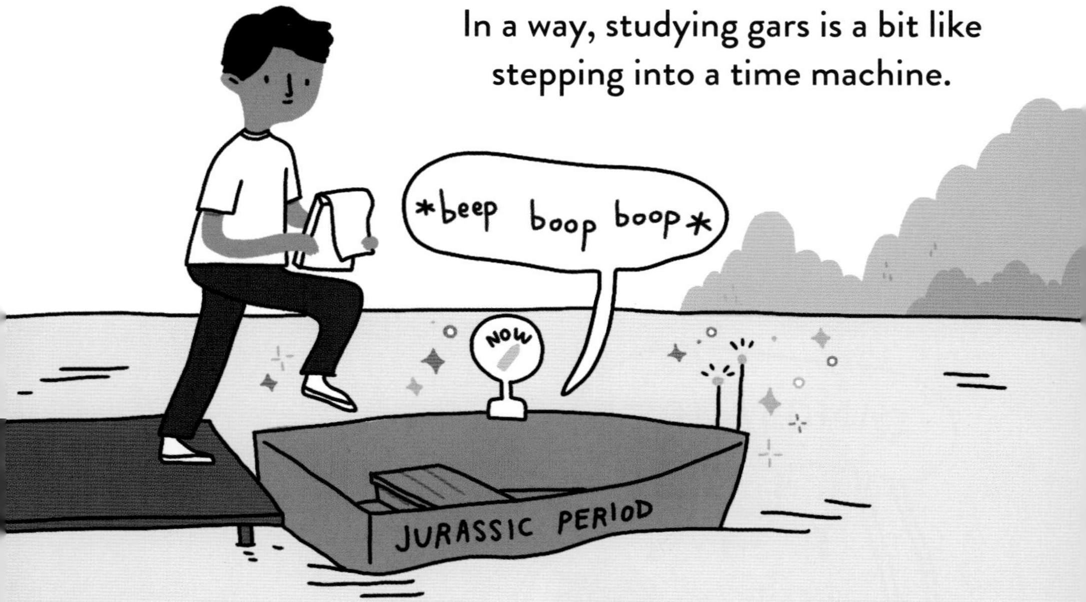
beep boop boop
NOW
JURASSIC PERIOD

It's a rare opportunity to study an animal from 157 million years ago that's still alive today.

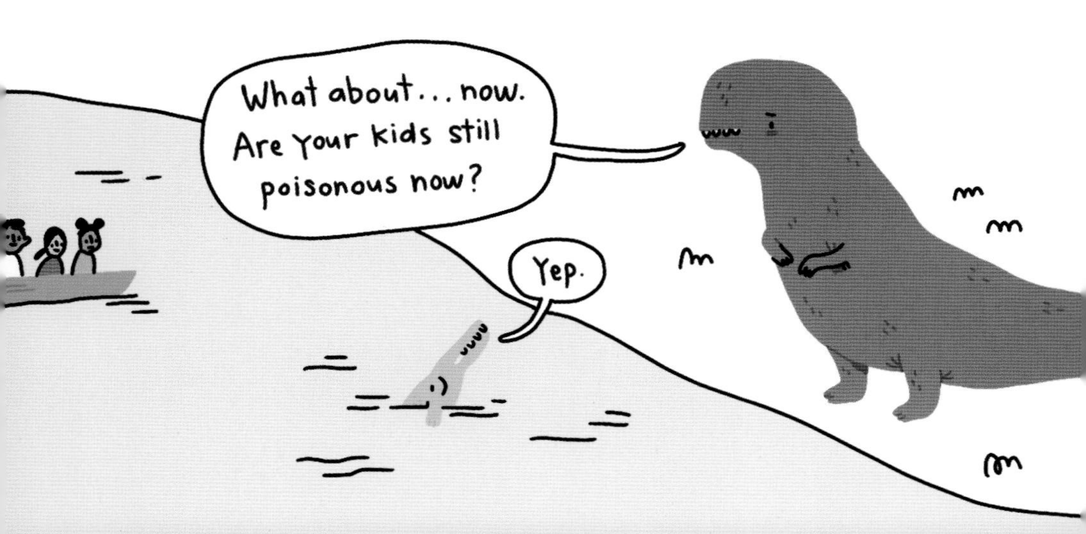
What about... now. Are your kids still poisonous now?
Yep.

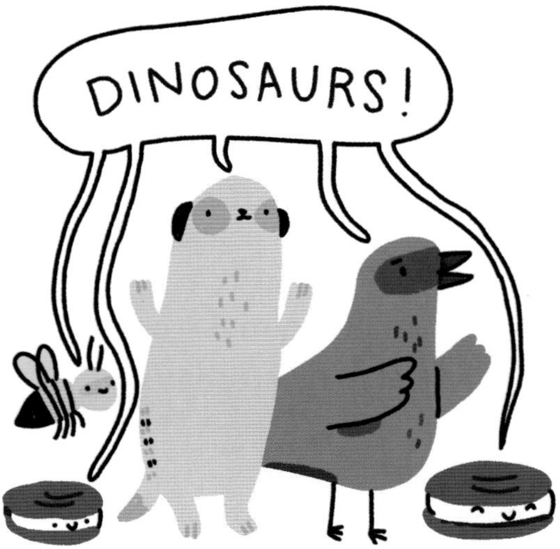
DINOSAURS!

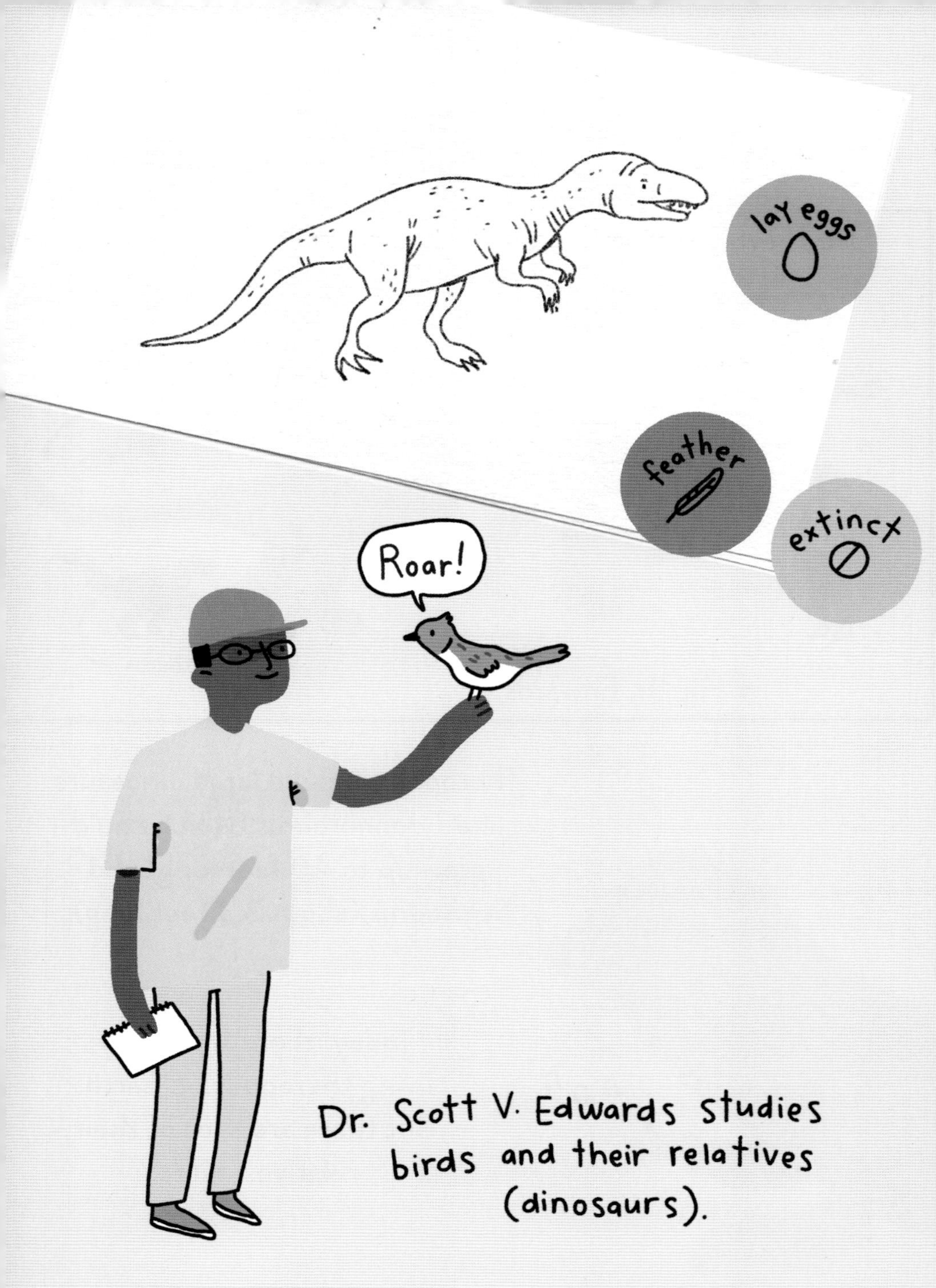
lay eggs
feather
extinct
Roar!

Dr. Scott V. Edwards studies birds and their relatives (dinosaurs).

DINOSAURS

Birds evolved from a group of dinosaurs called theropods.

ROAR*
Allosaurus
Dilophosaurus
Segisaurus

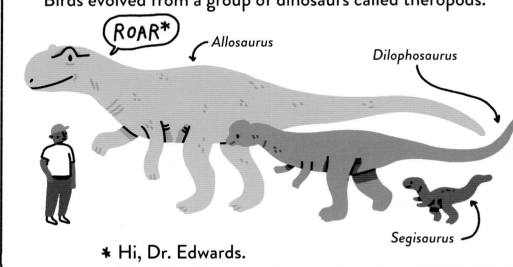

* Hi, Dr. Edwards.

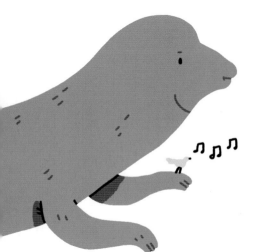

Theropods include large dinosaurs like *Tyrannosaurus* (which could grow up to 40 feet long) and *Segisaurus* (about 3.3 feet long).

Today, there aren't any living theropods on Earth. But there are a lot of their relatives: birds.

Even though a sparrow doesn't *look* very much like a *T. rex*, theropods and birds have a lot in common.

hollow bones

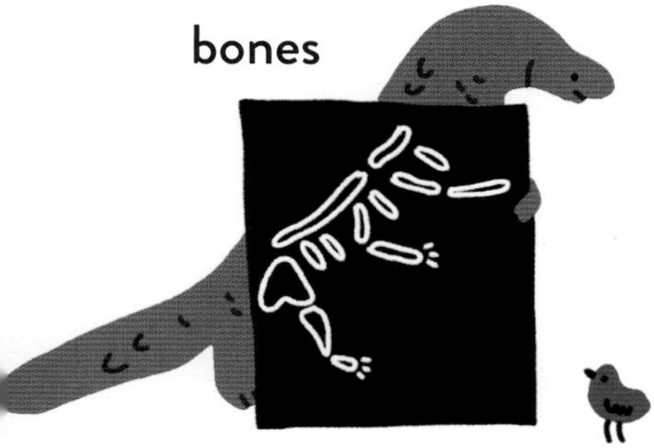

a furcula

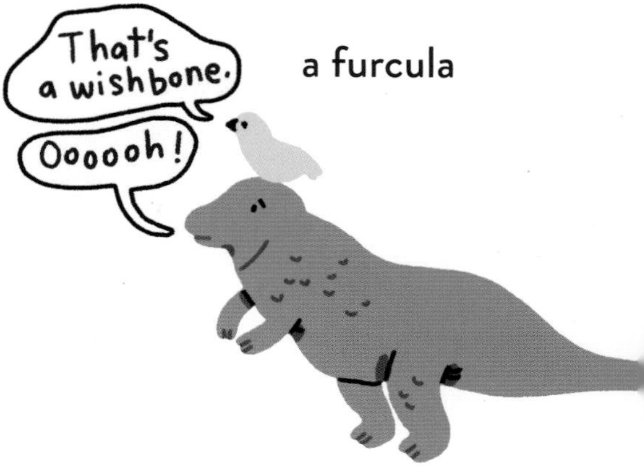
That's a wishbone.
Oooooh!

three main toes on their back limbs

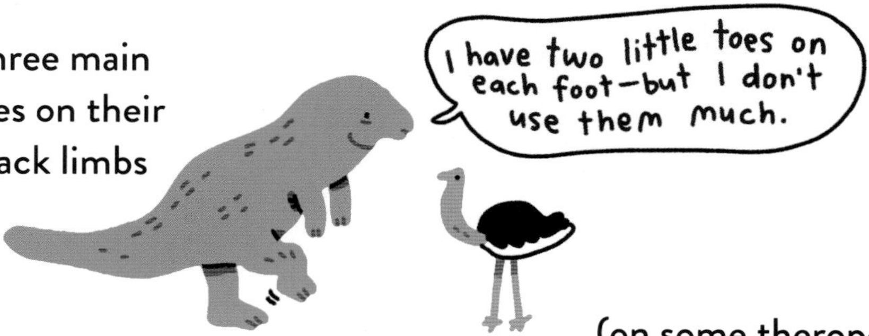
I have two little toes on each foot—but I don't use them much.

(on some theropods) feathers

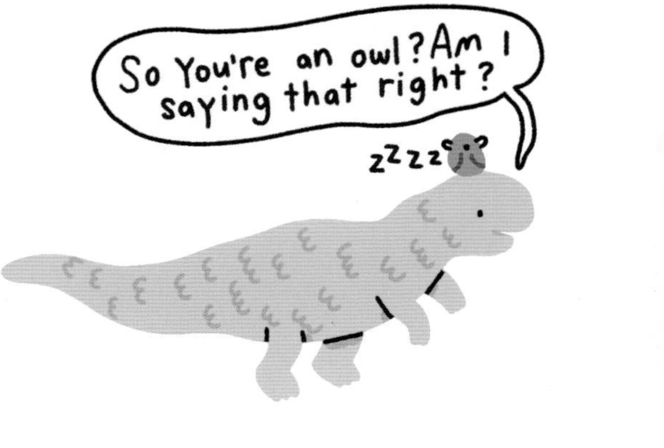
So You're an owl? Am I saying that right?
zzzz

and air sacs near their lungs to help them breathe.

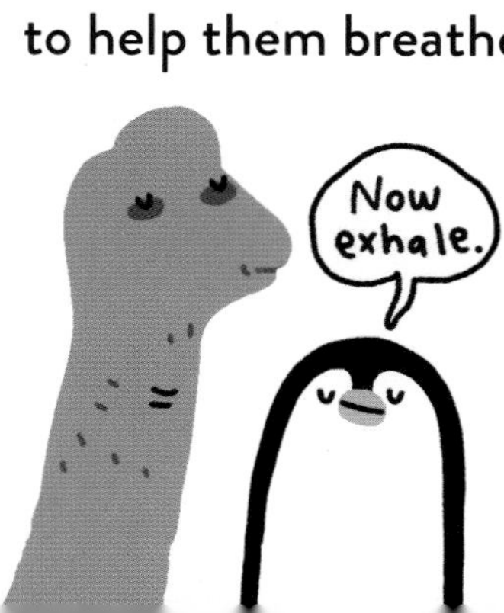
Now exhale.

Many scientists use fossils to study dinosaurs. Fossils exist because a dinosaur skeleton was buried in something wet, and turned to stone over thousands of years. There are fossilized bones, teeth, and even poop.

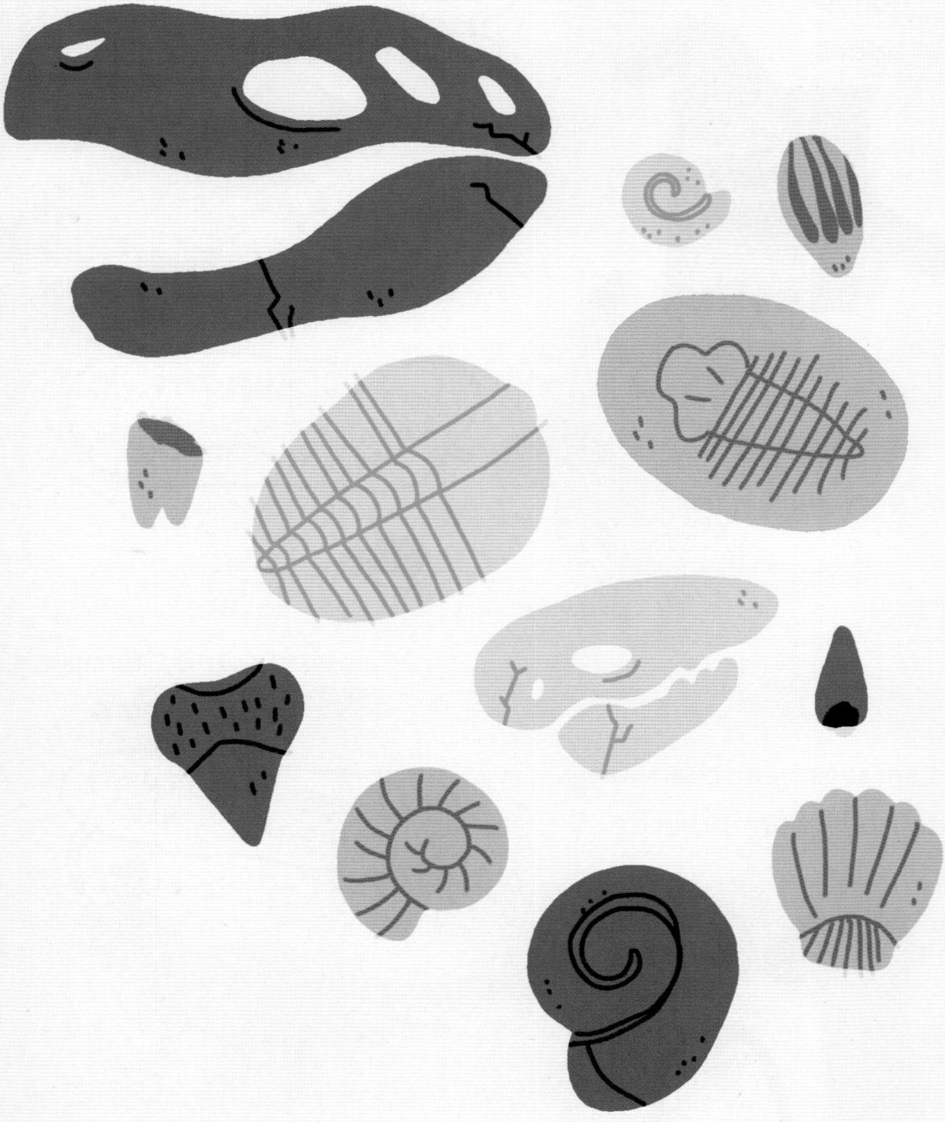

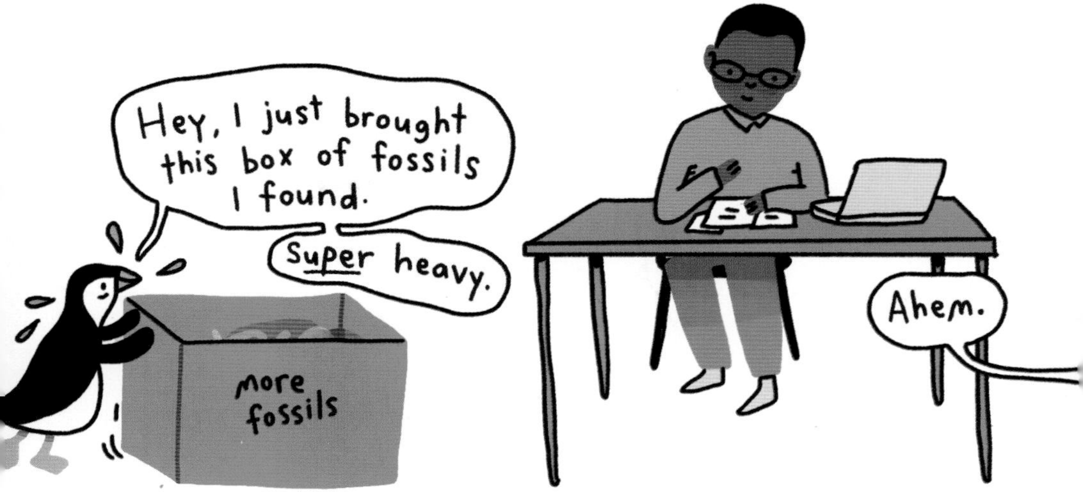
Hey, I just brought this box of fossils I found.
Super heavy.
more fossils
Ahem.

But Dr. Edwards and his team can learn new information by looking closely at the DNA of birds.

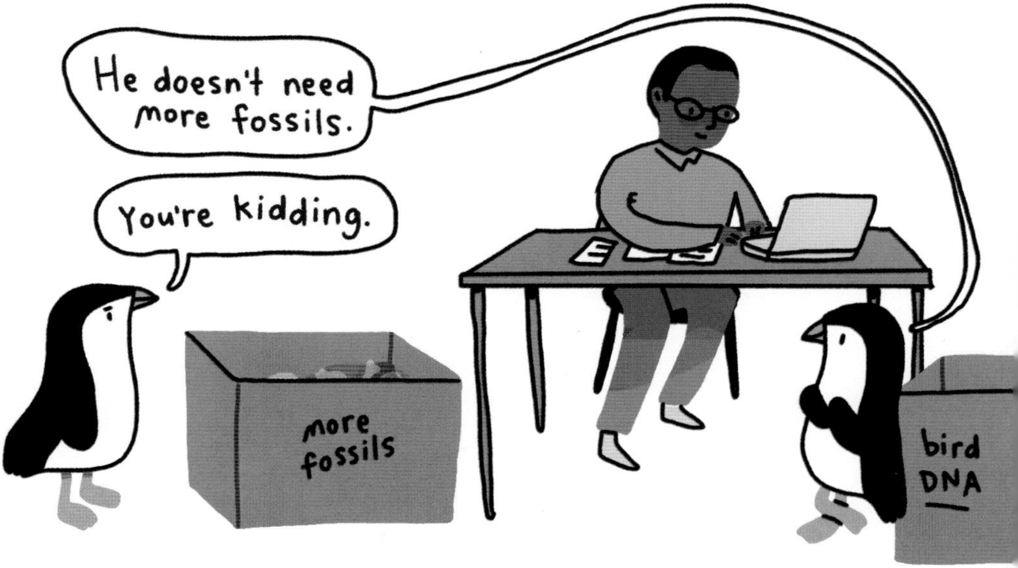
He doesn't need more fossils.
You're kidding.
more fossils
bird DNA

A bird's DNA (or a person's DNA or a plant's DNA) has all the information the bird (or person or plant) needs to grow and be a bird (or person or plant).

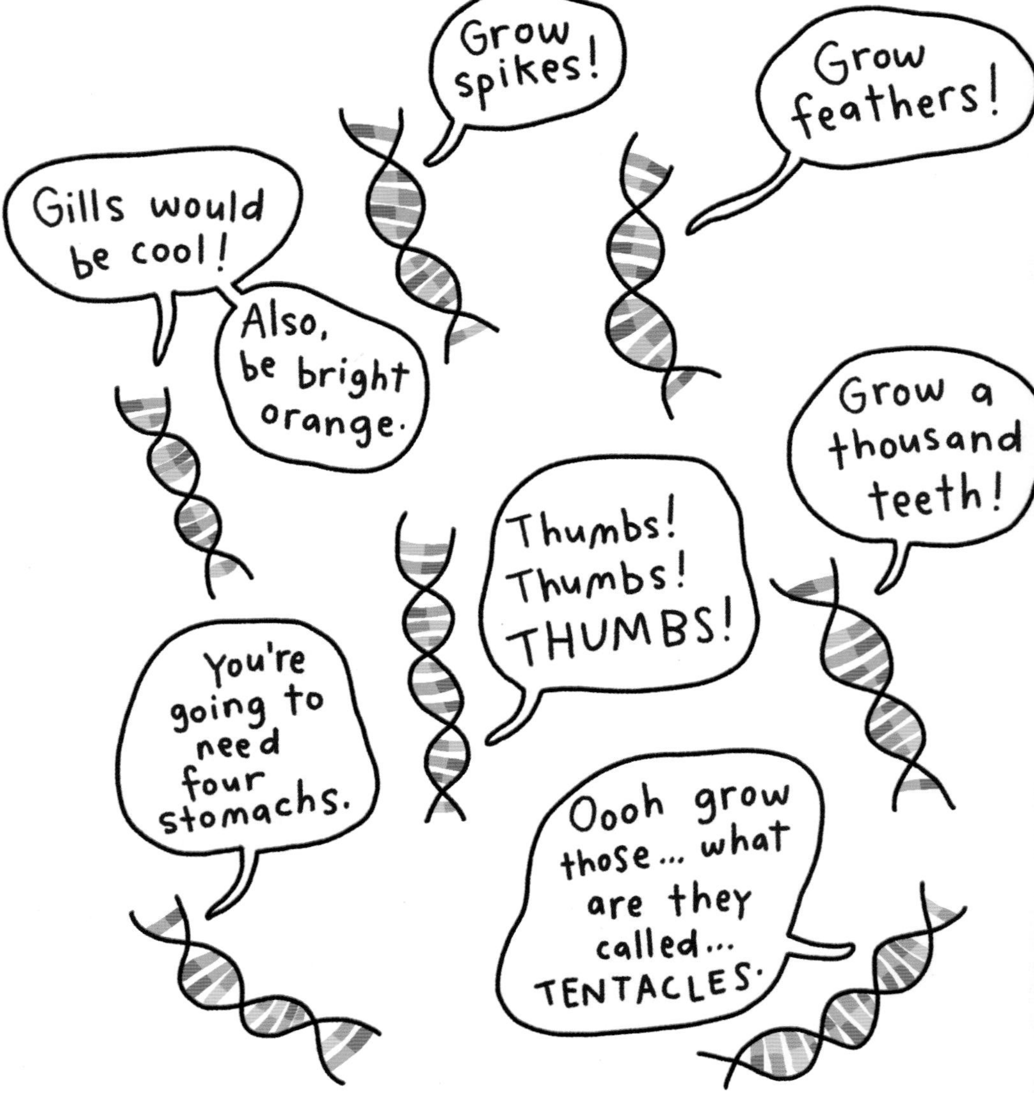
Grow spikes!
Grow feathers!
Gills would be cool!
Also, be bright orange.
Grow a thousand teeth!
Thumbs! Thumbs! THUMBS!
You're going to need four stomachs.
Oooh grow those... what are they called... TENTACLES.

The information is called a genome.

When Dr. Edwards looks at the DNA of birds, he looks for similarities and differences between bird genomes and theropod genomes.

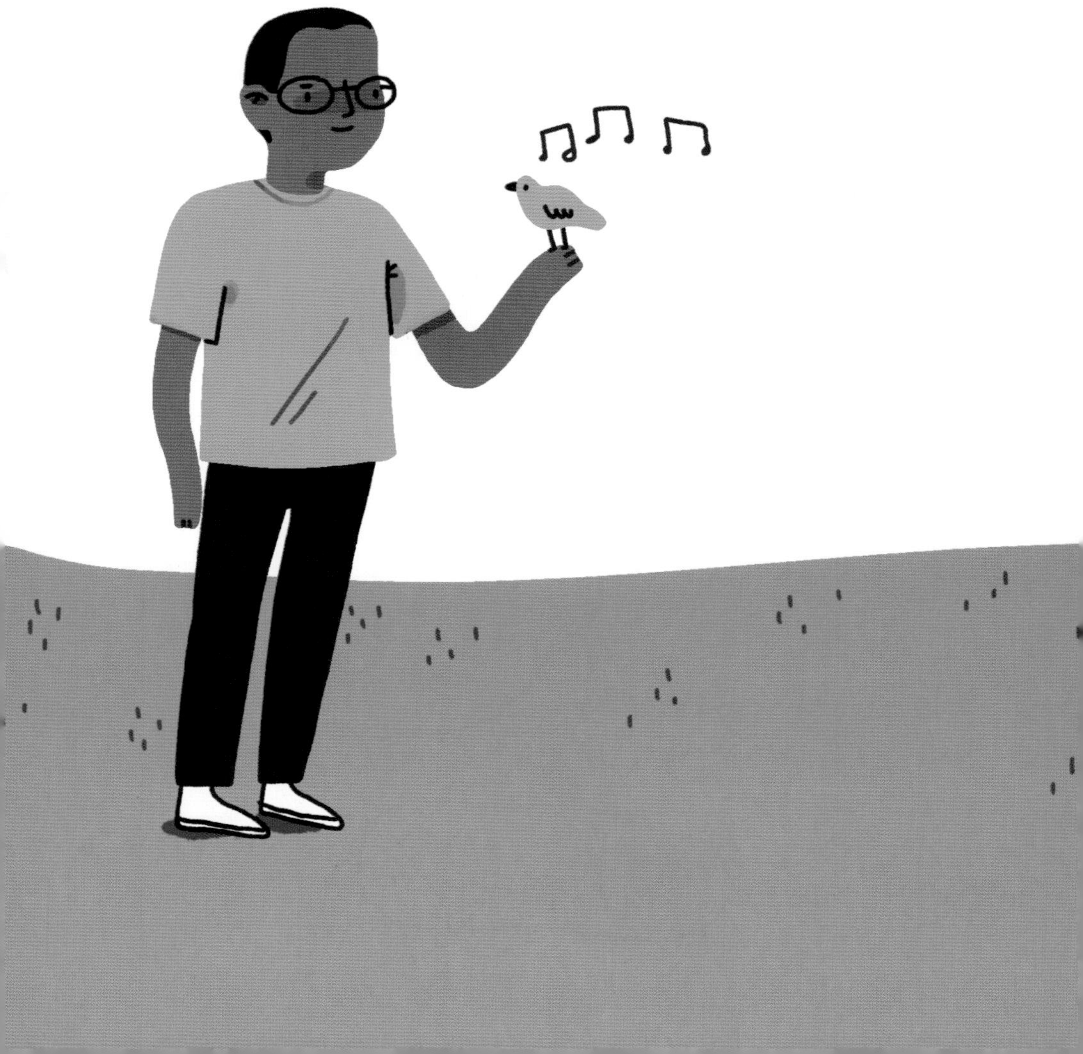

Genomes are made of blocks called base pairs.
A human genome has over 3 billion base pairs.

Dimples!
Eyelashes!
Look how sunburned I can get!

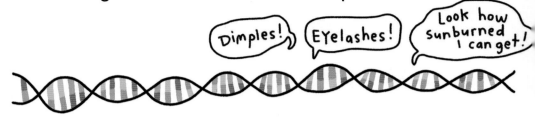

A humpback whale genome has fewer—
about 2.7 billion base pairs.

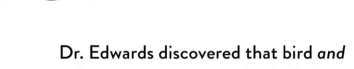

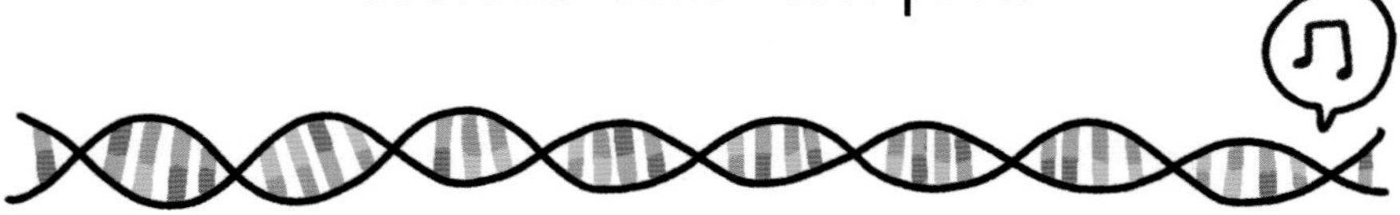

Dr. Edwards discovered that bird *and*
dinosaur genomes are both short,
only 1.5 billion base pairs.

Hey, 1.5 billion is still a lot actually.

A banana genome has
520 million base pairs.

And all of them are delicious.

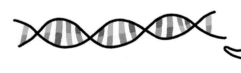

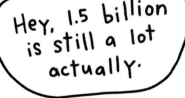

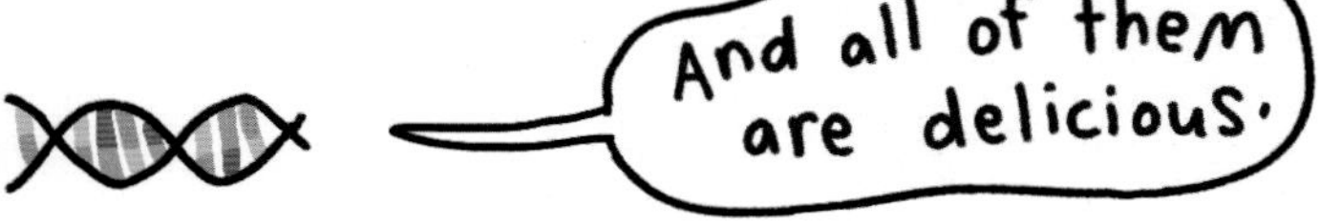

Studying bird genomes is another way to prove that birds and theropods are relatives.

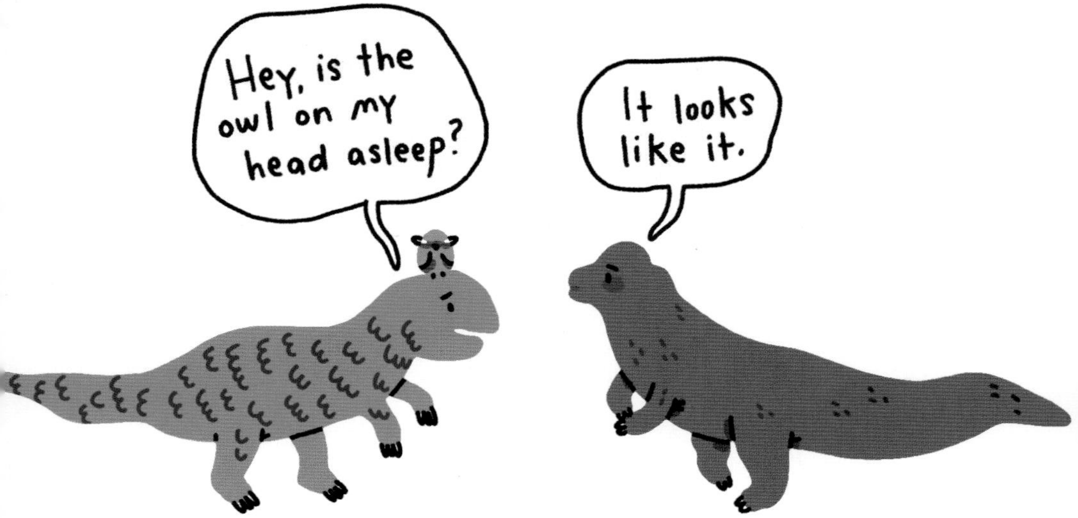
Hey, is the owl on my head asleep?
It looks like it.

And it helps Dr. Edwards learn about how these ancient creatures became the animal relatives we know today.

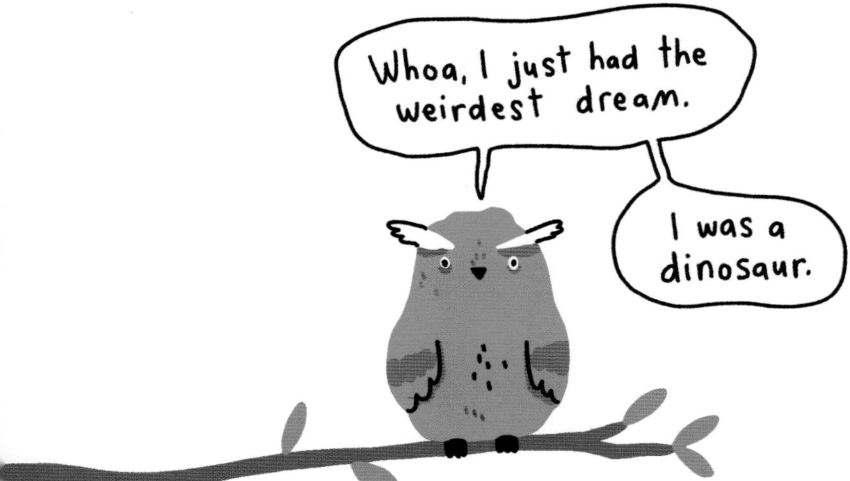
Whoa, I just had the weirdest dream.
I was a dinosaur.

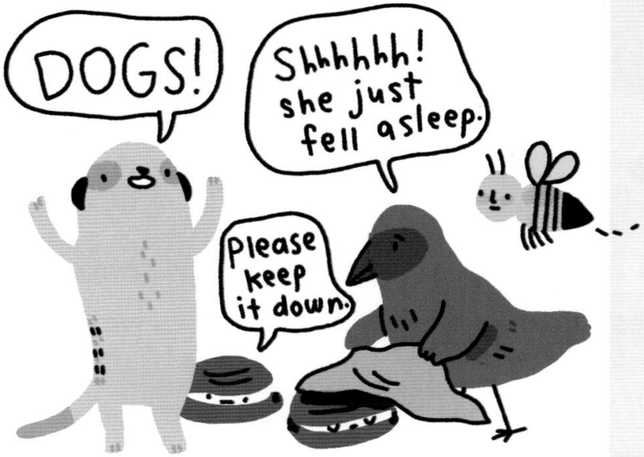
DOGS!
Shhhhhh! she just fell asleep.
Please keep it down.

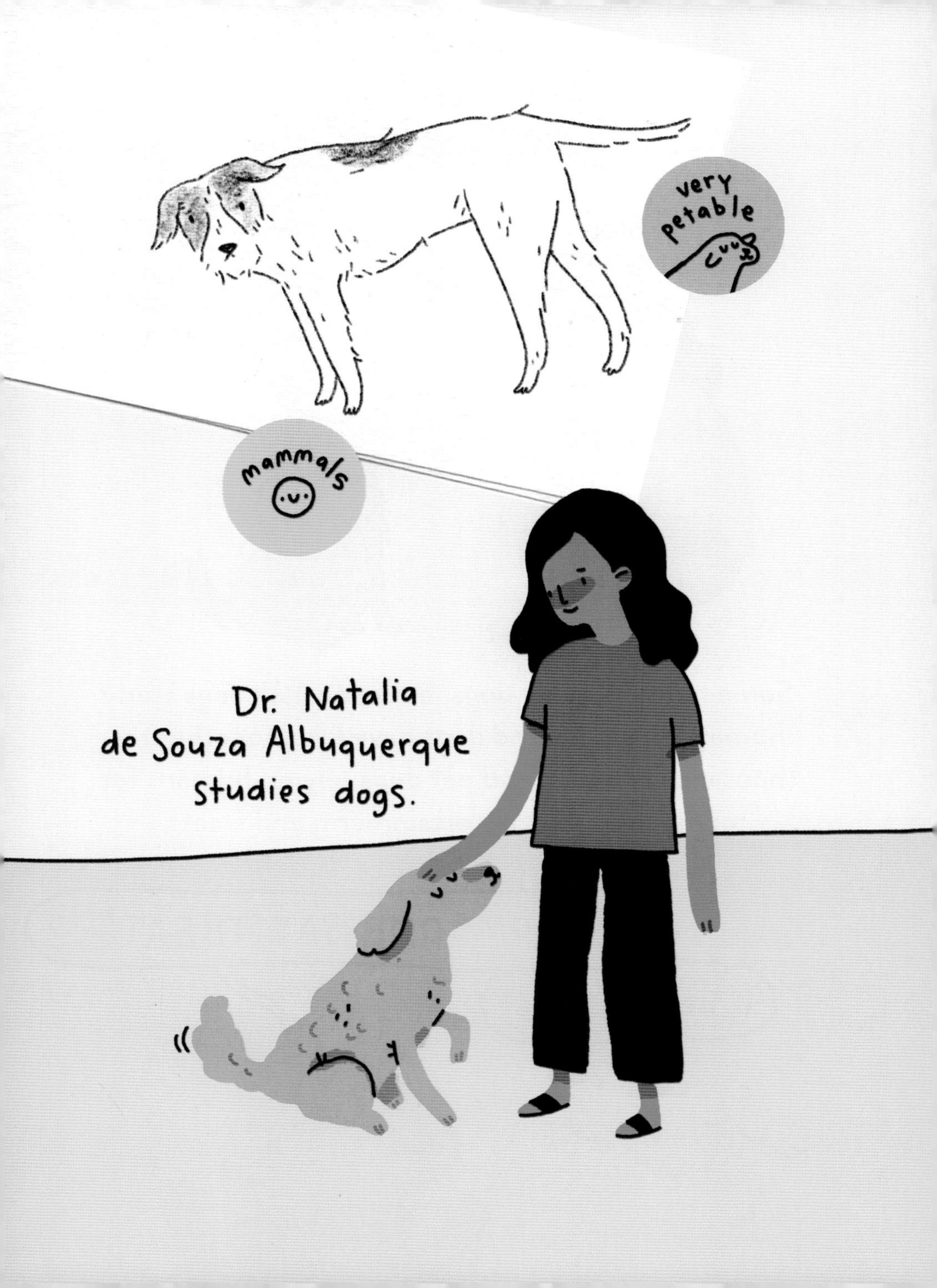
very petable
mammals

Dr. Natalia de Souza Albuquerque studies dogs.

DOGS

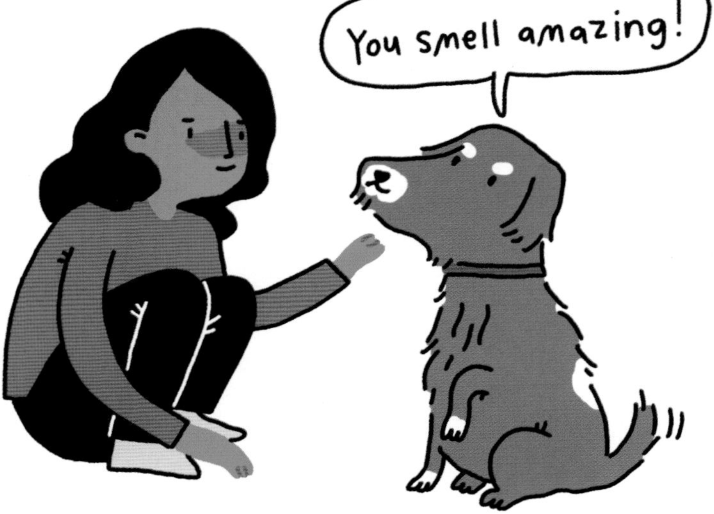
You smell amazing!

Some humans study dogs, but almost all dogs study humans. Humans and dogs have lived together for thousands of years, and pet dogs rely on humans for companionship, entertainment, and treats.

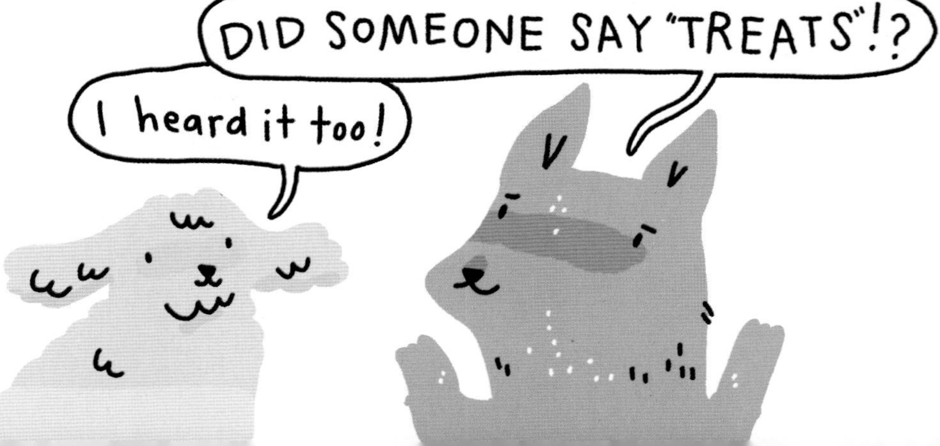
DID SOMEONE SAY "TREATS"!?
I heard it too!

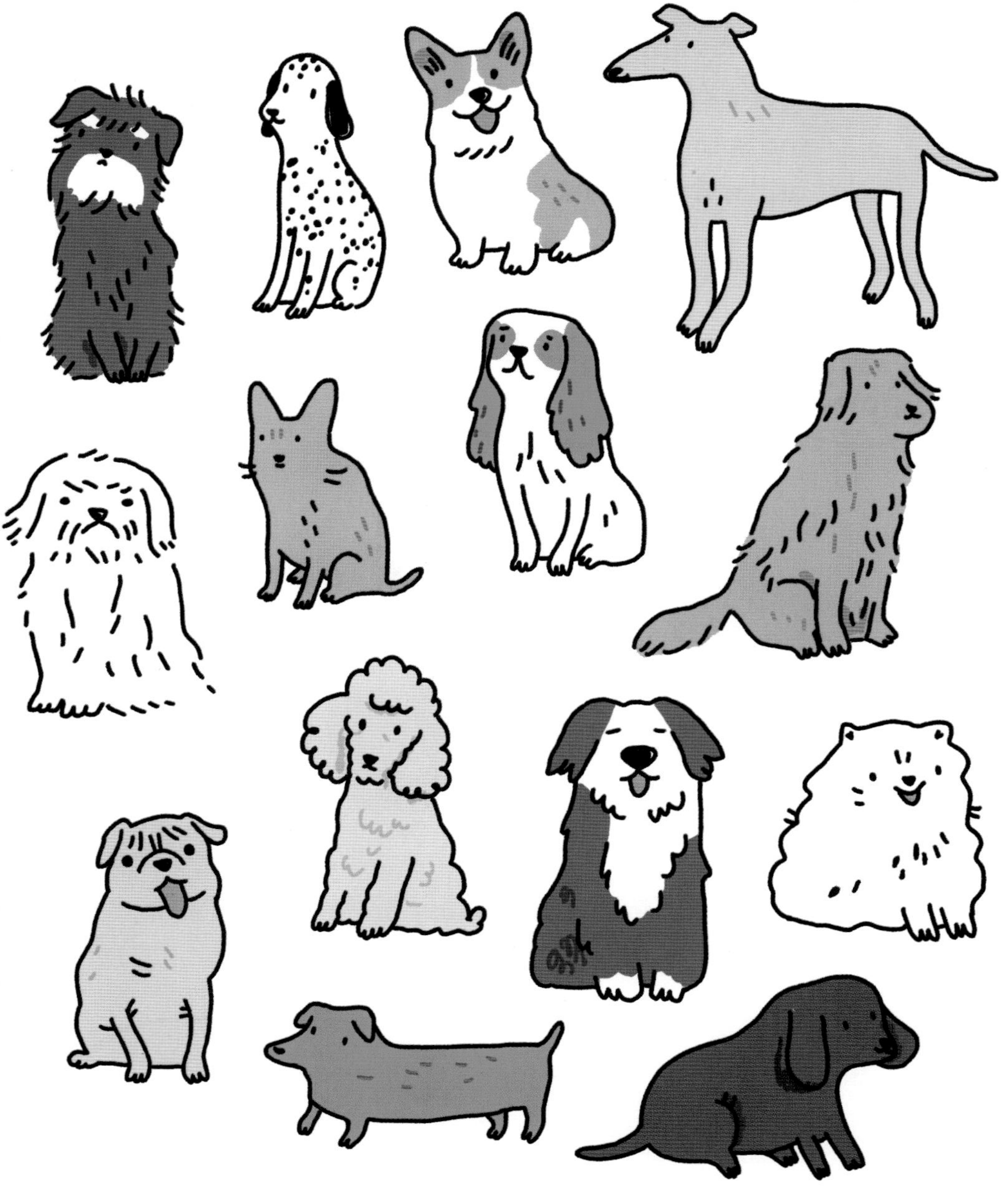

Dr. de Souza Albuquerque studies the way dogs understand human emotions.

Natalia has always loved animals. When she was a kid she carried around animal encyclopedias, and said when she grew up she wanted to understand what animals think and feel.

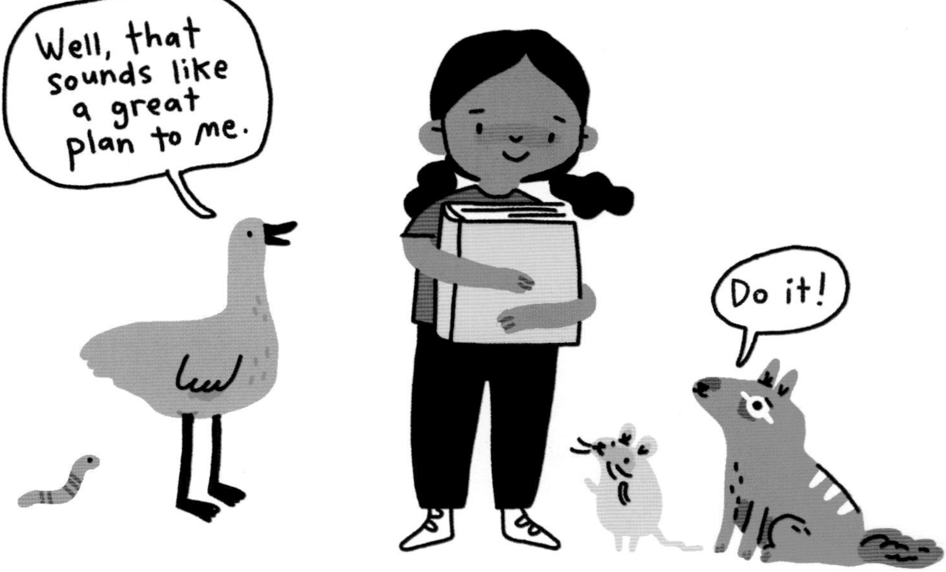
Well, that sounds like a great plan to me.
Do it!

She decided to study biology.

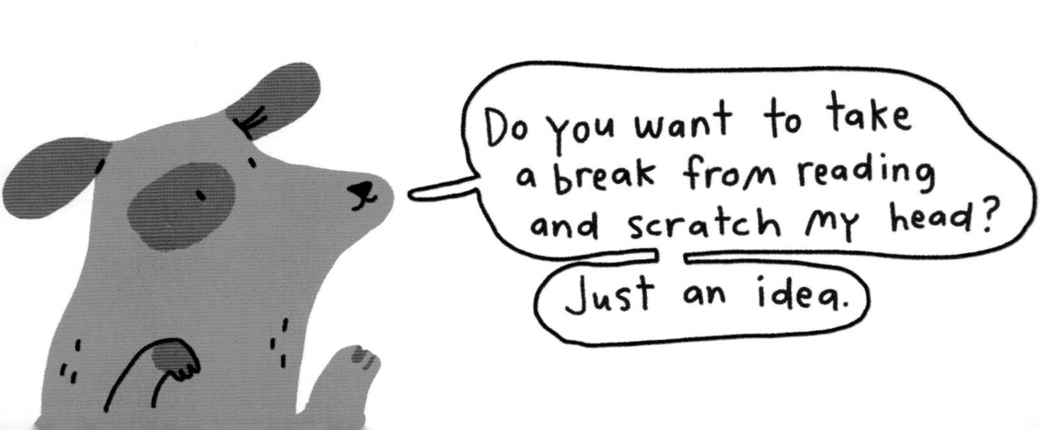
Do you want to take a break from reading and scratch my head?
Just an idea.

Her dog Polly, who lived with her for ten years, is the inspiration for her research.

And in the future, she'd also like to study the social and emotional skills of goats, cats, cows, and sea turtles.

Animals need to be able to recognize each other's moods to get along, and just survive.

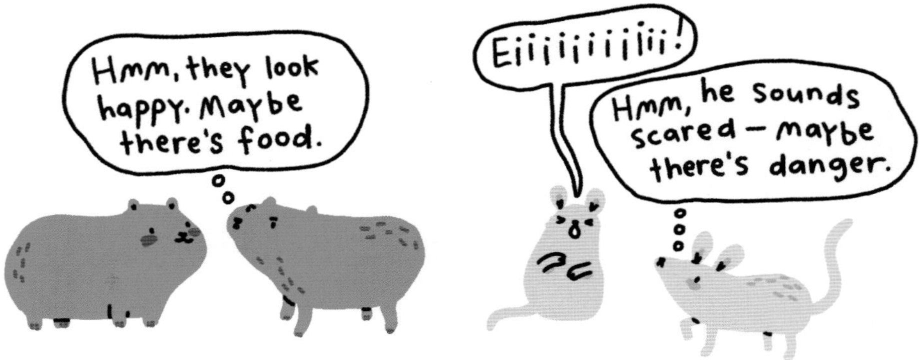
Hmm, they look happy. Maybe there's food.
Eiiiiiiiiiii!
Hmm, he sounds scared—maybe there's danger.

Animals use body language

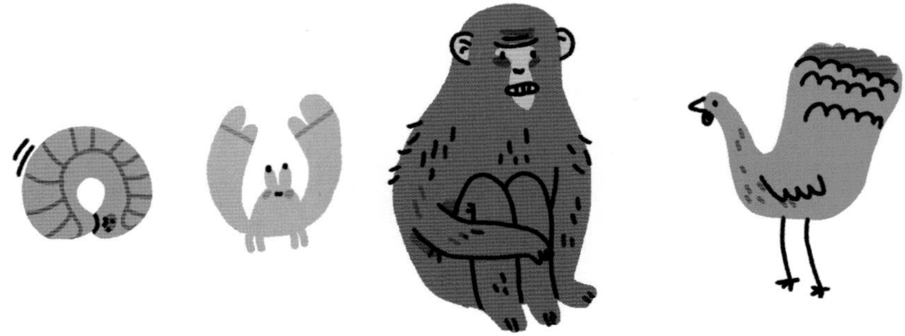

and sounds

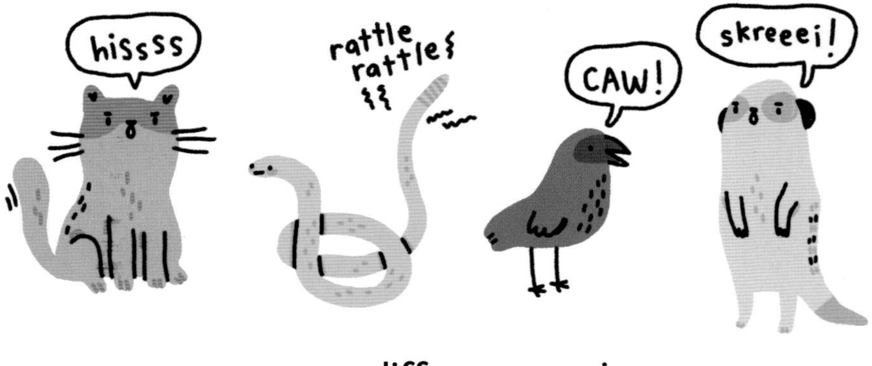
hissss
rattle rattle
CAW!
skreeei!

to express different emotions.

Some animals also use smell, but this isn't about smell.

And animals that can understand and *combine* a bunch of different clues can understand emotions faster and better.

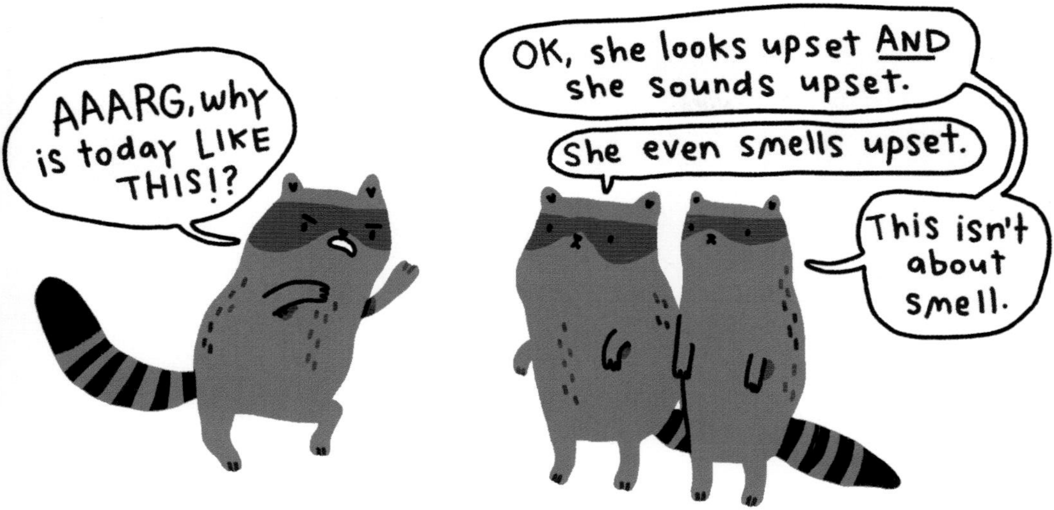
AAARG, why is today LIKE THIS!?
OK, she looks upset AND she sounds upset.
She even smells upset.
This isn't about smell.

Of course, it's not just animals that do this. Humans make happy and upset sounds and faces too.

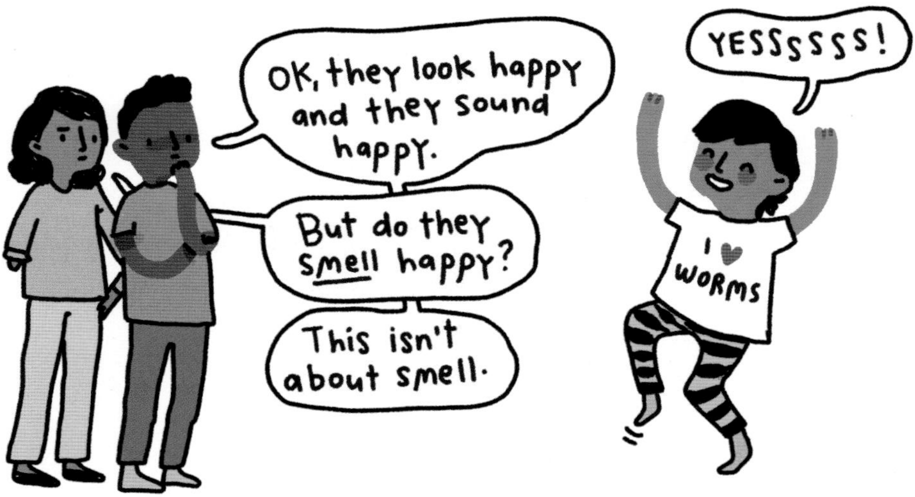
OK, they look happy and they sound happy.
But do they smell happy?
This isn't about smell.
YESSSSSS!
I ♥ WORMS

Dr. de Souza Albuquerque and her team wondered if dogs could *combine* these human clues.

Dr. de Souza Albuquerque's team chose photos of people and dogs making happy and upset faces.

same person   same dog

And they chose recordings of people and dogs that sounded happy or upset.

Let's go to the park!   What a great smell!

Where are my keys!?!   THIS LEAF SCARES ME!

To make sure that human words didn't give the dogs any clues, they used recordings of people speaking Portuguese, and did their study on dogs whose owners didn't speak Portuguese.

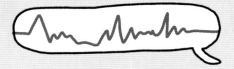

They also chose a recording of Brownian noise, a sound that doesn't sound happy or upset—just neutral.

Dr. de Souza Albuquerque and her team flew from Brazil to the United Kingdom to study the dogs there. They put each dog in a quiet room with two screens and a speaker . . .

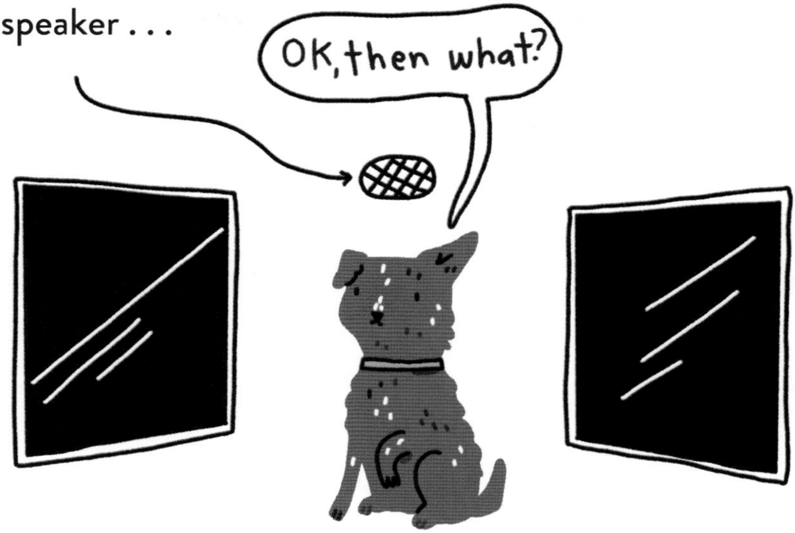
OK, then what?

and showed the dog two faces and played it one of the sounds.

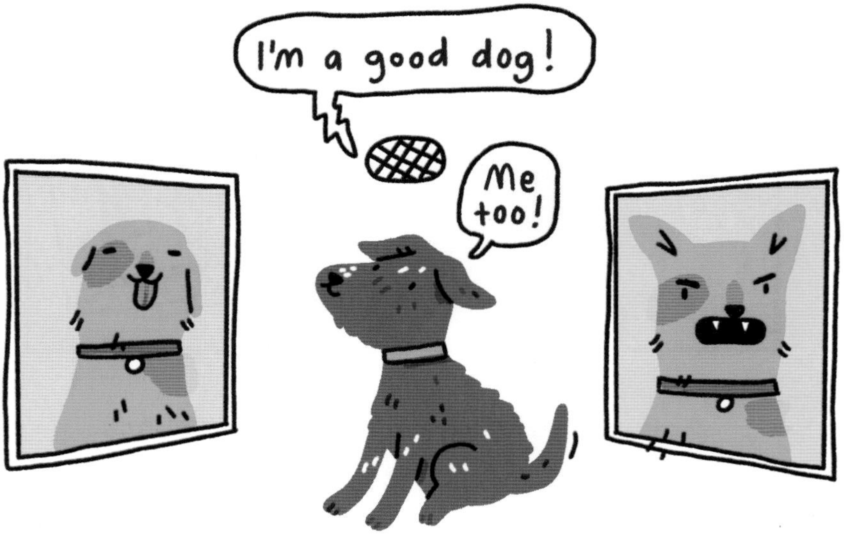
I'm a good dog!
Me too!

Dr. de Souza Albuquerque and her team recorded the dogs.

When she and other researchers watched the recordings, they saw that when happy sounds played, the dogs spent more time looking at the happy faces than the sad faces.

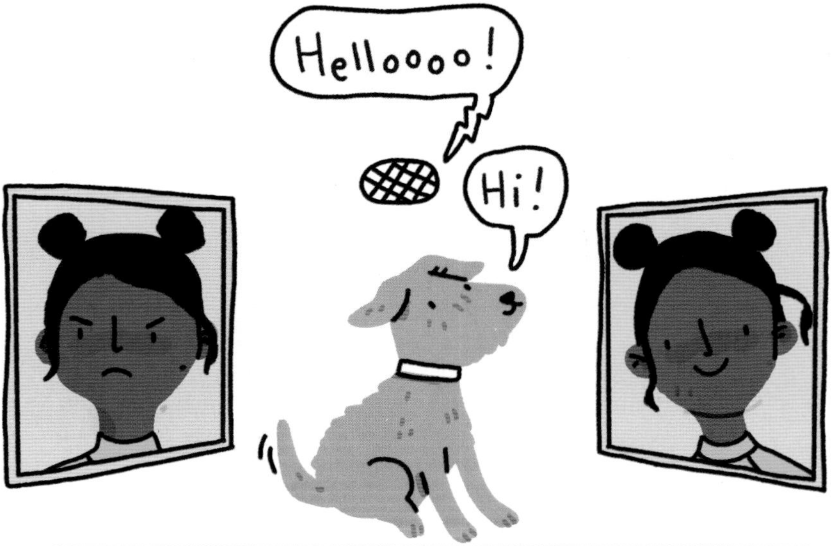
Helloooo!
Hi!

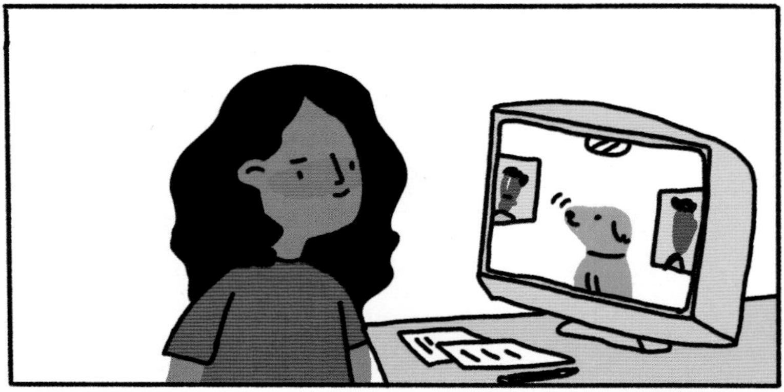

And when they heard the upset sounds,
the dog spent more time looking at upset faces.
This means dogs can combine visual and sound clues to
understand human emotions faster and better.

Before Dr. de Souza Albuquerque's research, no one knew for sure that any animal could combine human clues this way.

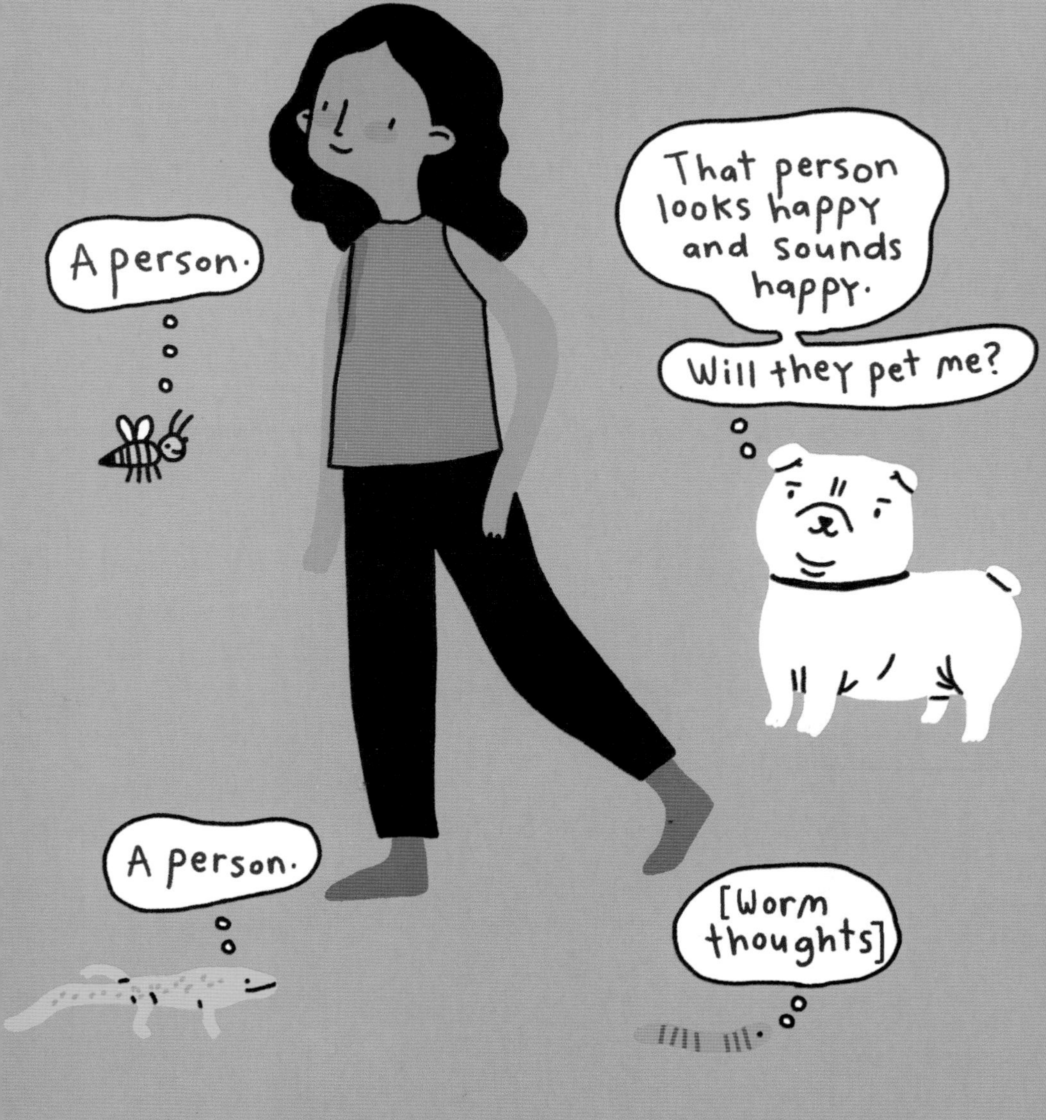
A person.
That person looks happy and sounds happy.
Will they pet me?
A person.
[Worm thoughts]

Should we wake her up? I don't want her to miss Dr. McGee.
ZZZZ

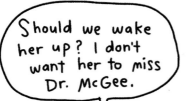

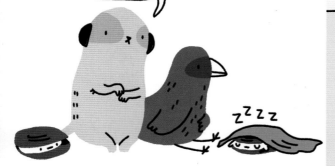

Dr. Earyn McGee studies lizards.

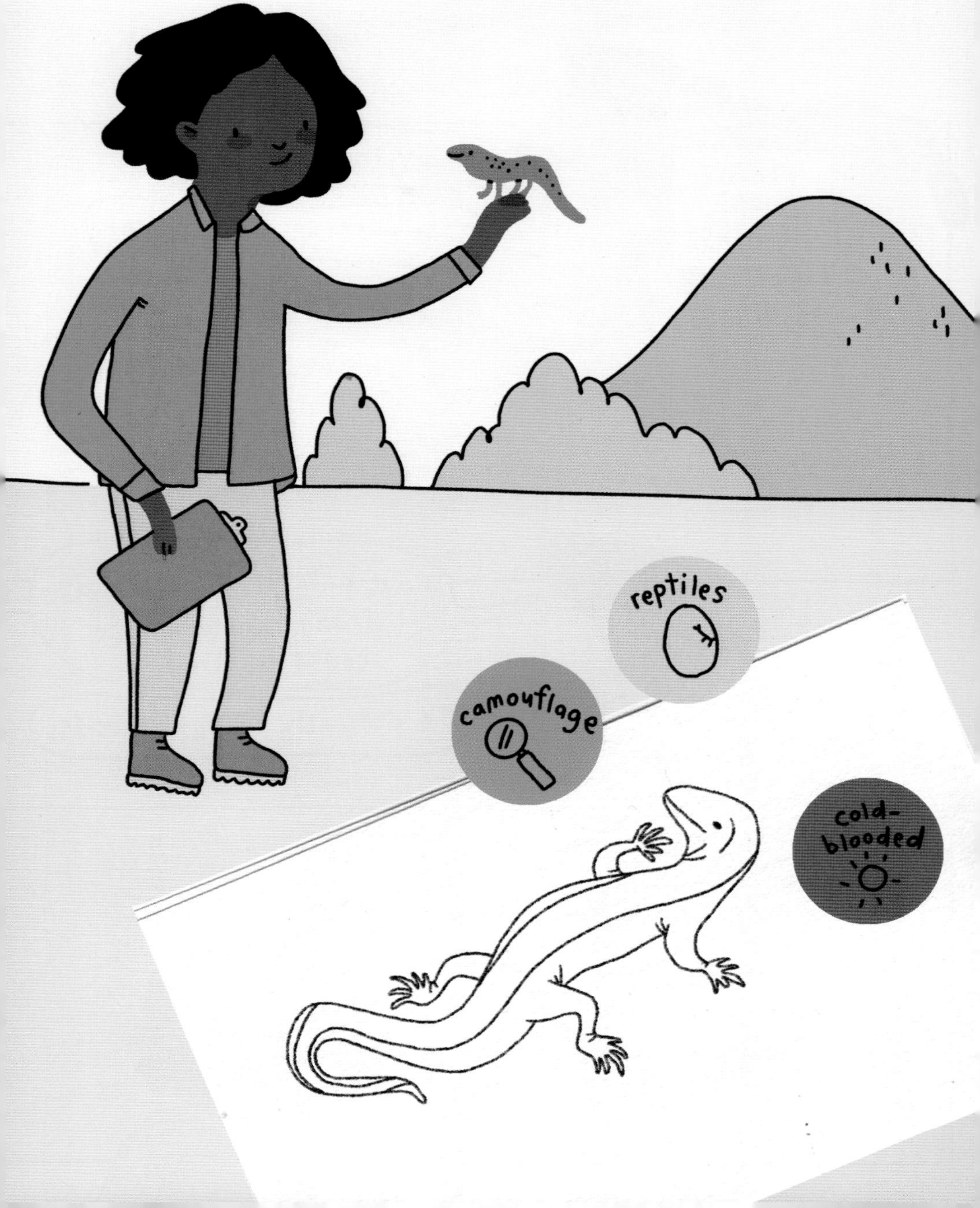
reptiles
camouflage
cold-blooded

LIZARDS

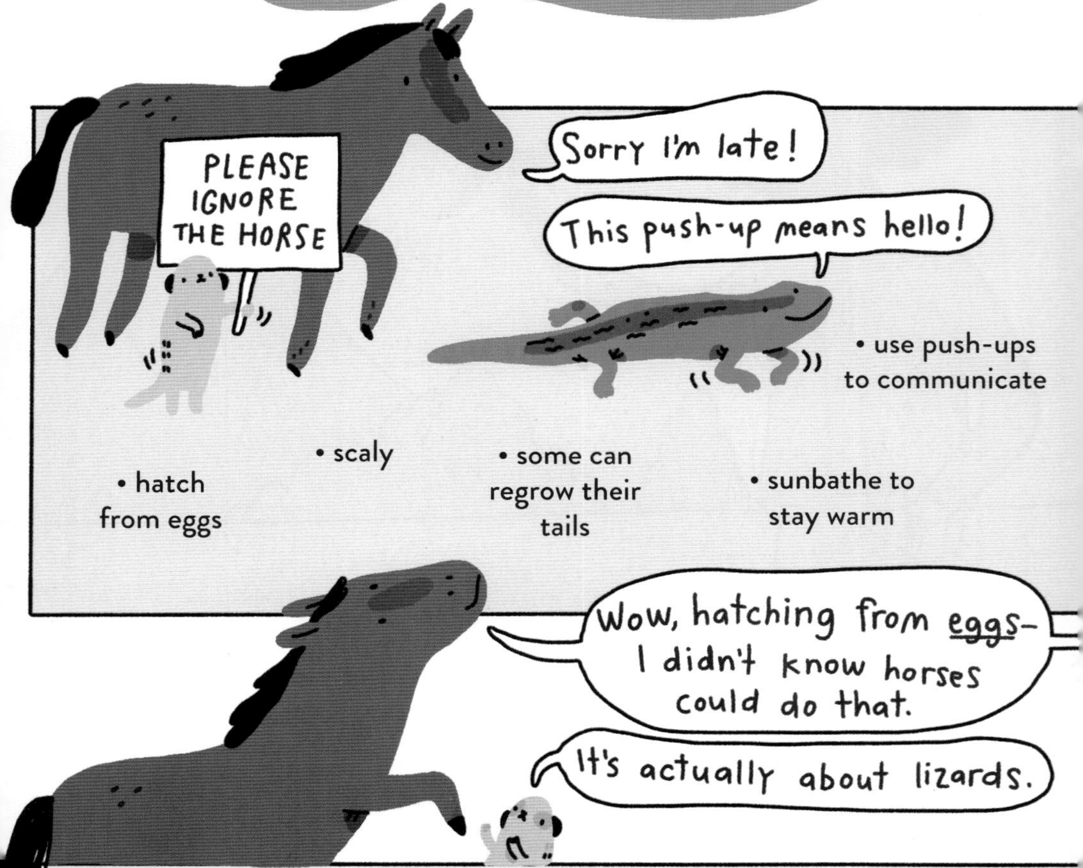
PLEASE IGNORE THE HORSE
Sorry I'm late!
This push-up means hello!
• use push-ups to communicate
• hatch from eggs
• scaly
• some can regrow their tails
• sunbathe to stay warm
Wow, hatching from eggs— I didn't know horses could do that.
It's actually about lizards.

She didn't realize she loved lizards until she met a herpetologist (that's a scientist who studies reptiles and amphibians). Now she's a lizard expert.

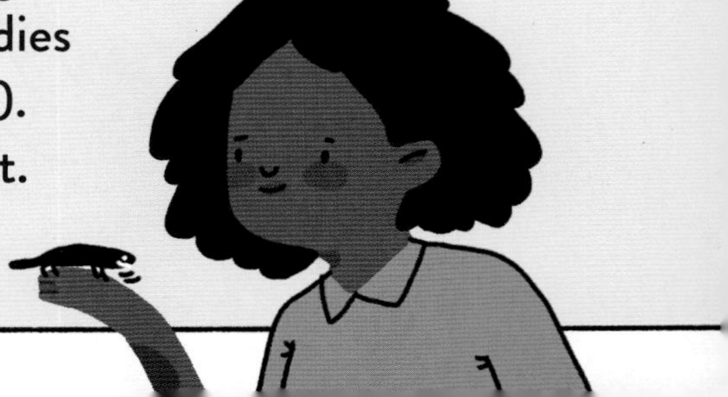

Lizards eat insects.

But scientists aren't sure *what kind* of insects they eat:
aquatic or *terrestrial*.

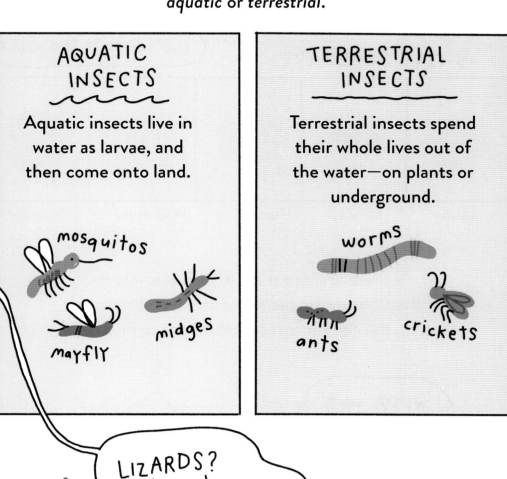

AQUATIC INSECTS

Aquatic insects live in water as larvae, and then come onto land.

mosquitos

mayfly

midges

TERRESTRIAL INSECTS

Terrestrial insects spend their whole lives out of the water—on plants or underground.

worms

ants

crickets

LIZARDS? What am I doing here then?

I don't know.

As the climate changes, there is more and more drought, and the streams where these lizards live are shrinking. That means there are fewer places for aquatic insects to lay their eggs.

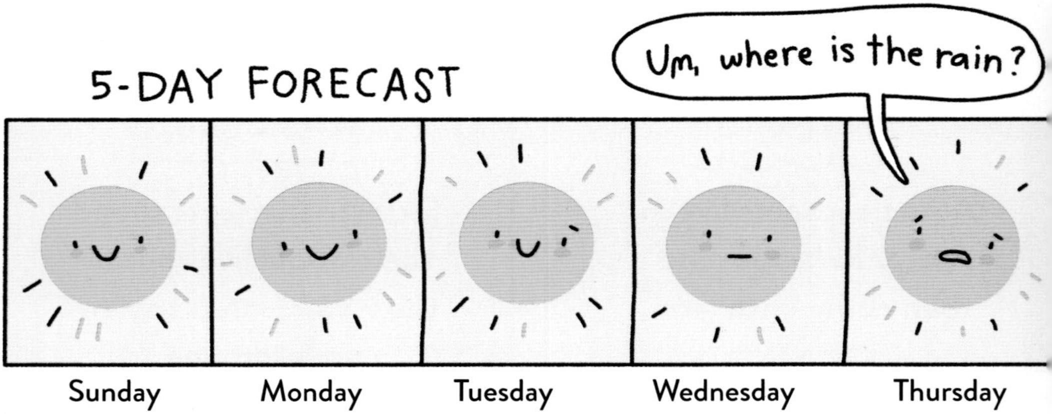
Um, where is the rain?
5-DAY FORECAST
Sunday
Monday
Tuesday
Wednesday
Thursday

If these lizards eat mostly aquatic insects, they'll be in trouble as the streams shrink and the aquatic insects are harder to find.

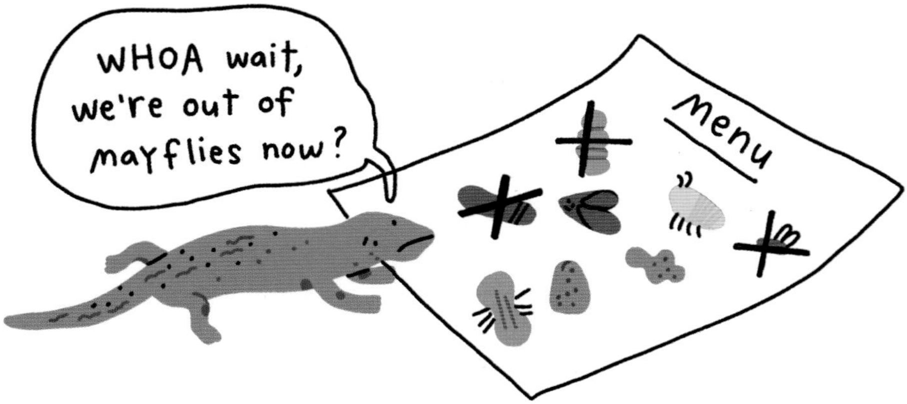
WHOA wait, we're out of mayflies now?
menu

But if the lizards eat mostly insects that lay their eggs on dry land, it won't be as big a problem.

Dr. McGee is studying lizard diets to discover whether aquatic insects are an important food source.

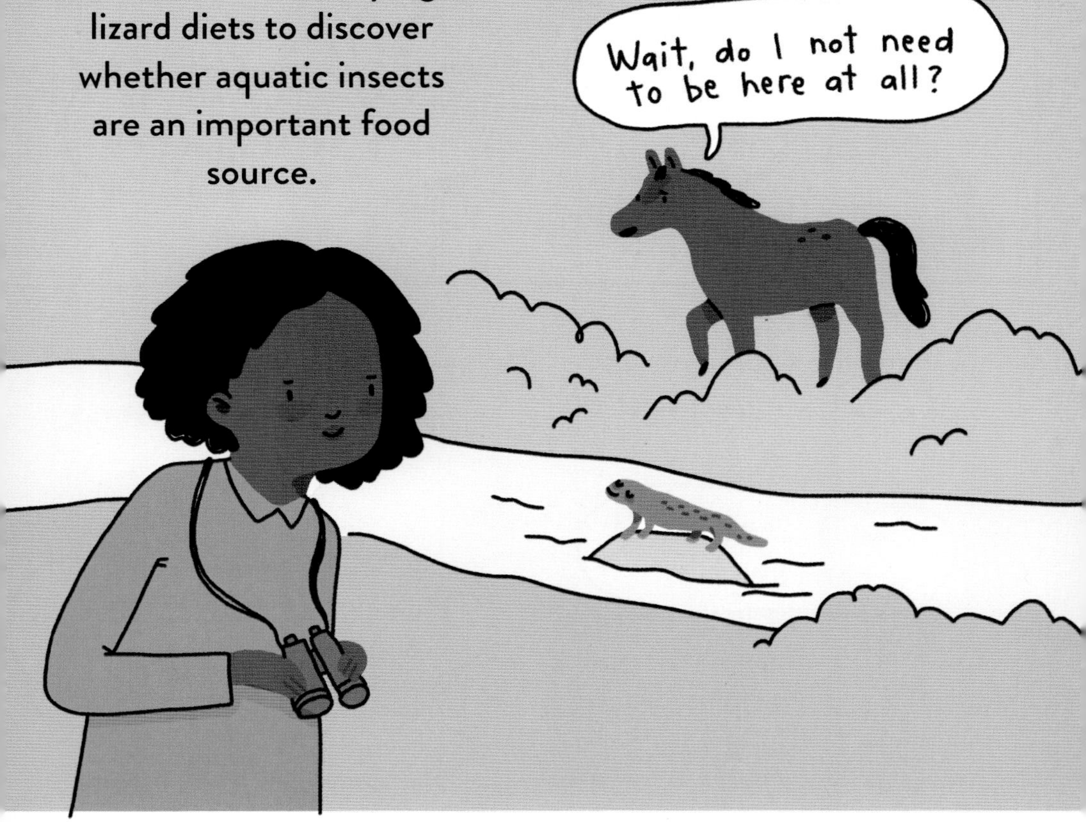
Wait, do I not need to be here at all?

She and her team visit streams to look for lizards, and study the lizard poop to discover what they're eating.

Lizards are great at camouflage.
But Dr. McGee is great at seeing them.

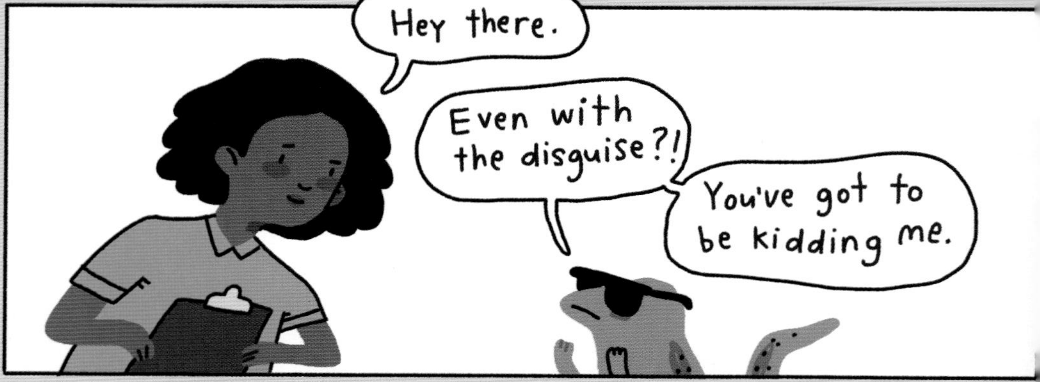
Hey there.
Even with the disguise?!
You've got to be kidding me.

Once, she took a photo of a well-hidden lizard.

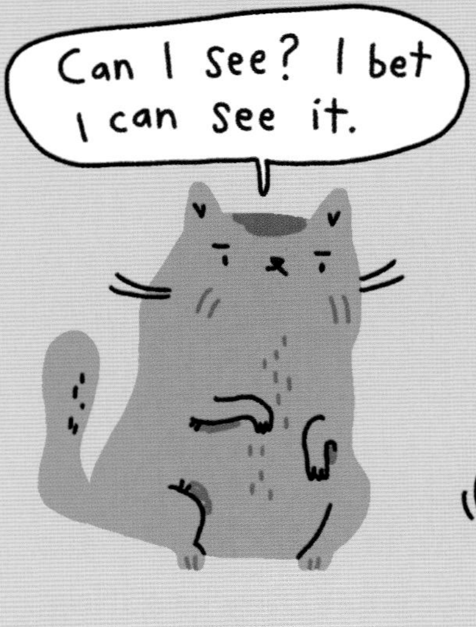
Can I see? I bet I can see it.

And when she shared the photo online, almost no one could see it.

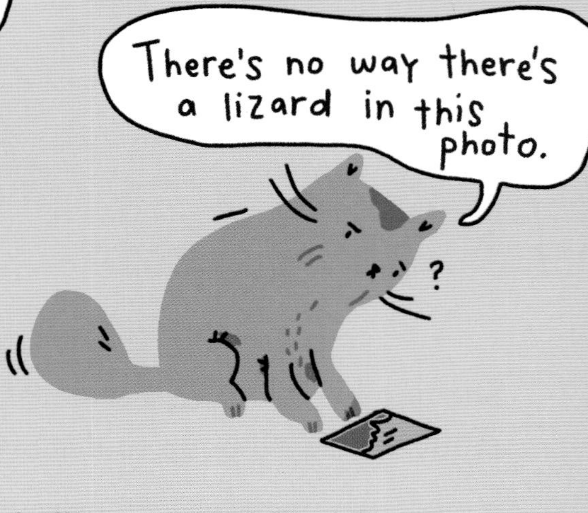
There's no way there's a lizard in this photo.
?

Now she hosts a weekly challenge called Find That Lizard.

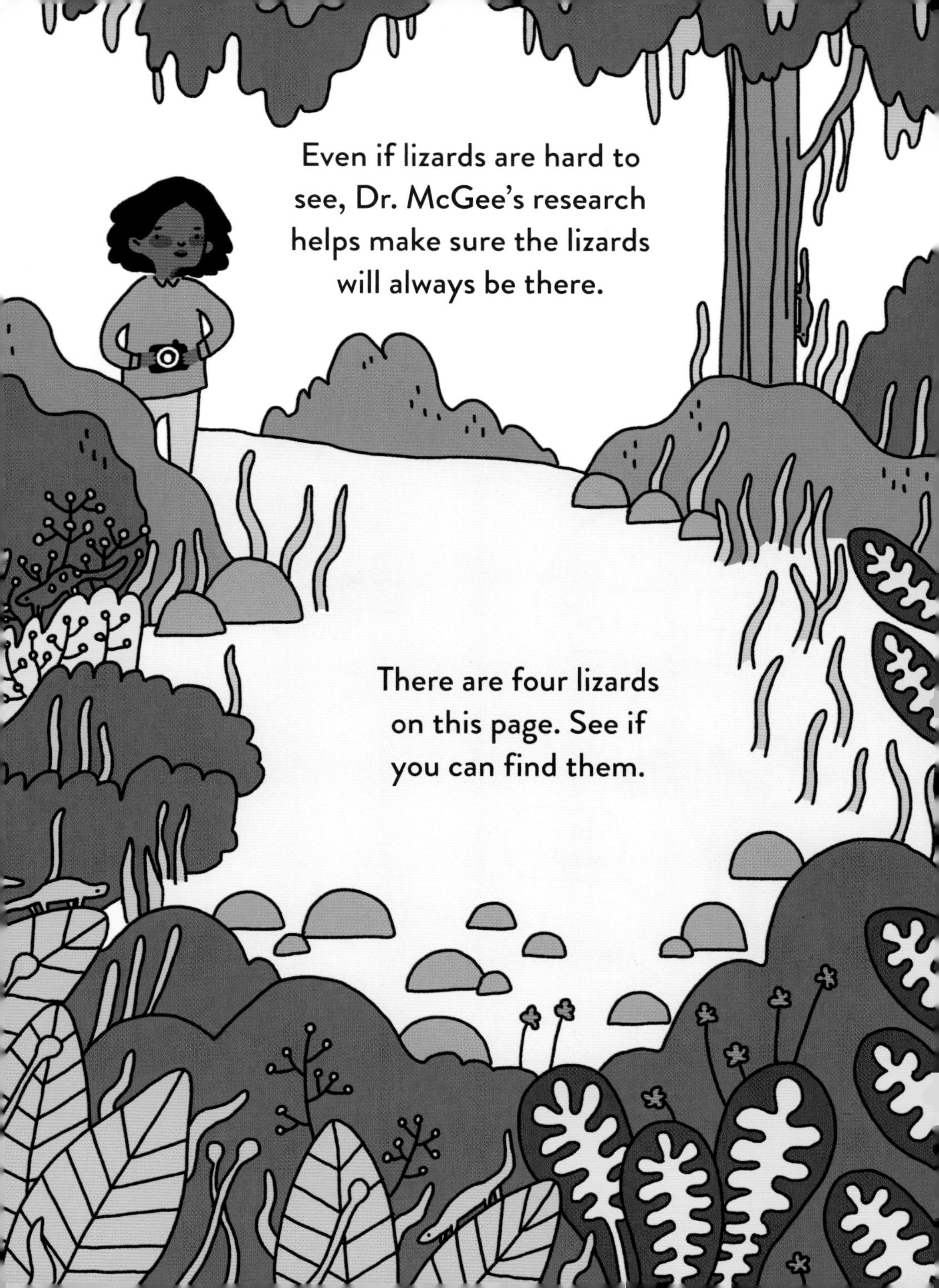

Even if lizards are hard to see, Dr. McGee's research helps make sure the lizards will always be there.

There are four lizards on this page. See if you can find them.

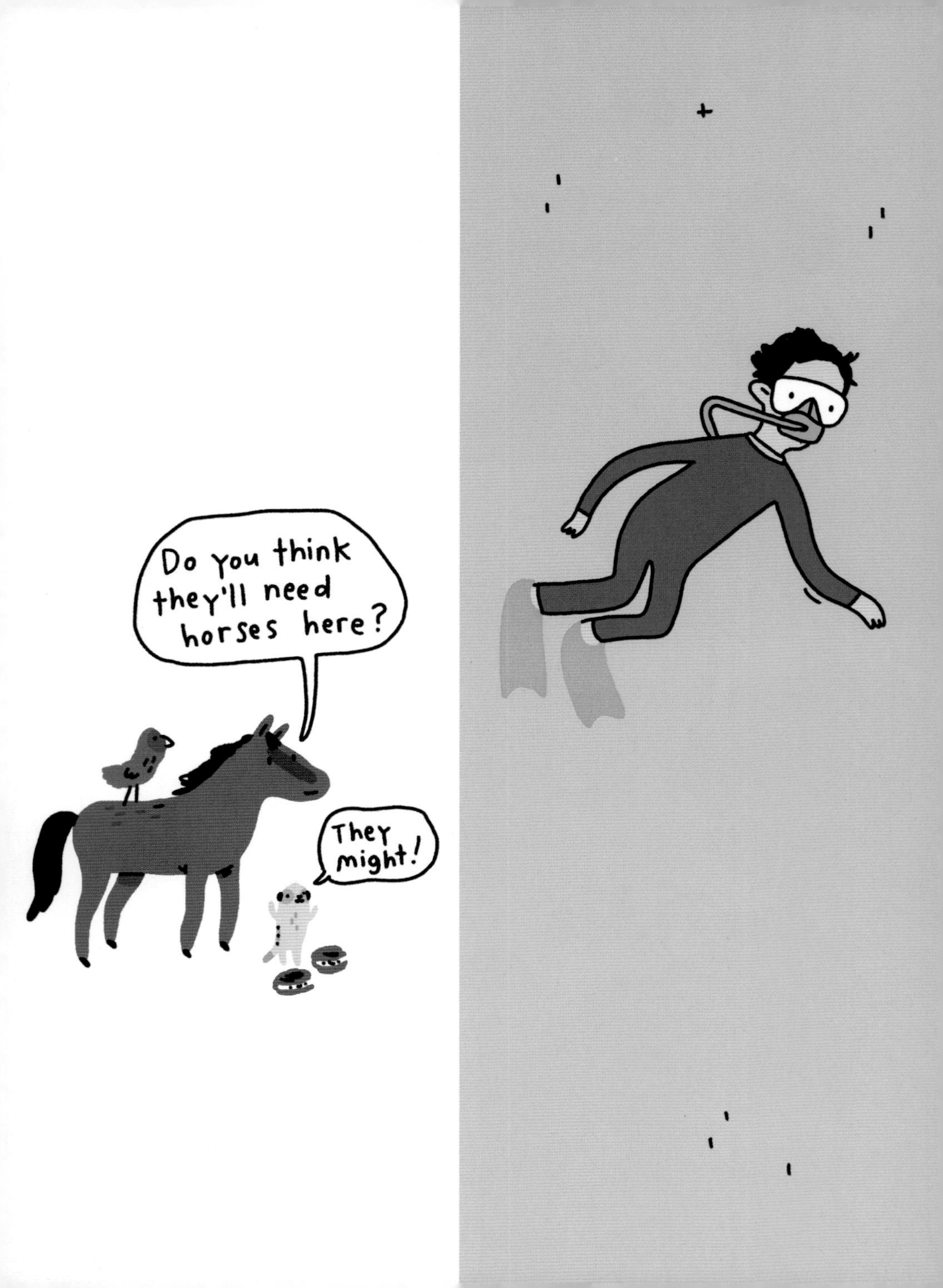
Do you think they'll need horses here?
They might!

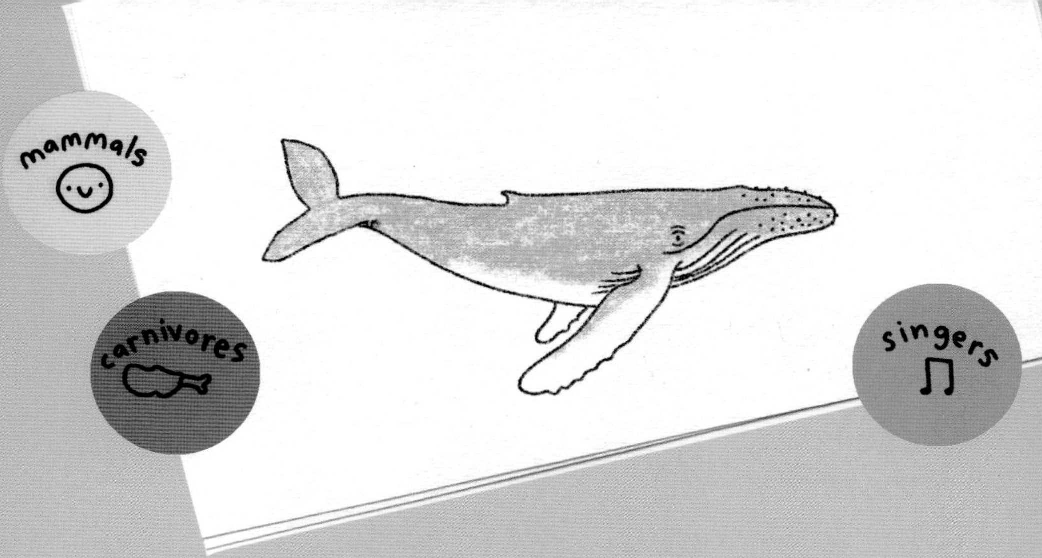
mammals
carnivores
singers

Dr. Ellen Garland studies humpback whales.

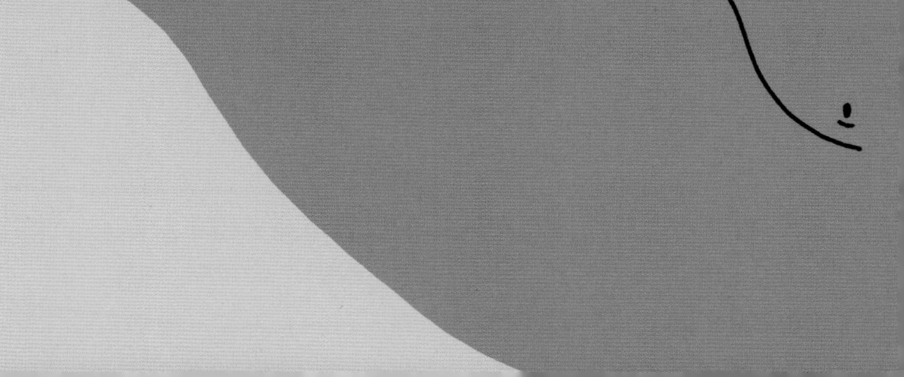

HUMPBACK WHALES

Humpback whales are migratory—that means they move to different places as the seasons change. A group of whales is called a pod.

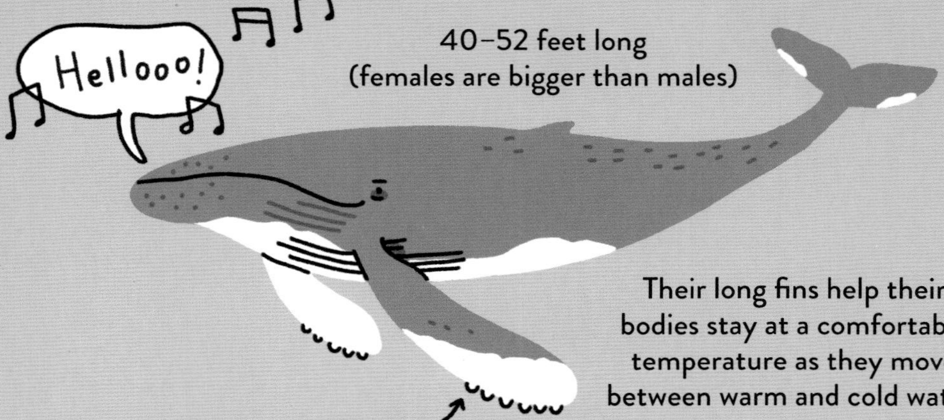
Hellooo!

40–52 feet long
(females are bigger than males)

Their long fins help their bodies stay at a comfortable temperature as they move between warm and cold water.

Barnacles grow on their fins, which helps them defend themselves against orcas.

A humpback whale eats 2,000 pounds of krill and fish every day.

Every humpback whale's tail has a slightly different pattern. Scientists use tail photos to tell whales apart.

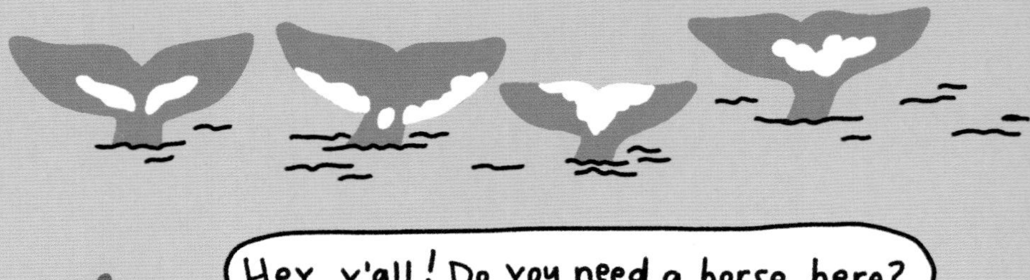

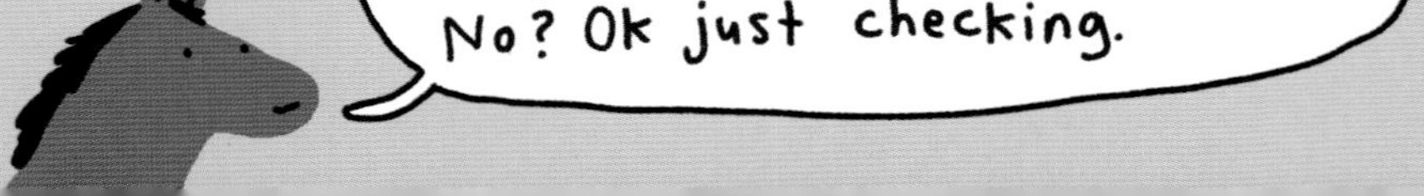
Hey y'all! Do you need a horse here? No? Ok just checking.

Humpback whales are very friendly. They're sometimes seen hanging out with other animals, like blue whales, minke whales, gray whales, right whales, and bottlenose dolphins.

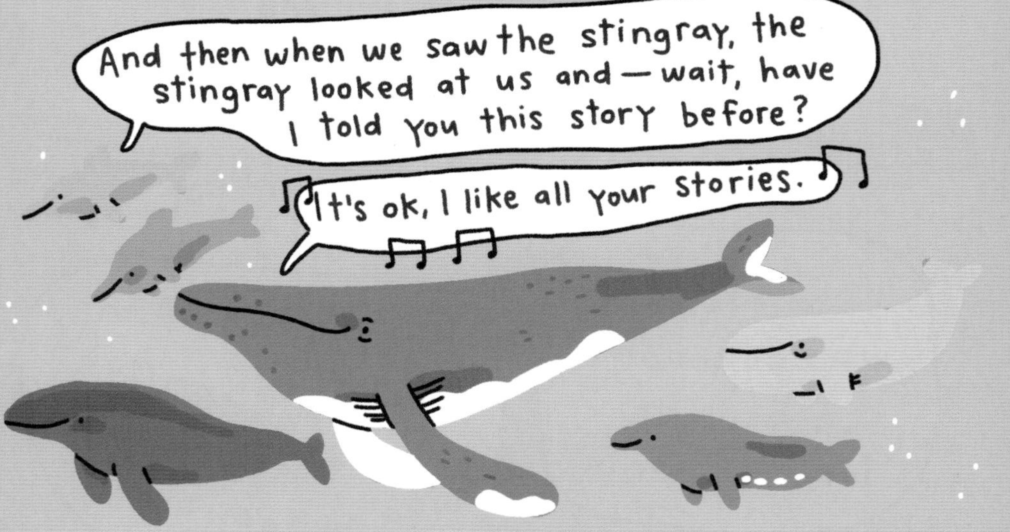
And then when we saw the stingray, the stingray looked at us and—wait, have I told you this story before?
It's ok, I like all your stories.

They're also amazing swimmers.
But Dr. Garland is most interested in their songs.

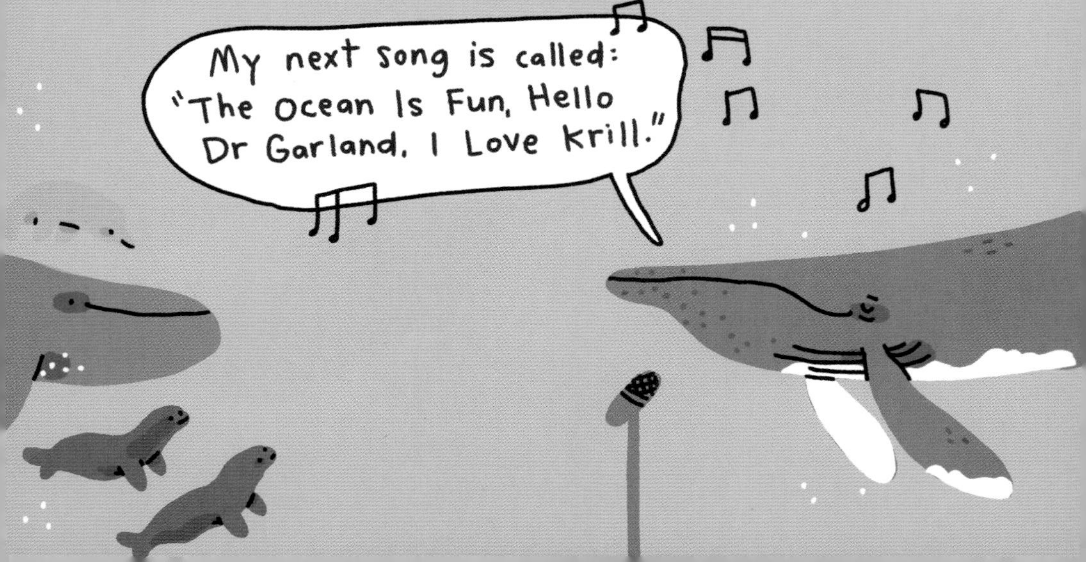
My next song is called: "The Ocean Is Fun, Hello Dr Garland, I Love Krill."

The males sing songs that can be five to thirty minutes long, and they sing them over and over again for hours.

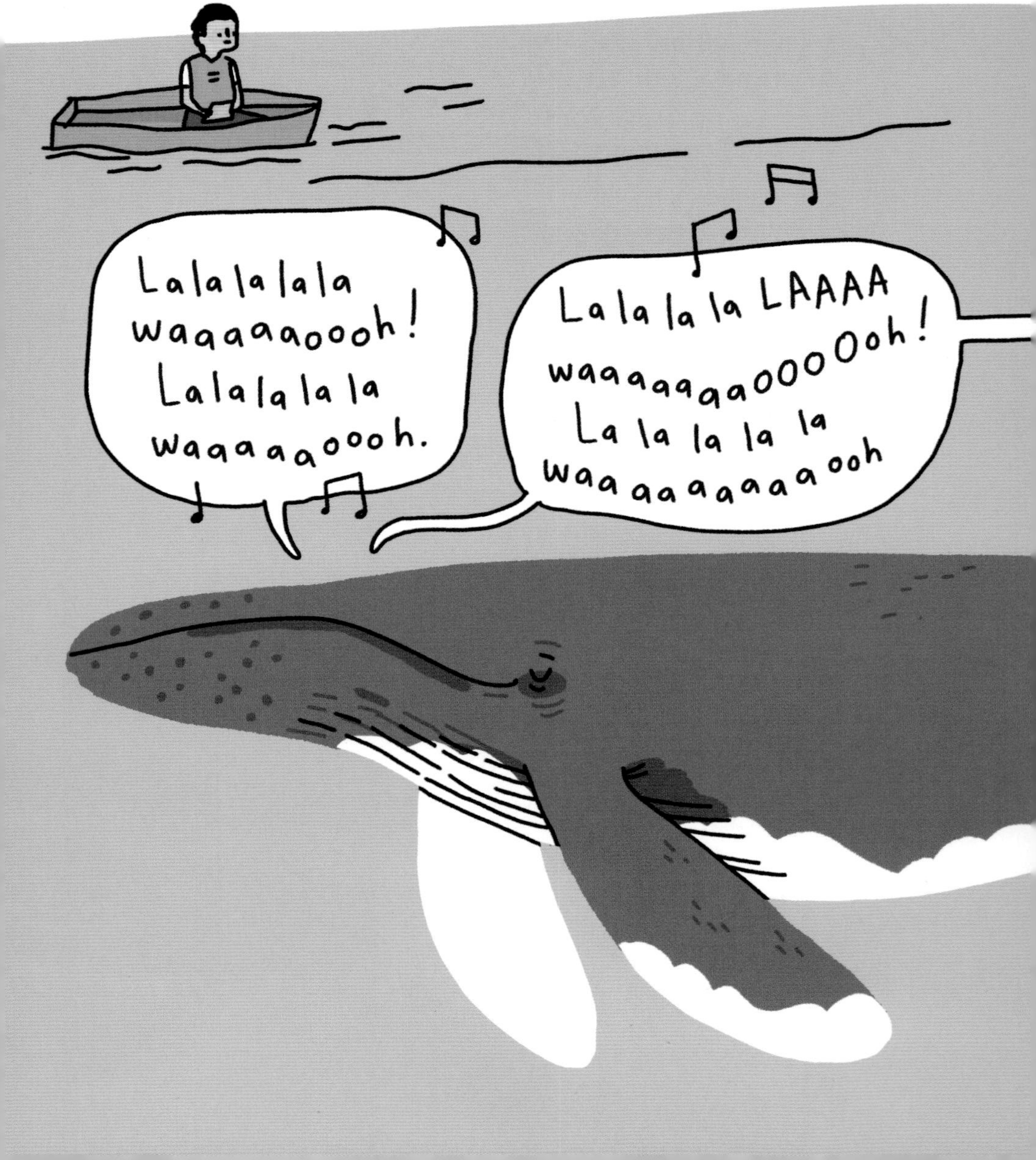

Lalalalala waaaaaoooh! Lalalalala waaaaaoooh.
La la la la LAAAA waaaaaaaaOOOOoh! La la la la la waaaaaaaaaaooh

The songs have noises that sound like violins, trumpets, crying cats, and the strangest sounds your stomach has ever made. There are very high and super-low notes.

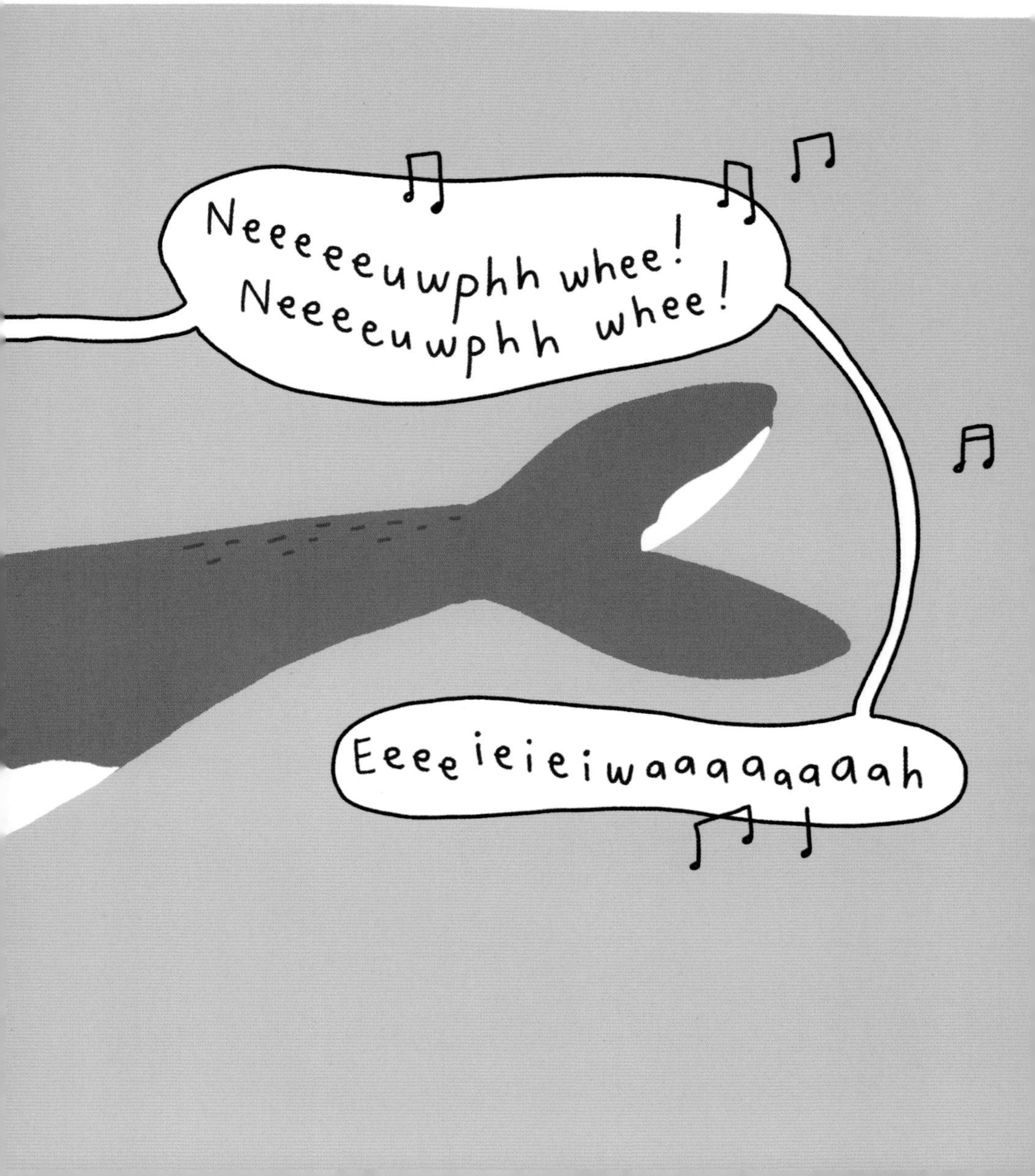
Neeeeeeuwphh whee!
Neeeeeuwphh whee!
Eeeeieieiwaaaaaaaah

Humans haven't learned as much about whale songs as we have about bird songs and frog songs.

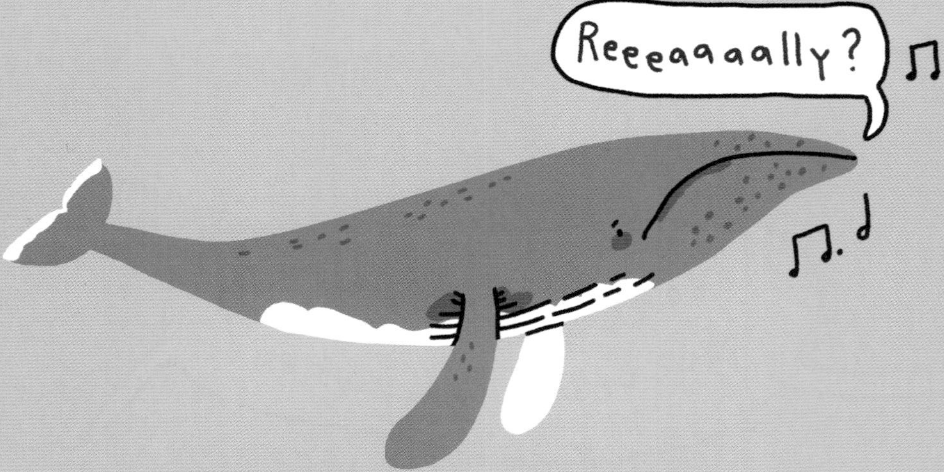
Reeeaaaaally?

This is because a fifty-foot-long animal is much harder to study in a small space—scientists like Dr. Garland have to follow the whales.

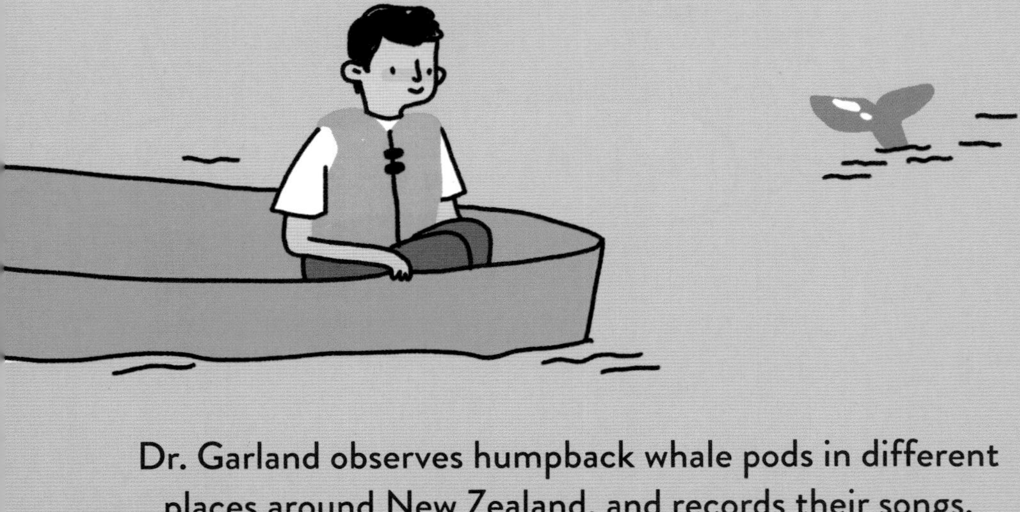

Dr. Garland observes humpback whale pods in different places around New Zealand, and records their songs.

Scientists aren't sure exactly why humpback whales sing. They might sing to show other whales how strong and smart they are.

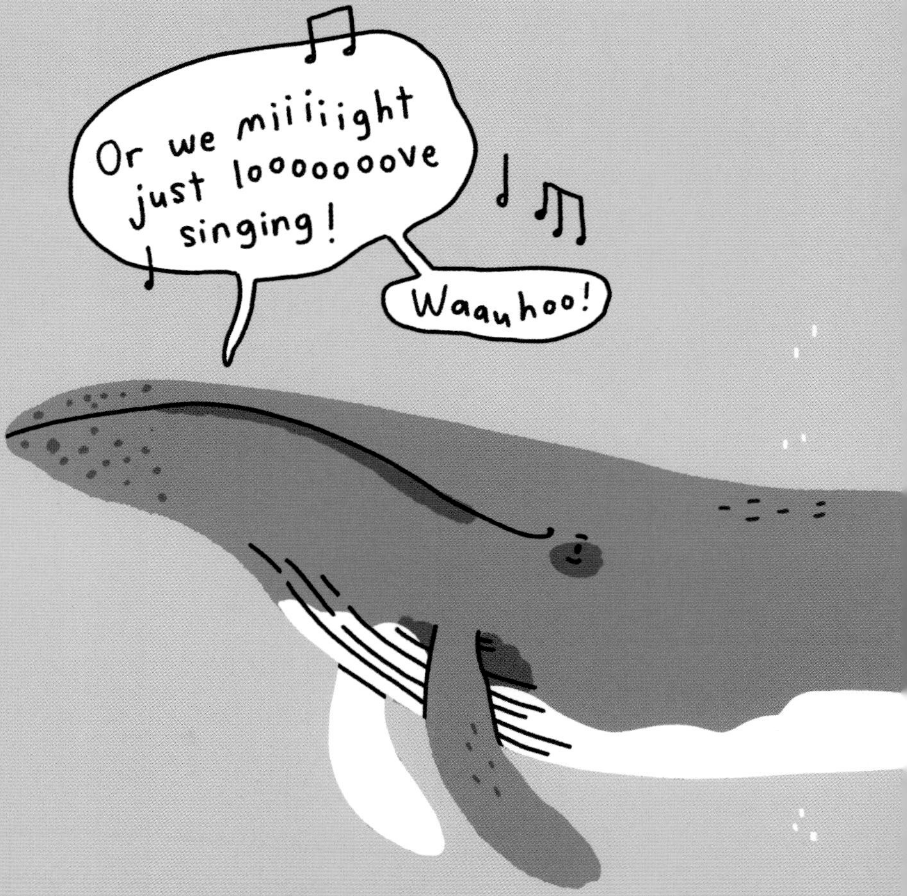
Or we miiiiight just looooooove singing!
Waauhoo!

It's probably not just because they love singing.

Every male in one pod sings the same song.

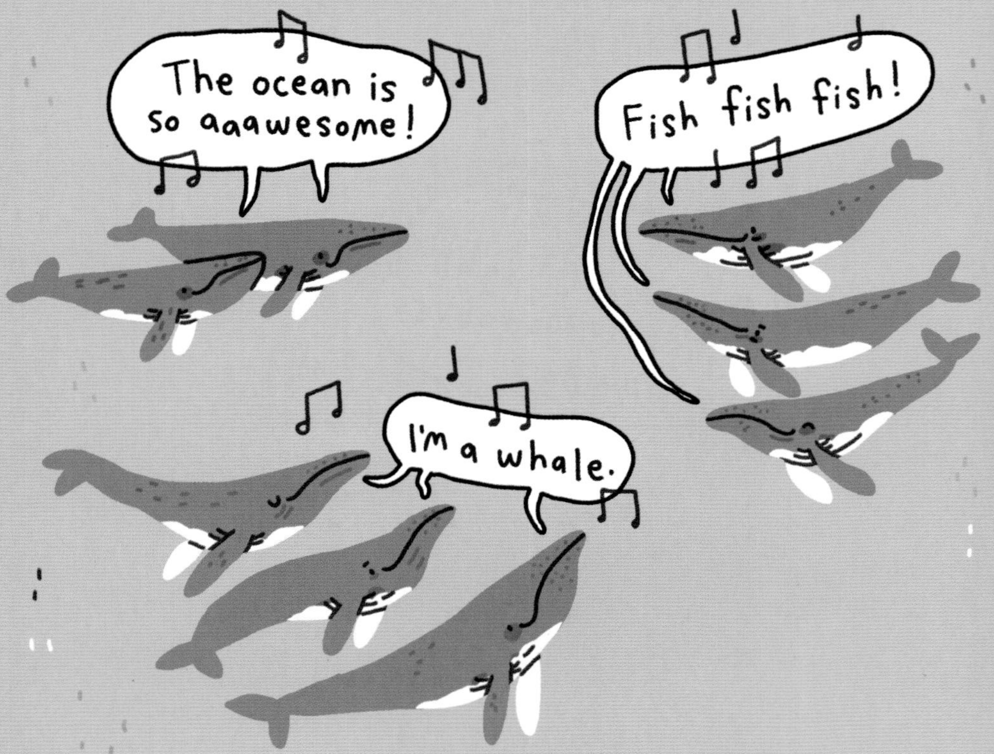
The ocean is so aaawesome!
Fish fish fish!
I'm a whale.

But when Dr. Garland studied the songs closely, she realized some whale songs combined parts of two other songs.

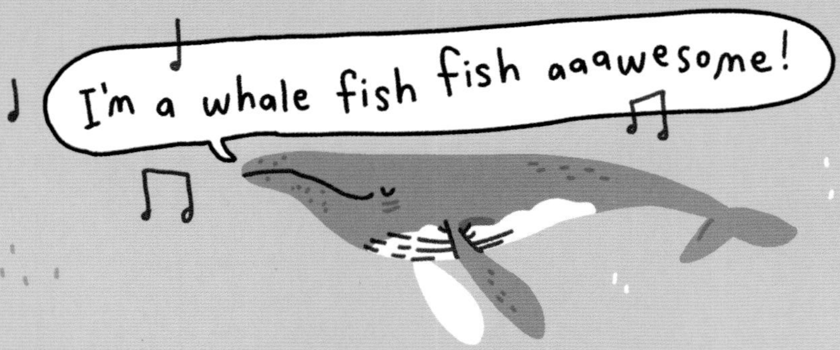
I'm a whale fish fish aaawesome!

Dr. Garland was able to use all her recordings to prove that when whales travel and meet other pods, they learn new songs, and they start to sing them too.

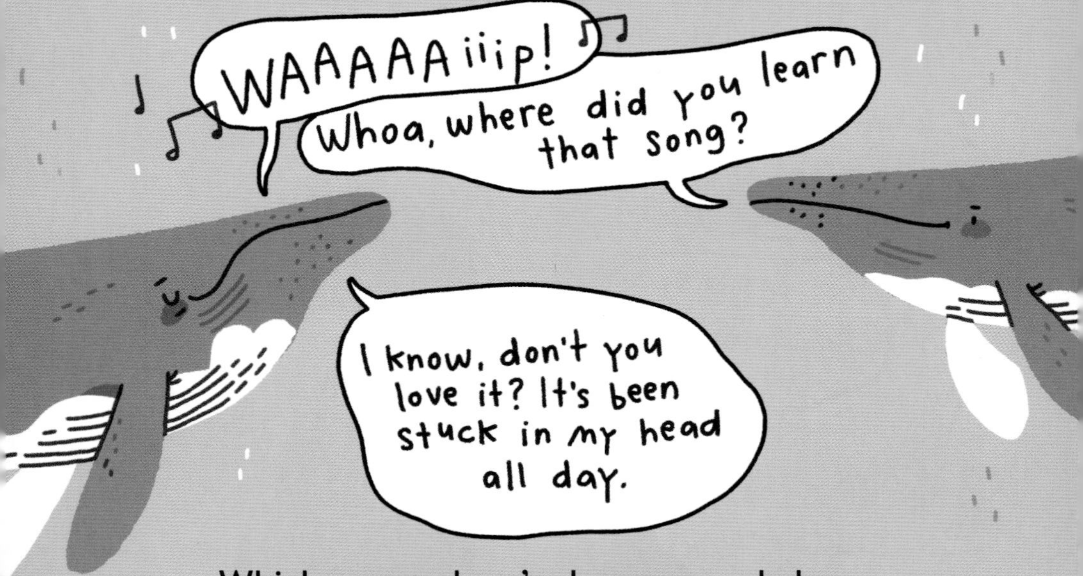
WAAAAAiiip!
Whoa, where did you learn that song?
I know, don't you love it? It's been stuck in my head all day.

Which means there's always new whale music being made and shared and sung.

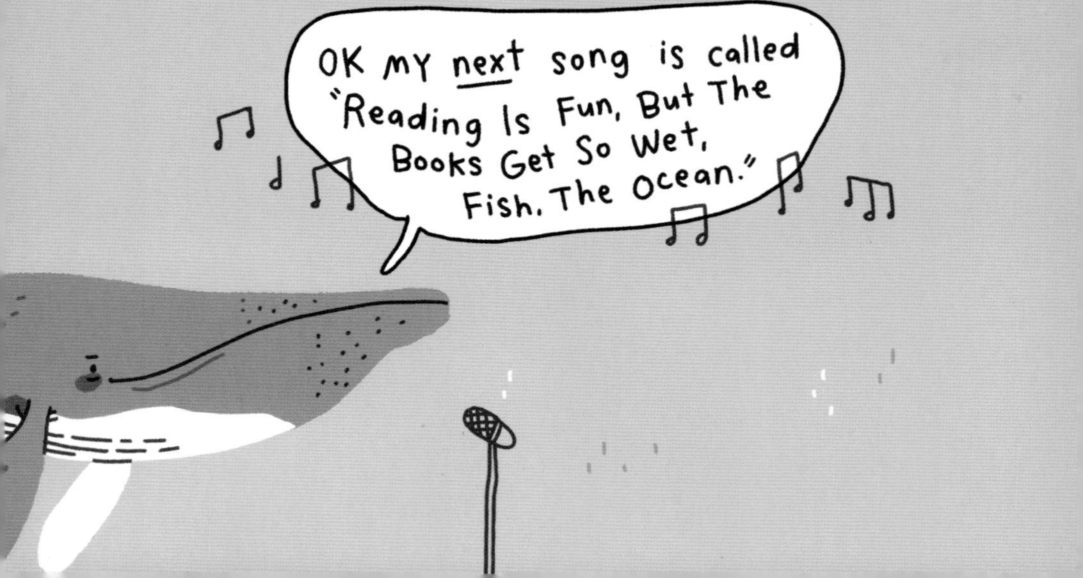
OK my next song is called "Reading Is Fun, But The Books Get So Wet, Fish, The Ocean."

Ok, I'm back! What did I miss?
Um, it depends- How long were You gone?
z z z z

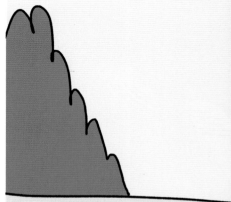

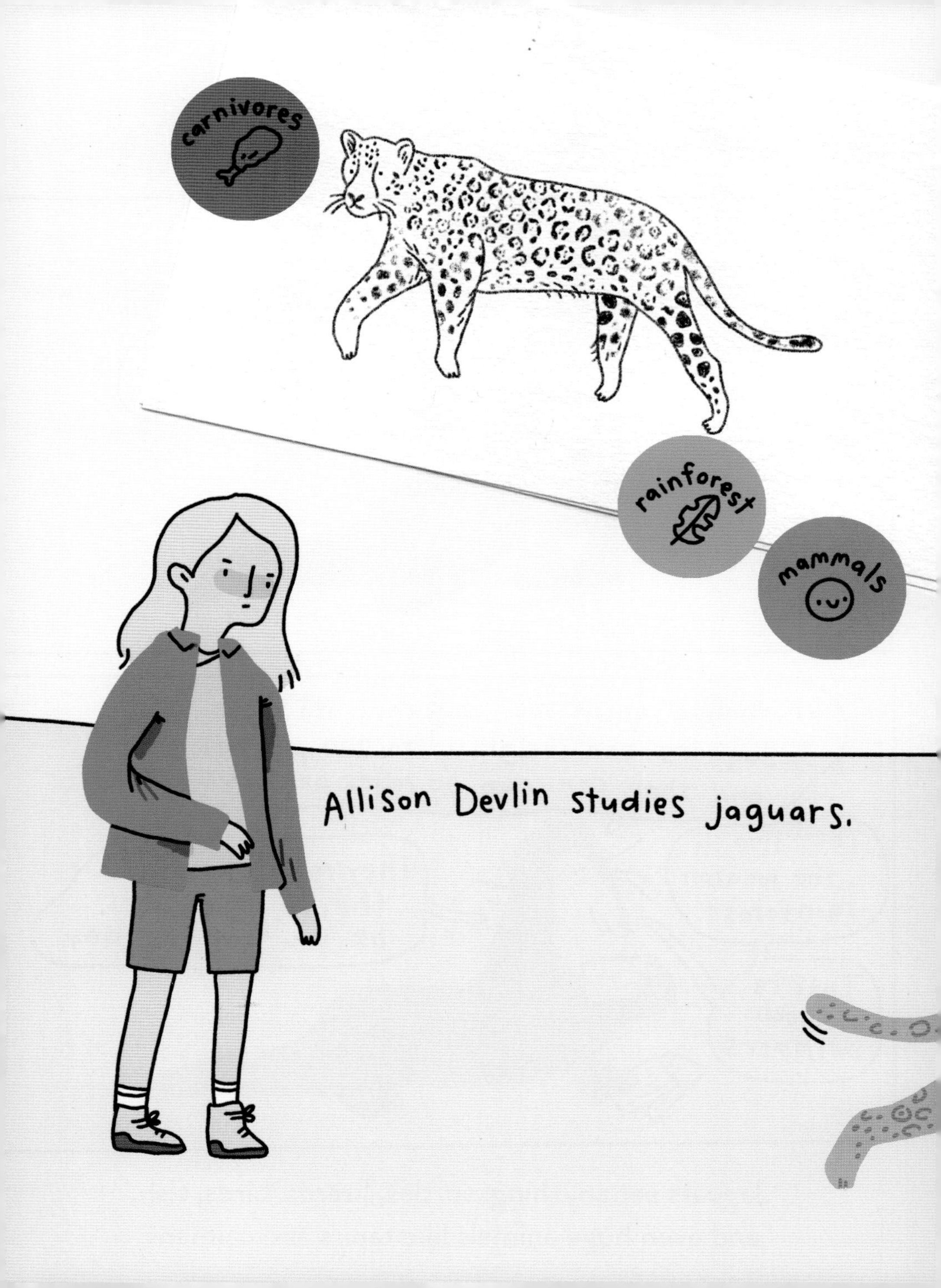
carnivores
rainforest
mammals

Allison Devlin studies jaguars.

JAGUARS

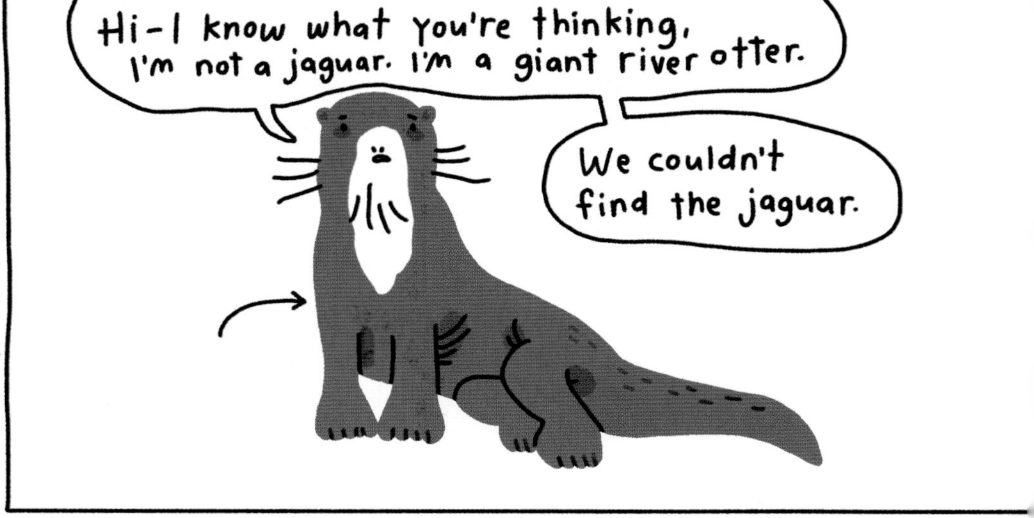

Hi-I know what you're thinking, I'm not a jaguar. I'm a giant river otter.
We couldn't find the jaguar.

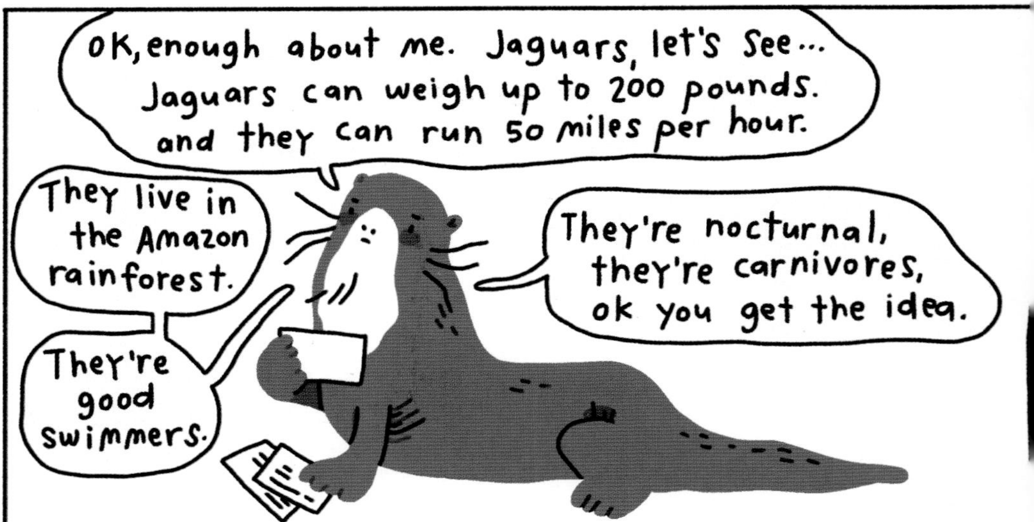

OK, enough about me. Jaguars, let's see... Jaguars can weigh up to 200 pounds. and they can run 50 miles per hour.
They live in the Amazon rainforest.
They're good swimmers.
They're nocturnal, they're carnivores, ok you get the idea.

Jaguars eat anything: turtles, lizards, birds, fish, and even huge animals like tapirs and caimans.

Jaguars are very secretive.

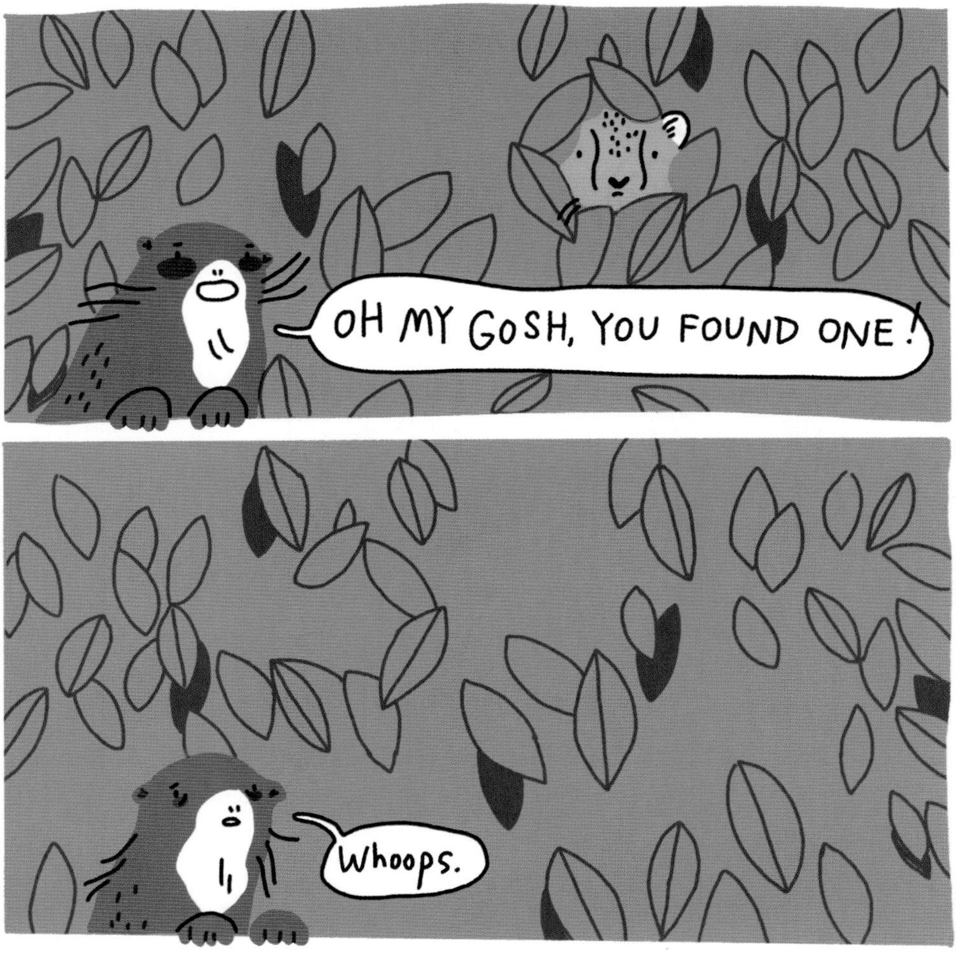
OH MY GOSH, YOU FOUND ONE!
Whoops.

They're also endangered. Today there are fewer than 170,000 jaguars in the world. They're threatened by habitat loss—jaguars used to be found all over Central and South America. Dr. Allison Devlin and other experts are trying to help them. But it's so difficult to see the jaguars that it's hard to know what's working.

Dr. Devlin has been researching big cats since she was a teenager. One of her first jobs was working with a special scat-sniffing dog to collect jaguar poop.

Scat is another word for "poop."

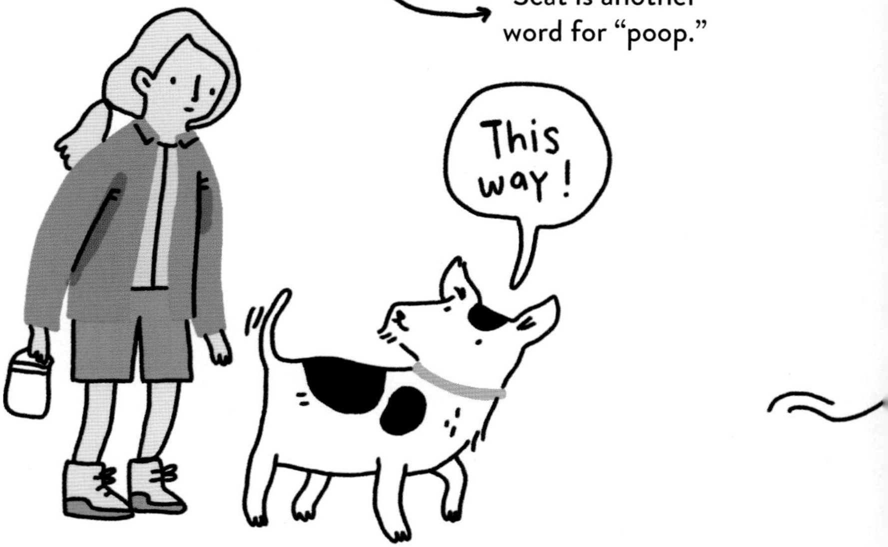
This way!

The scat not only tells Dr. Devlin that jaguars have been here—scientists can also study the scat to find out:

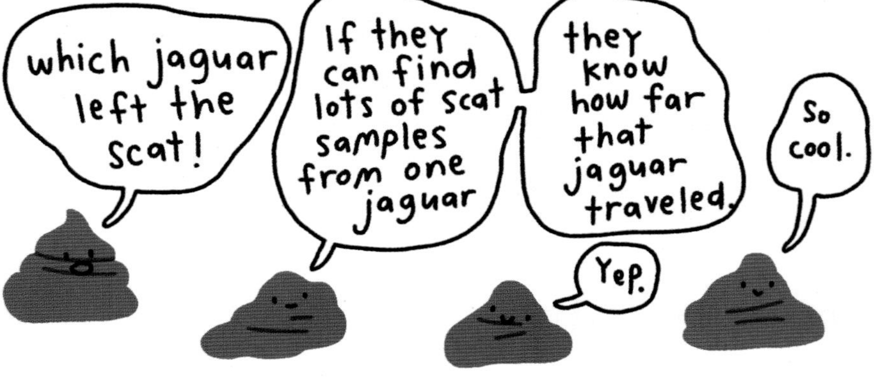
which jaguar left the scat!
If they can find lots of scat samples from one jaguar
they know how far that jaguar traveled.
Yep.
So cool.

Now Dr. Devlin uses motion-activated cameras to study the jaguars.

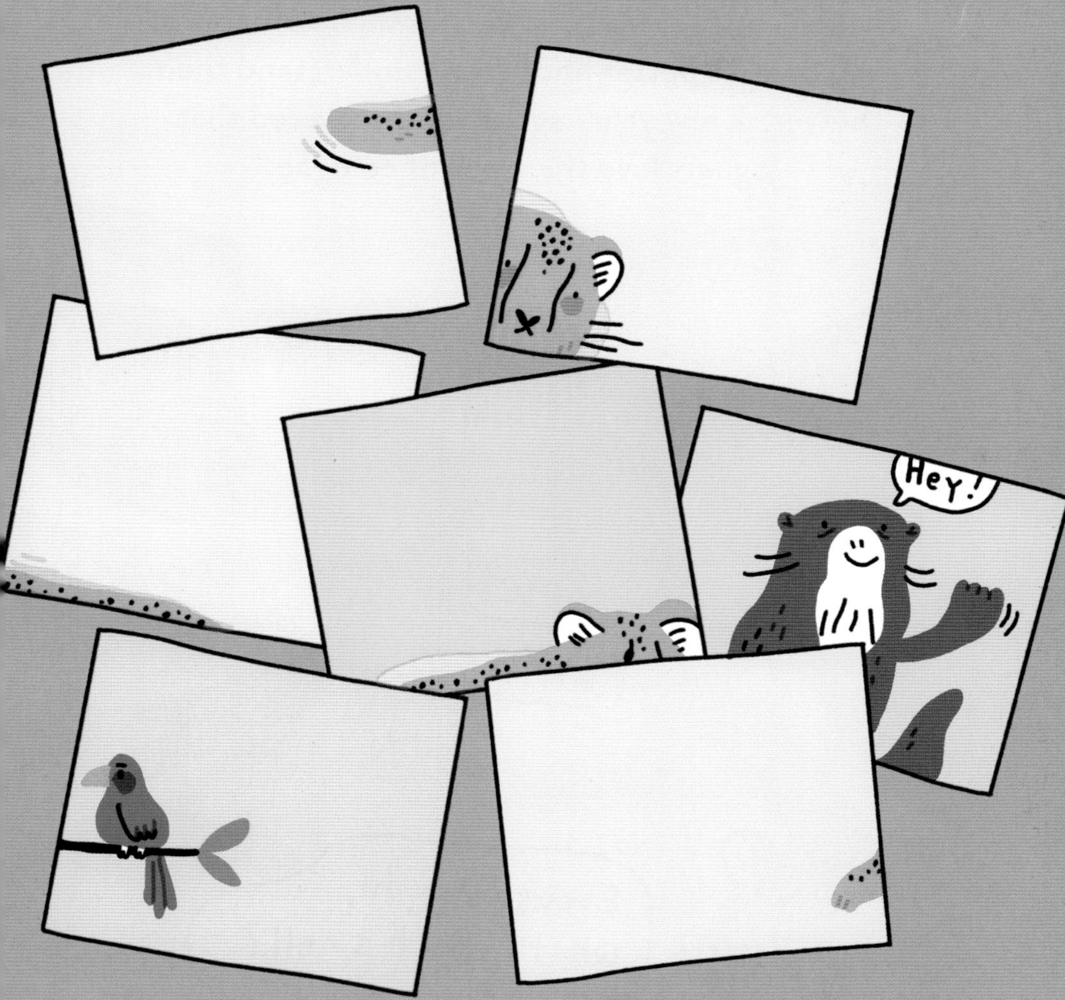
Hey!

The cameras take a photo every time an animal (hopefully a jaguar) sets them off.

Dr. Devlin's team is always looking for things that will attract more jaguars to their cameras so they can get better photos and understand them better. A few years ago, they discovered that jaguars love the smell of cologne.

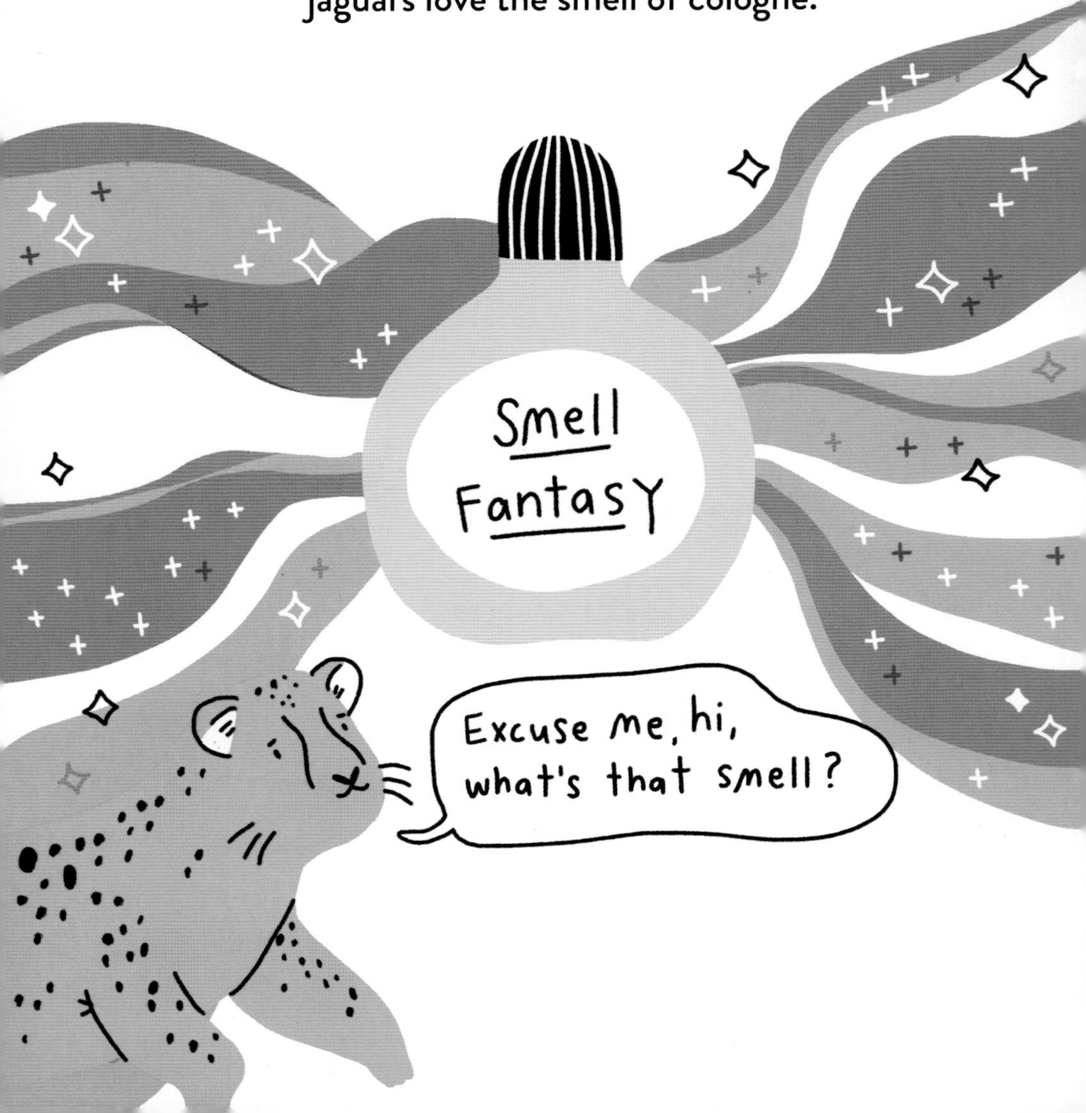
Smell Fantasy
Excuse me, hi, what's that smell?

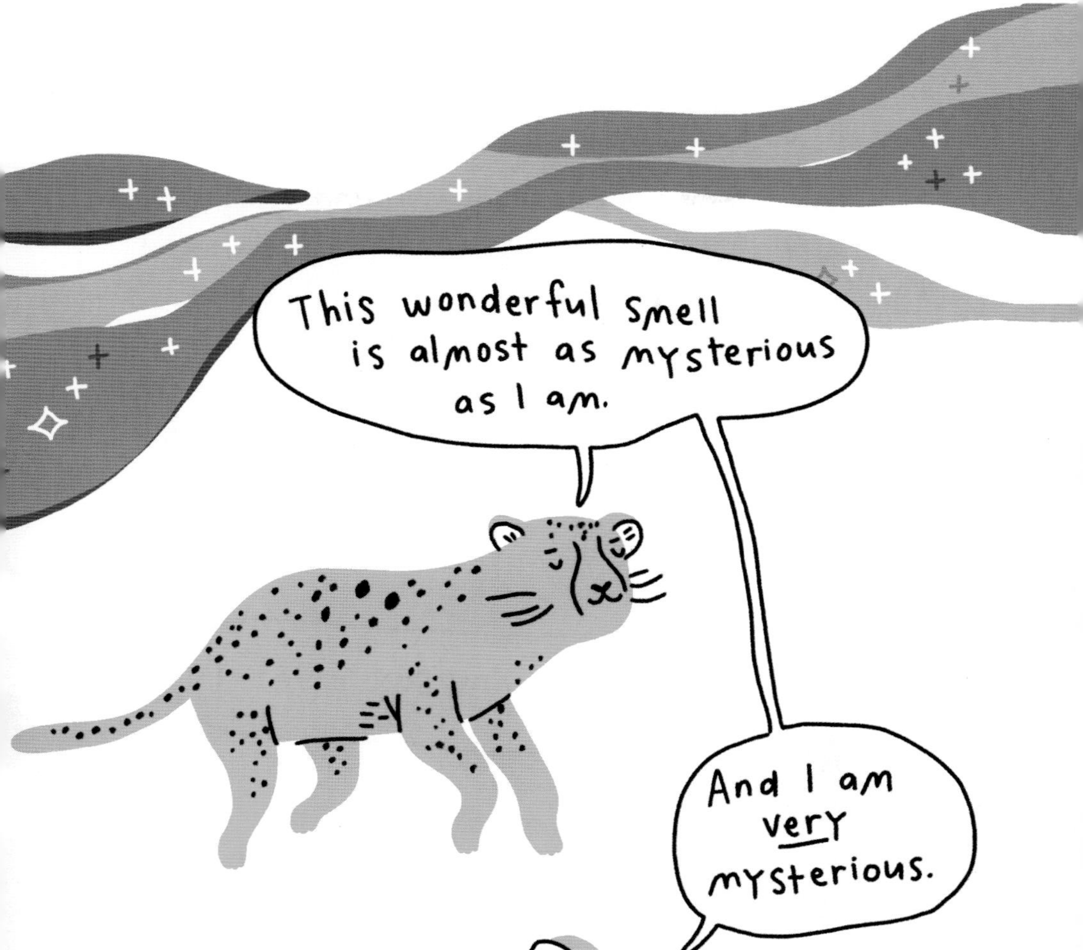
This wonderful smell is almost as mysterious as I am.
And I am very mysterious.

A 6.7-ounce bottle costs about $28. Researchers spray a little near the cameras and at night the jaguars come to investigate.

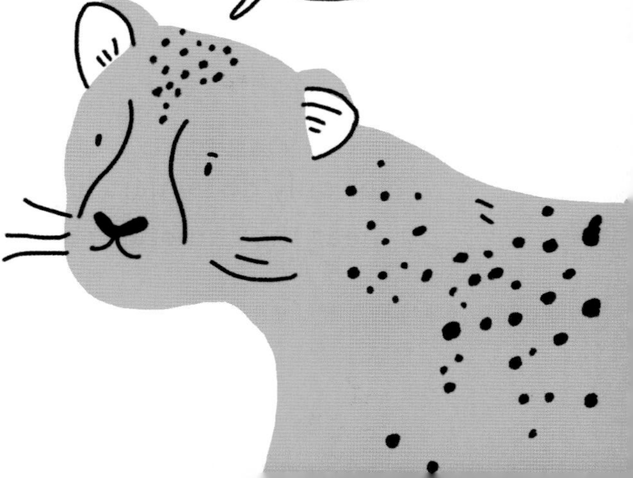

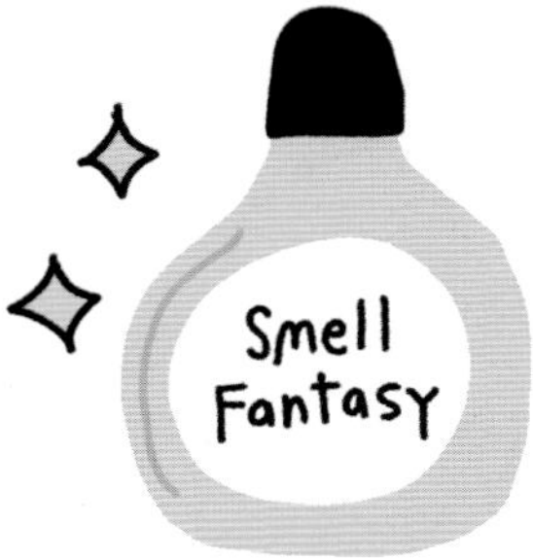
Smell
Fantasy

The cologne was made for humans to wear, but the jaguars are probably interested in the synthetic *civetone*, which smells like the sticky, smelly goo that a civet rubs onto trees to mark their territory and attract other civets.

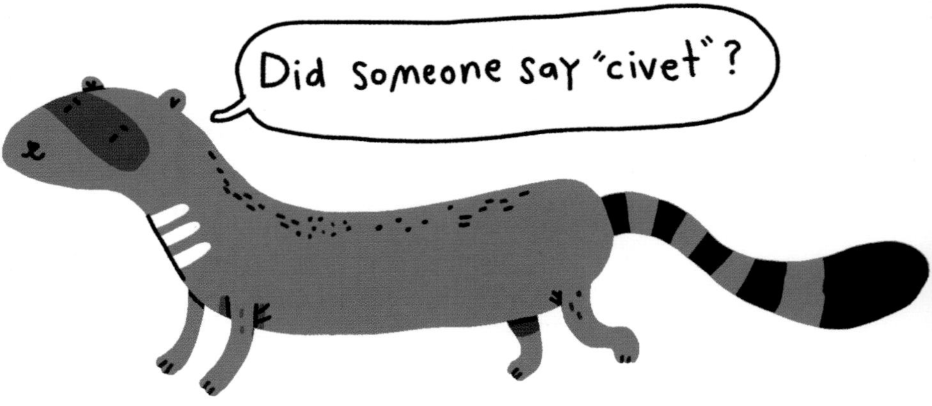
Did someone say "civet"?

Not only do jaguars like getting a good sniff near the cameras—they also stay longer.

Thanks to the new smell, Dr. Devlin has even seen two jaguars together in one photo, which researchers hadn't been able to see before.

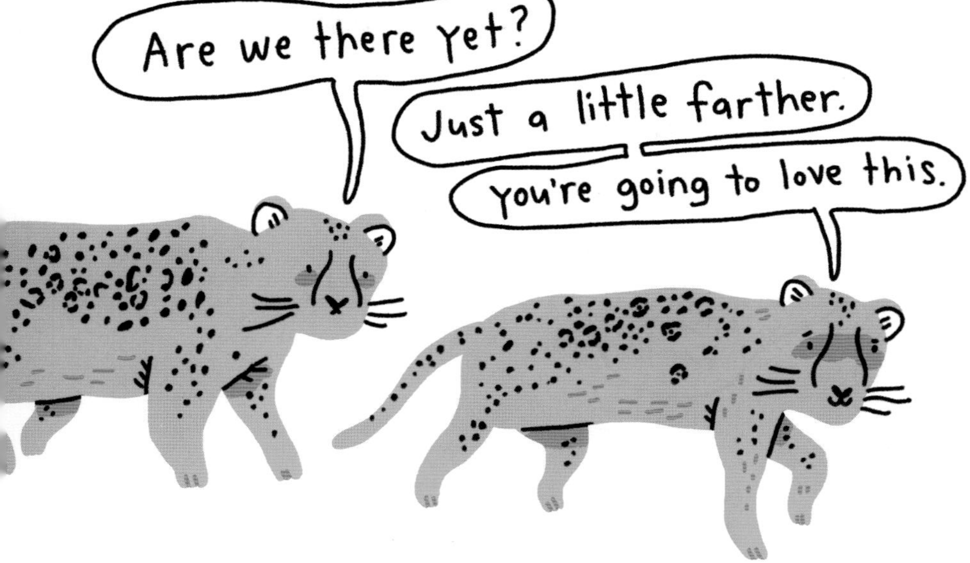
Are we there yet?
Just a little farther.
You're going to love this.

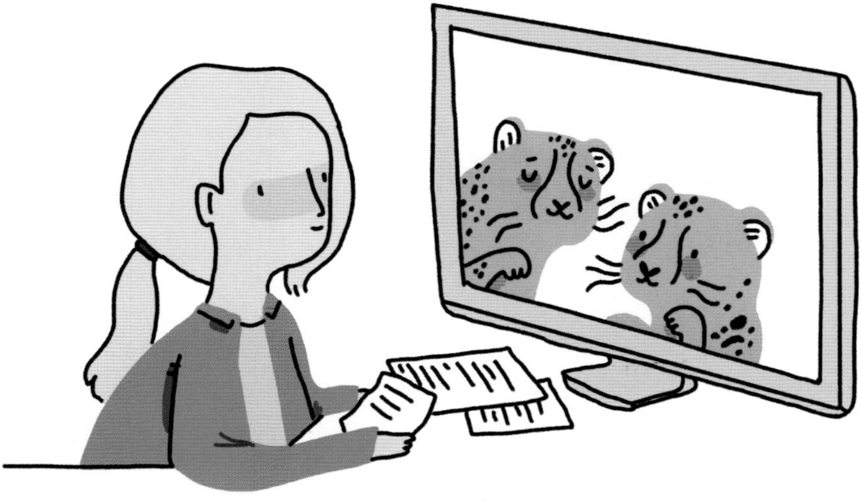

The photos are helping the scientists learn more about these super-secretive animals.

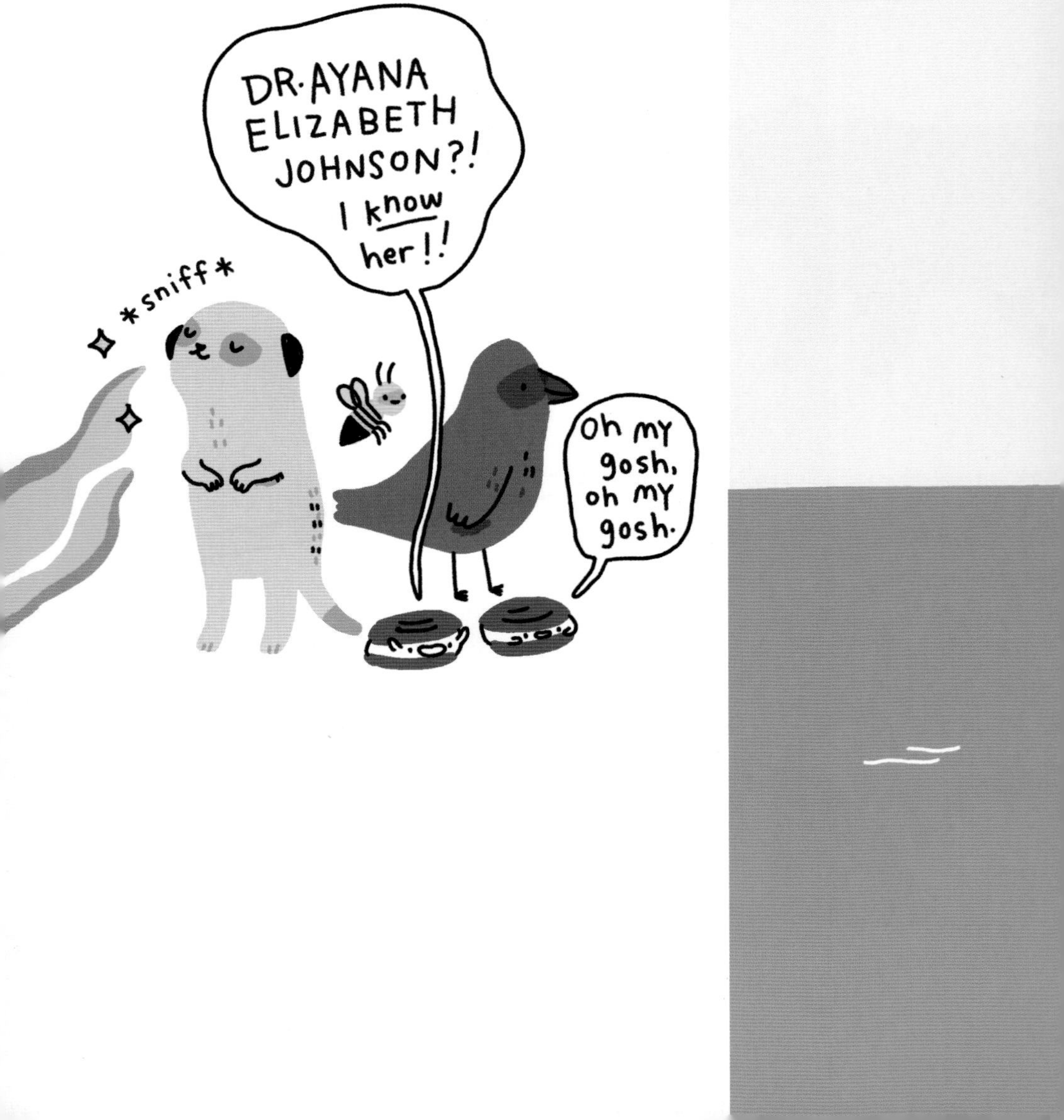
DR. AYANA ELIZABETH JOHNSON?! I know her!!
sniff
Oh my gosh, oh my gosh.

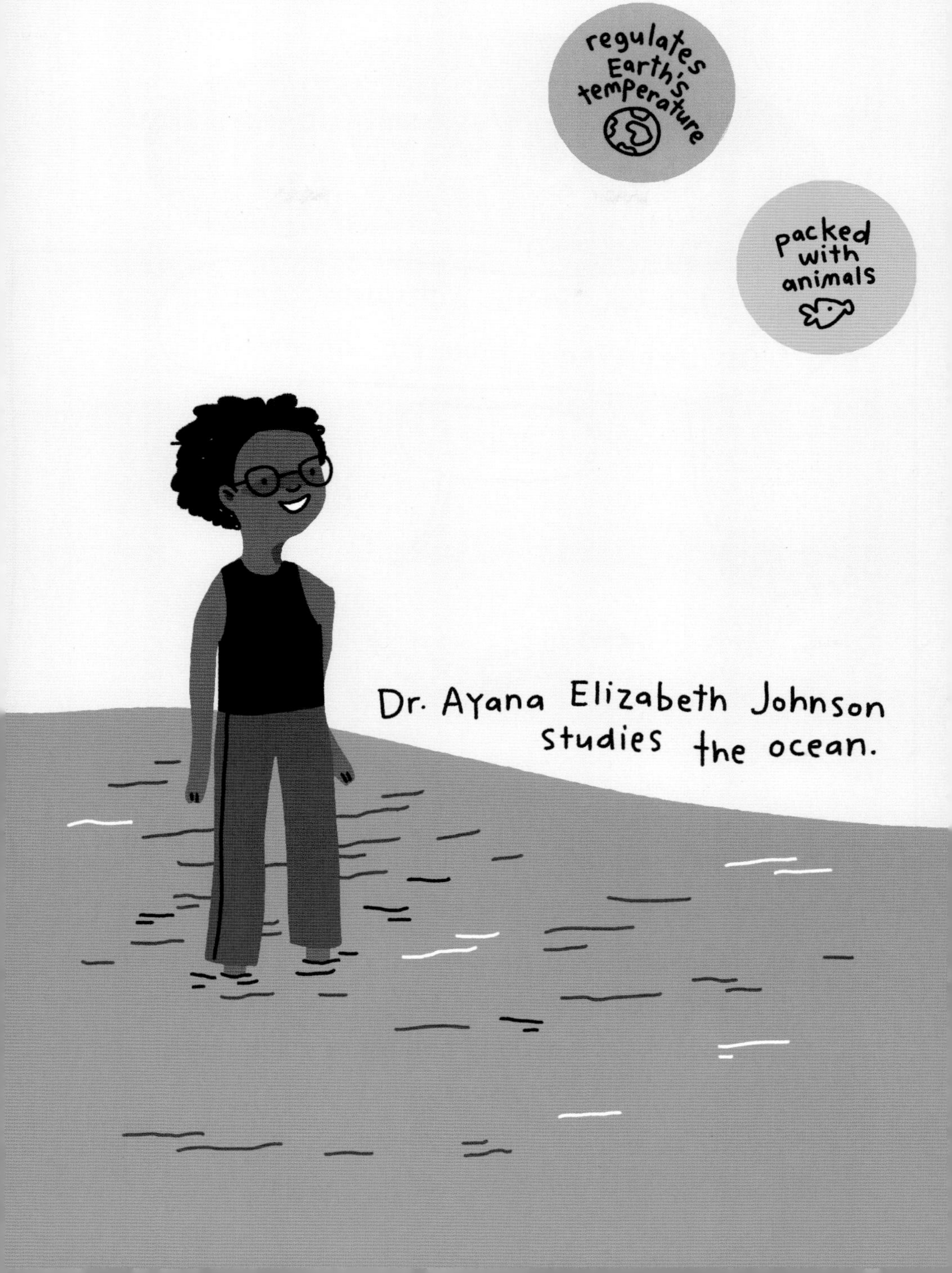
regulates Earth's temperature
packed with animals

Dr. Ayana Elizabeth Johnson studies the ocean.

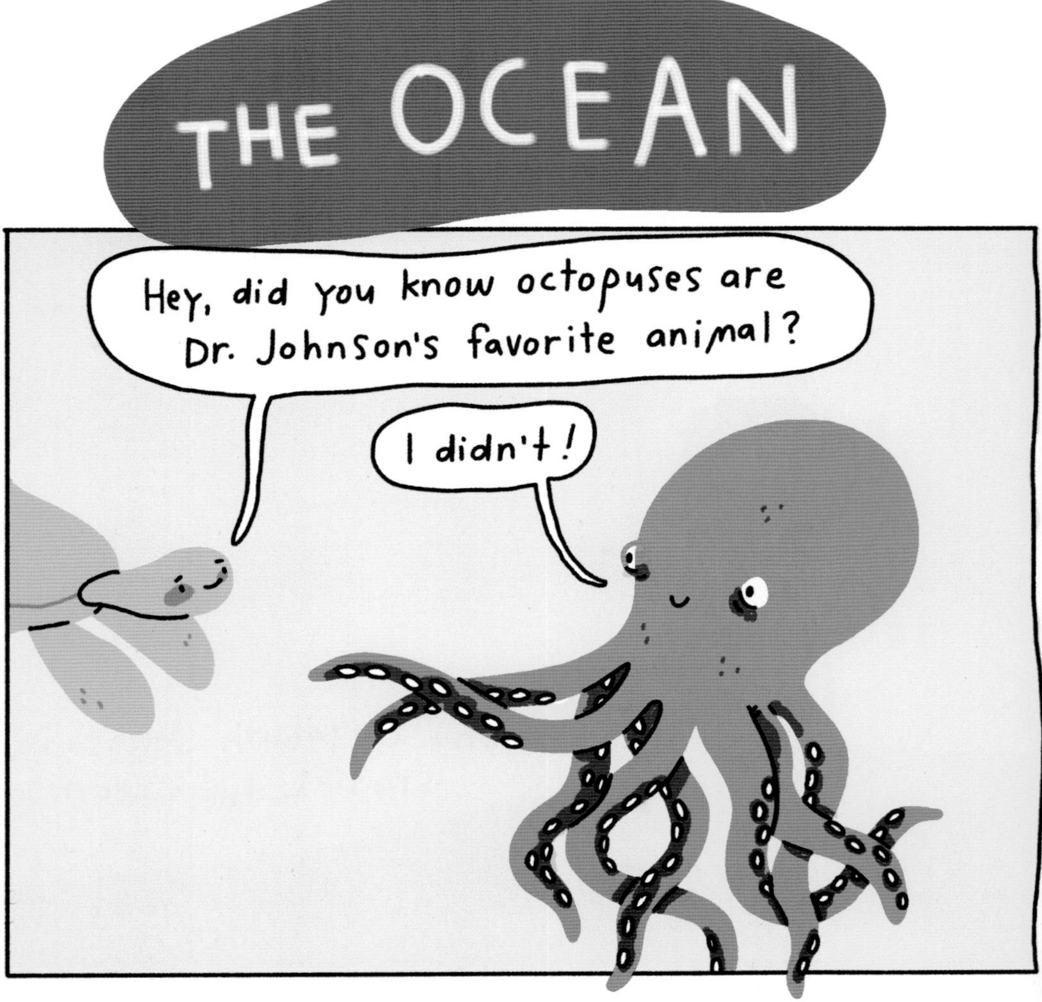
THE OCEAN
Hey, did you know octopuses are Dr. Johnson's favorite animal?
I didn't!

Oceans cover 68 percent of the planet. They're home to one million species and they absorb heat and pollution, making life safer for everyone on land.

Ayana grew up loving animals *and* the ocean.

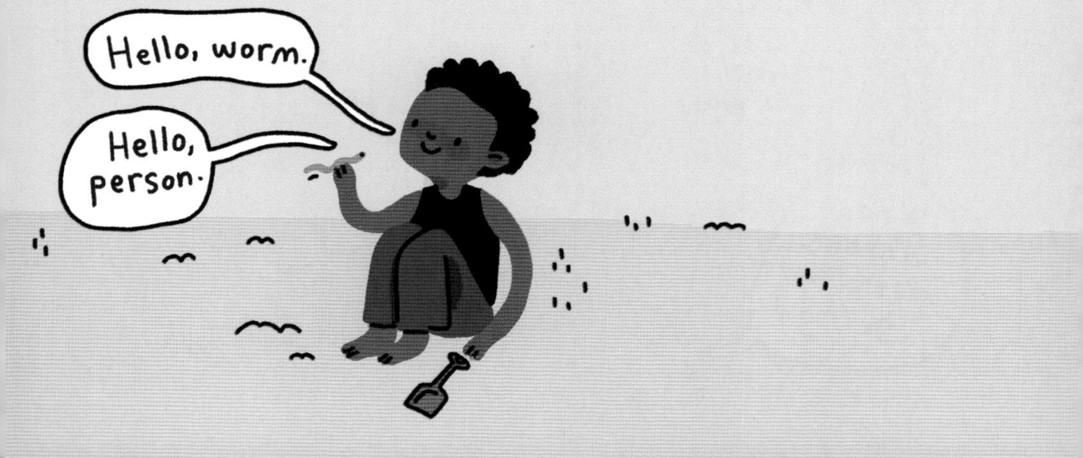
Hello, worm.
Hello, person.

When she was ten, she saw a coral reef for the first time.

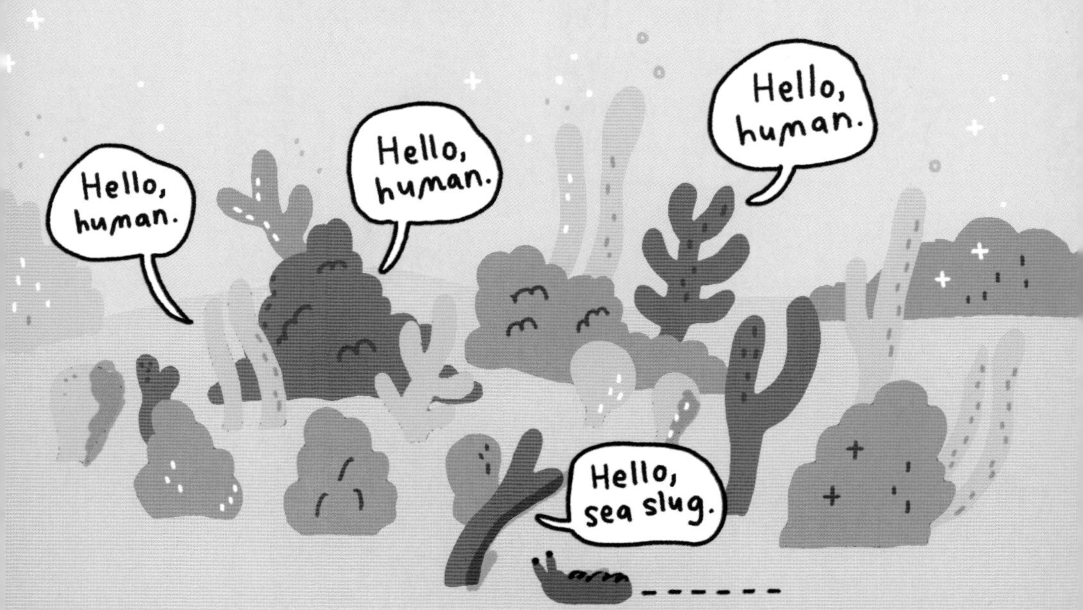
Hello, human.
Hello, human.
Hello, human.
Hello, sea slug.

As a scientist, Dr. Johnson has learned about the reasons the ocean is in danger:

things like overfishing

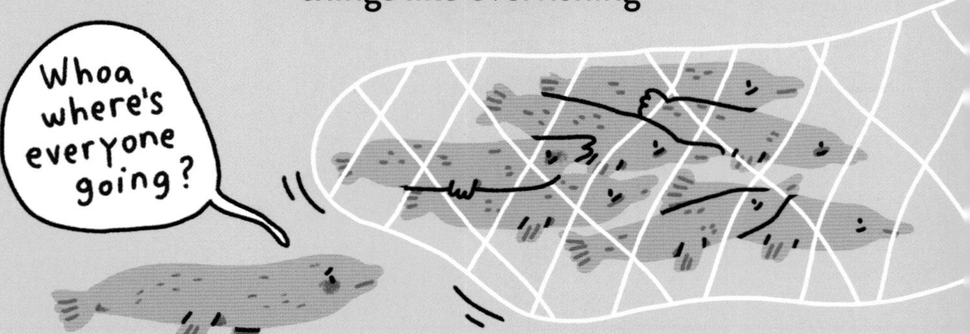
Whoa where's everyone going?

and pollution.

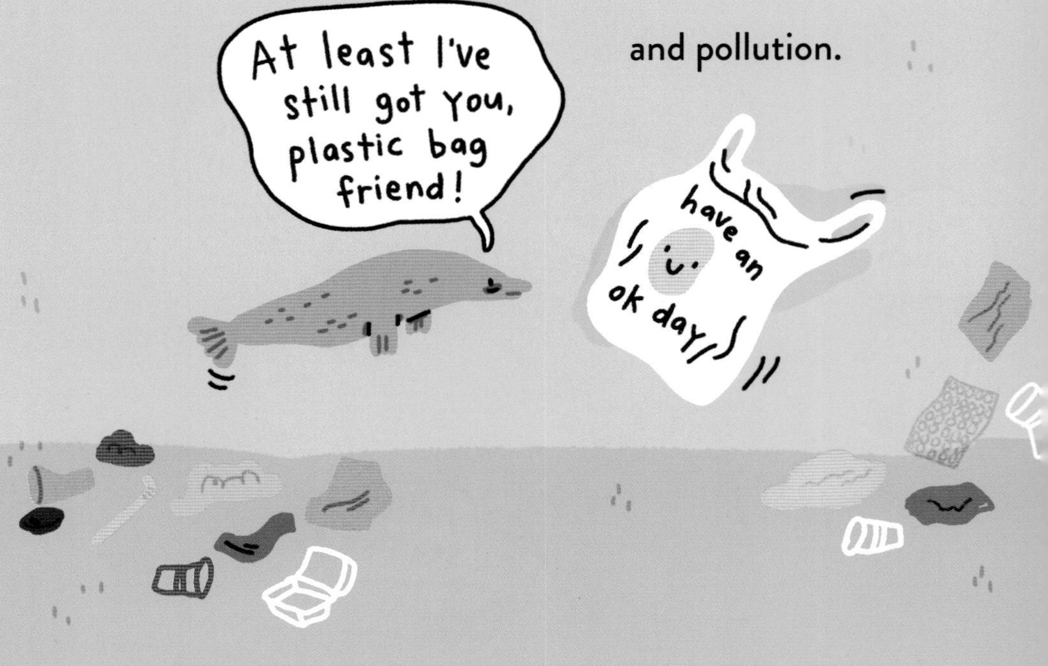
At least I've still got you, plastic bag friend!
have an ok day

She works to come up with plans to protect the ocean and the planet, and then she makes sure as many people as possible know about the plan and how they can help.

Dr. Johnson meets with politicians . . .

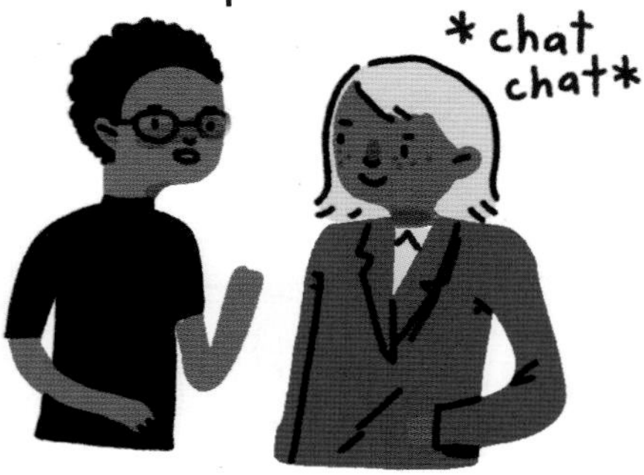
chat chat

she gives speeches . . .

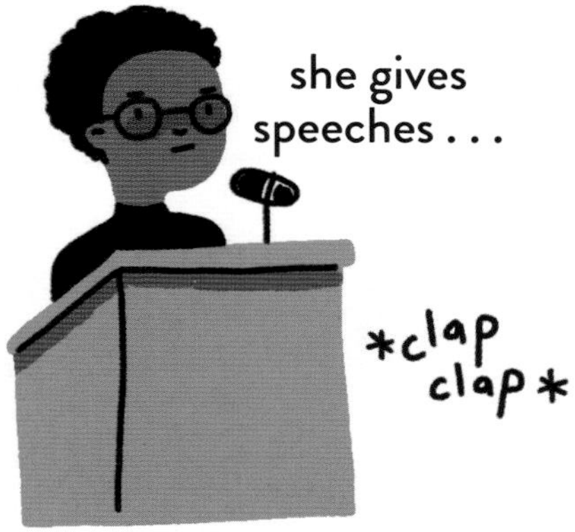
clap clap

she writes books . . .

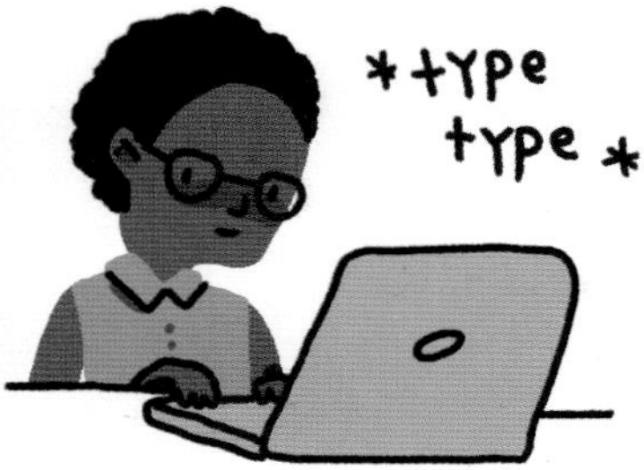
type type

she does interviews . . .

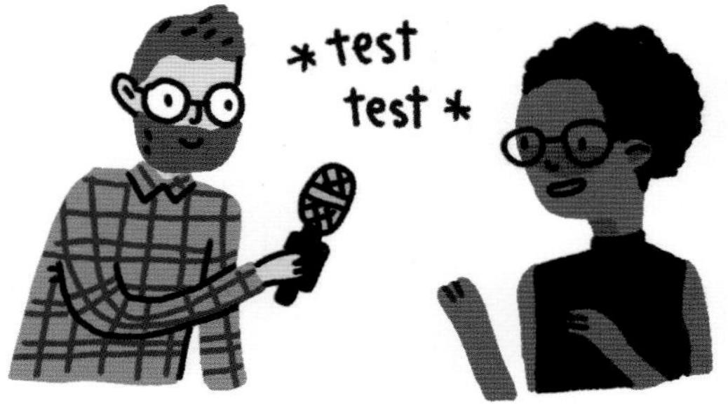
test test

and she meets with experts around the world.

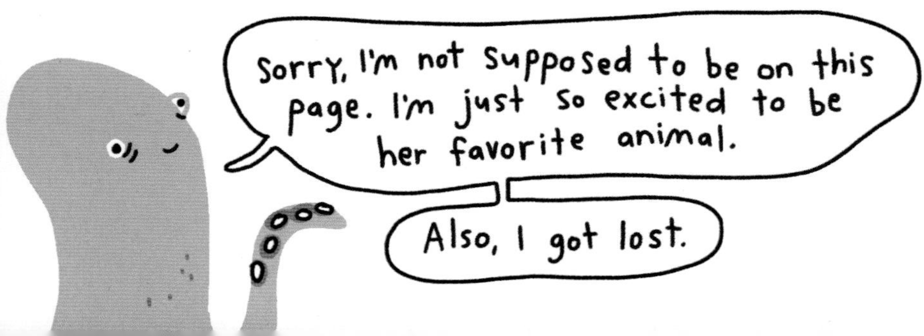
Sorry, I'm not supposed to be on this page. I'm just so excited to be her favorite animal.
Also, I got lost.

To do her work, Dr. Johnson uses her science skills, but she also uses her public speaking skills, her creativity, her writing skills, and her sense of humor.

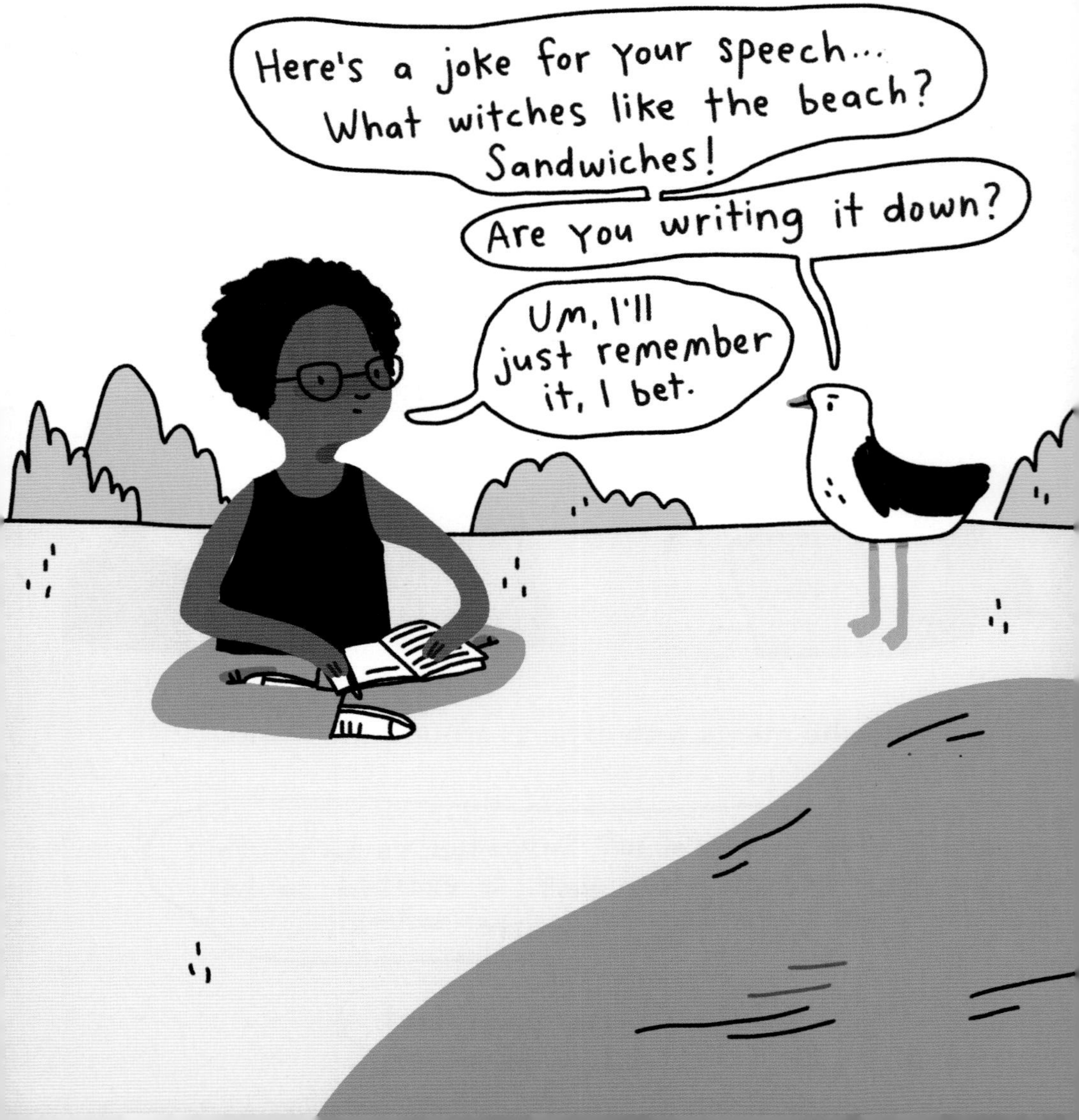
Here's a joke for your speech... What witches like the beach? Sandwiches!
Are you writing it down?
Um, I'll just remember it, I bet.

Even though our oceans aren't as healthy as they used to be, Dr. Johnson says if we all work together, there's still a lot we can do to save them, and our planet.

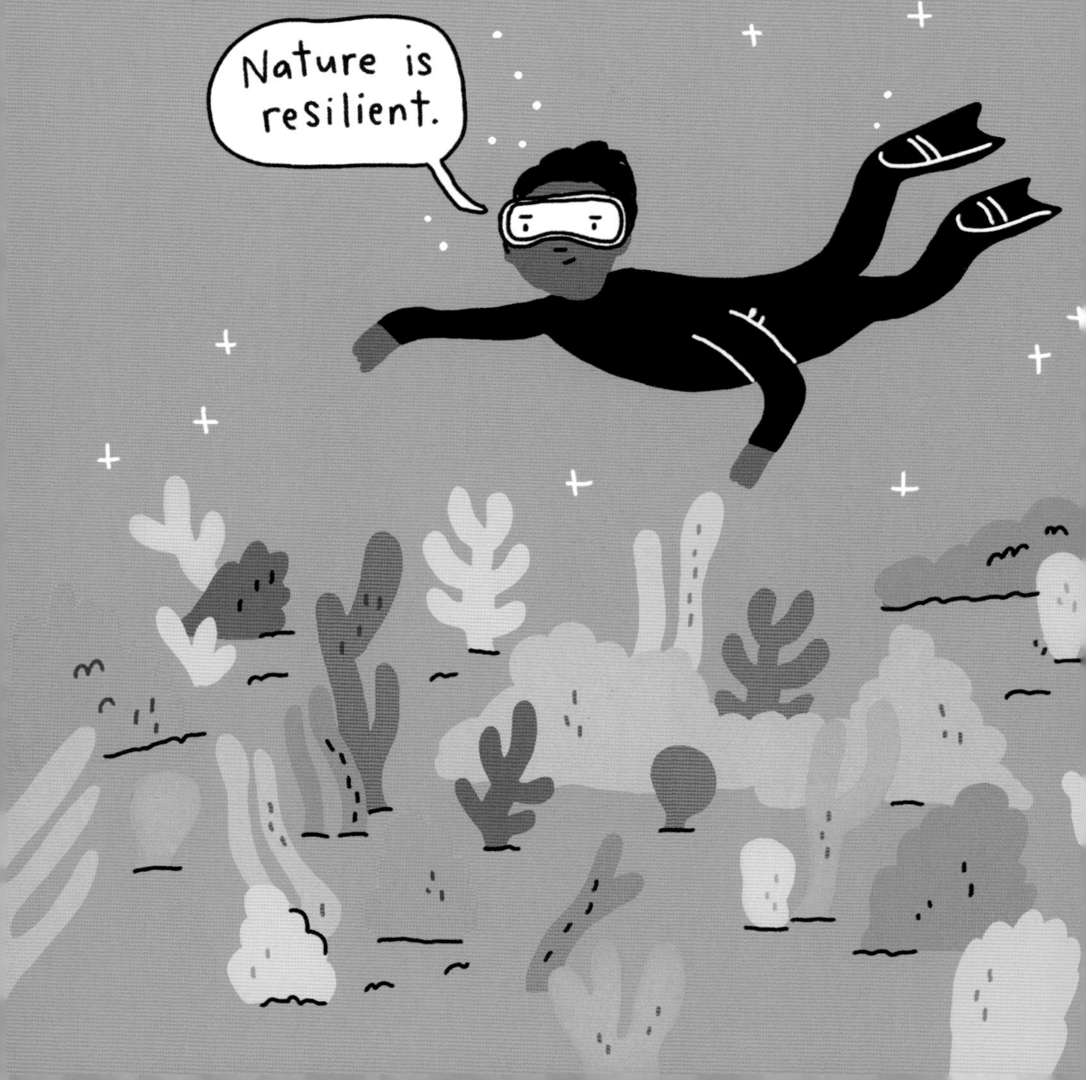
Nature is resilient.

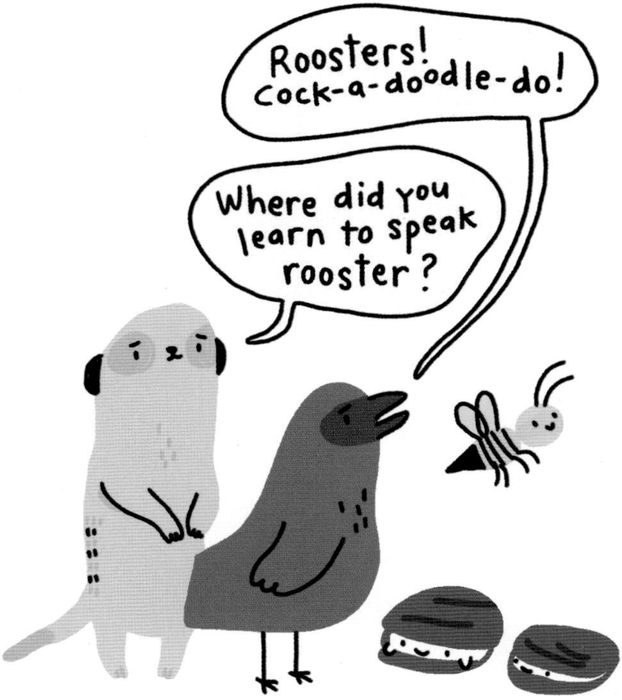
Roosters! Cock-a-doodle-do!
Where did you learn to speak rooster?

Dr. Tsuyoshi Shimmura studies roosters.

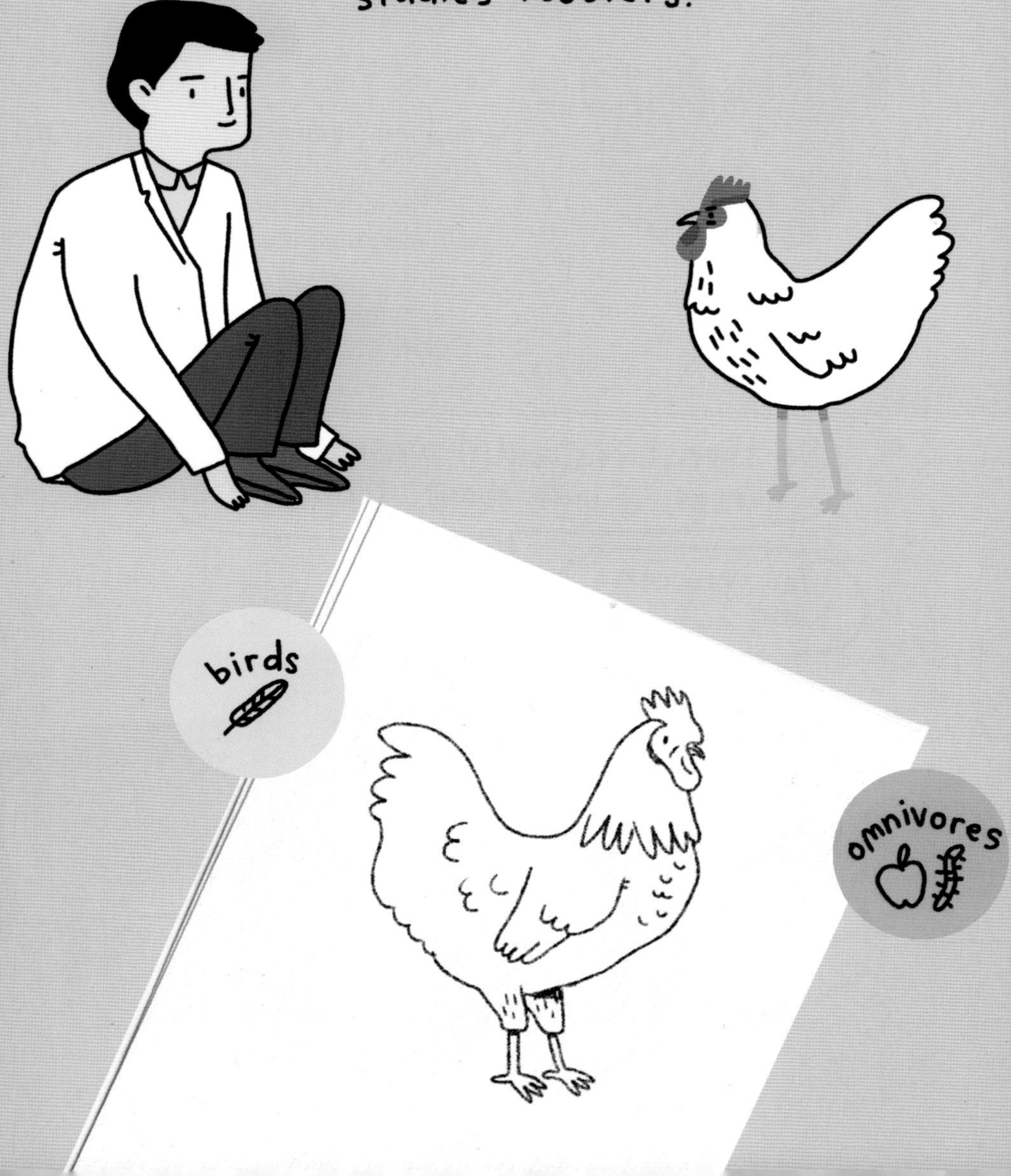
birds
omnivores

ROOSTERS

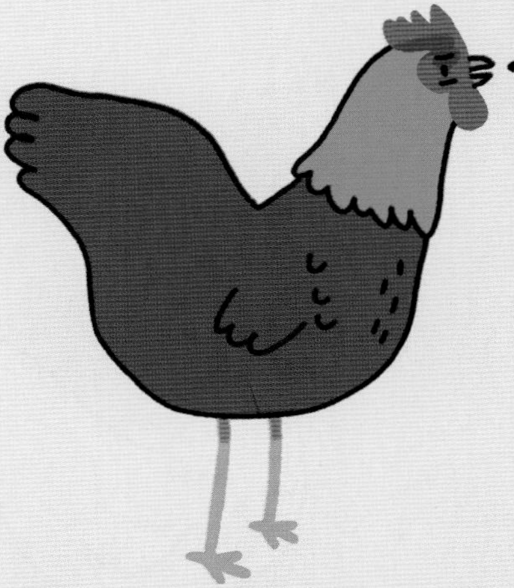
Just love to roost.

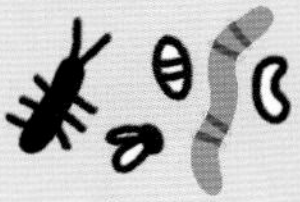

Omnivores (they eat insects and seeds).

They can fly, but not very far and only for a few seconds.

There are more chickens on earth than any other species of bird.

A rooster is a male chicken.

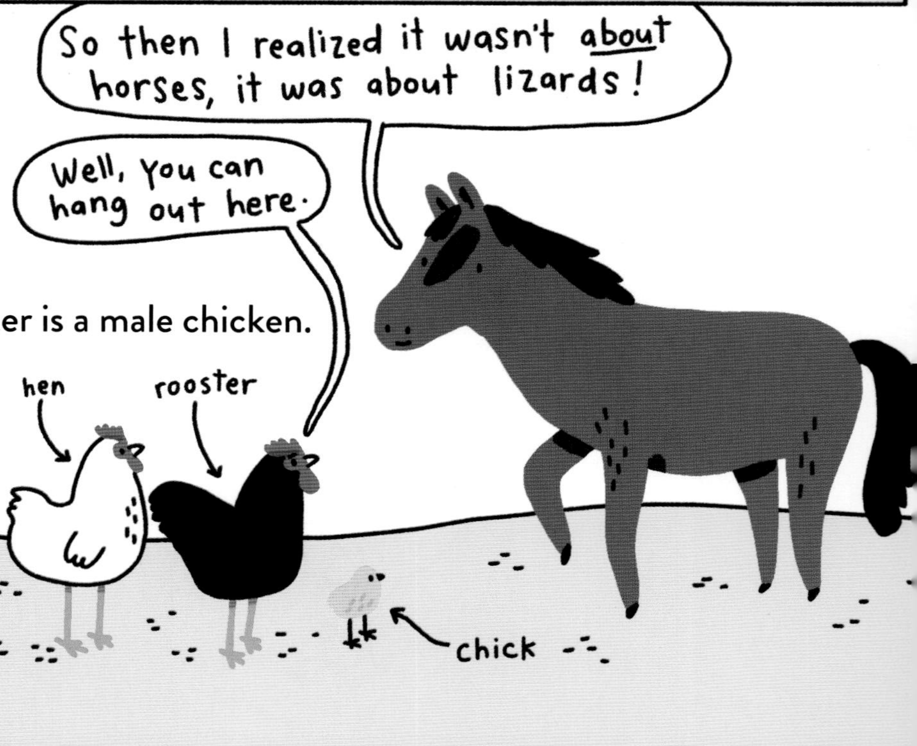
So then I realized it wasn't about horses, it was about lizards!
Well, you can hang out here.
hen
rooster
chick

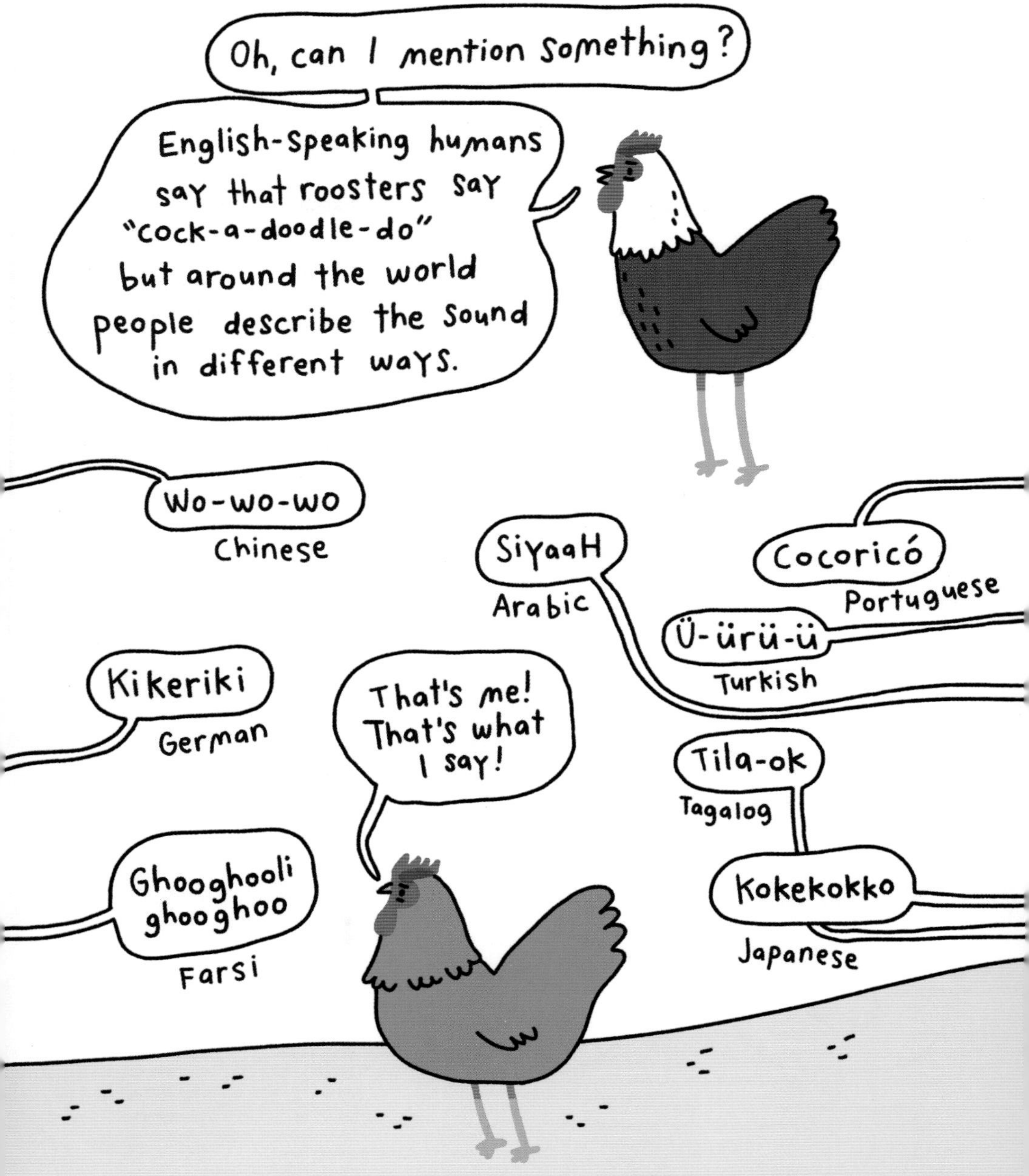

Oh, can I mention something?
English-speaking humans say that roosters say "cock-a-doodle-do" but around the world people describe the sound in different ways.
Wo-wo-wo
Chinese
SiyaaH
Arabic
Cocoricó
Portuguese
Ü-ürü-ü
Turkish
Kikeriki
German
That's me! That's what I say!
Tila-ok
Tagalog
Ghooghooli ghooghoo
Farsi
Kokekokko
Japanese

Chickens live all over the world (except Antarctica). And everywhere they live, roosters crow every morning, just before dawn.

They crow to mark their territory—the top-ranking rooster crows first, announcing that anything in the area belongs to him.

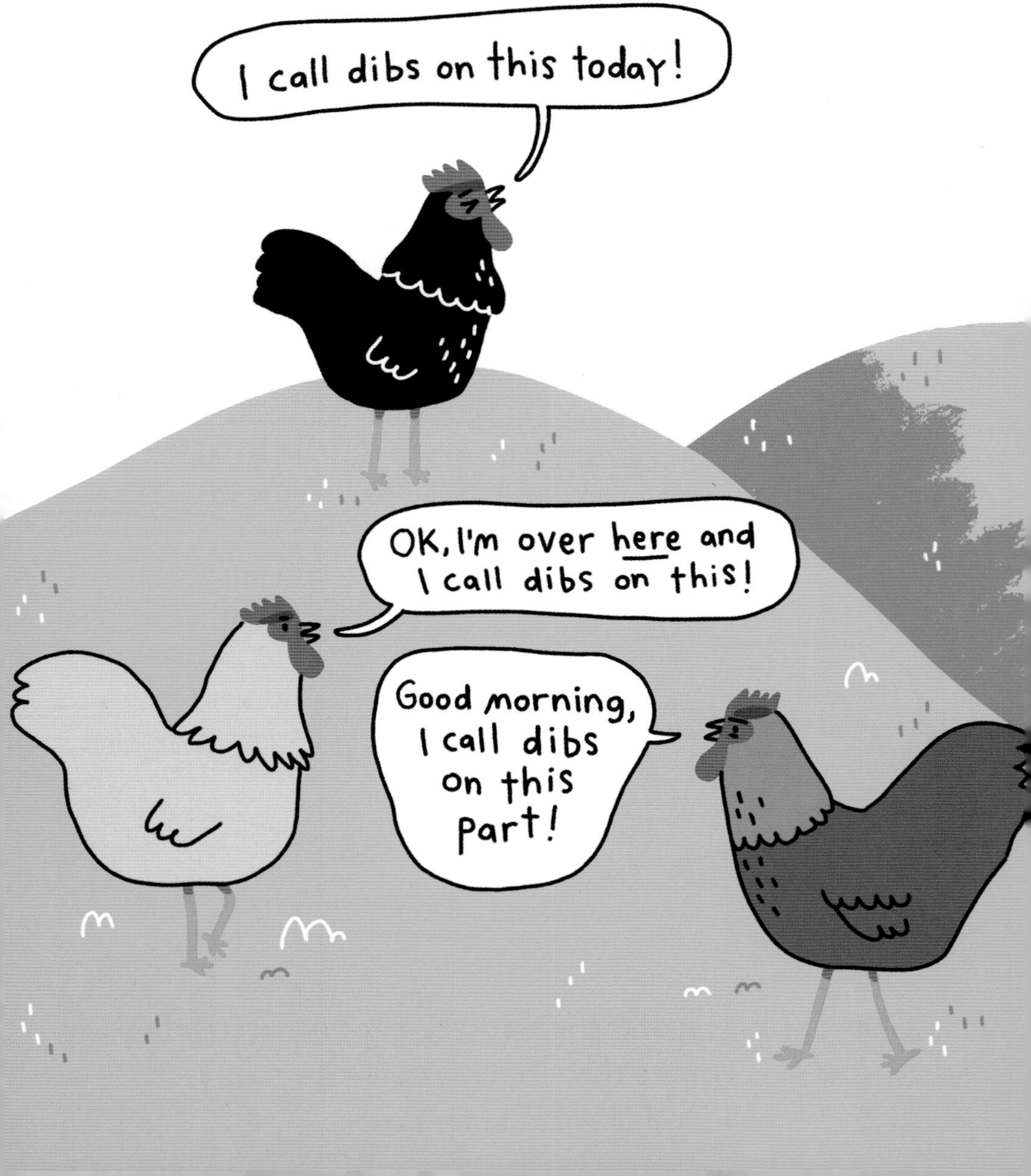
I call dibs on this today!
OK, I'm over here and I call dibs on this!
Good morning, I call dibs on this part!

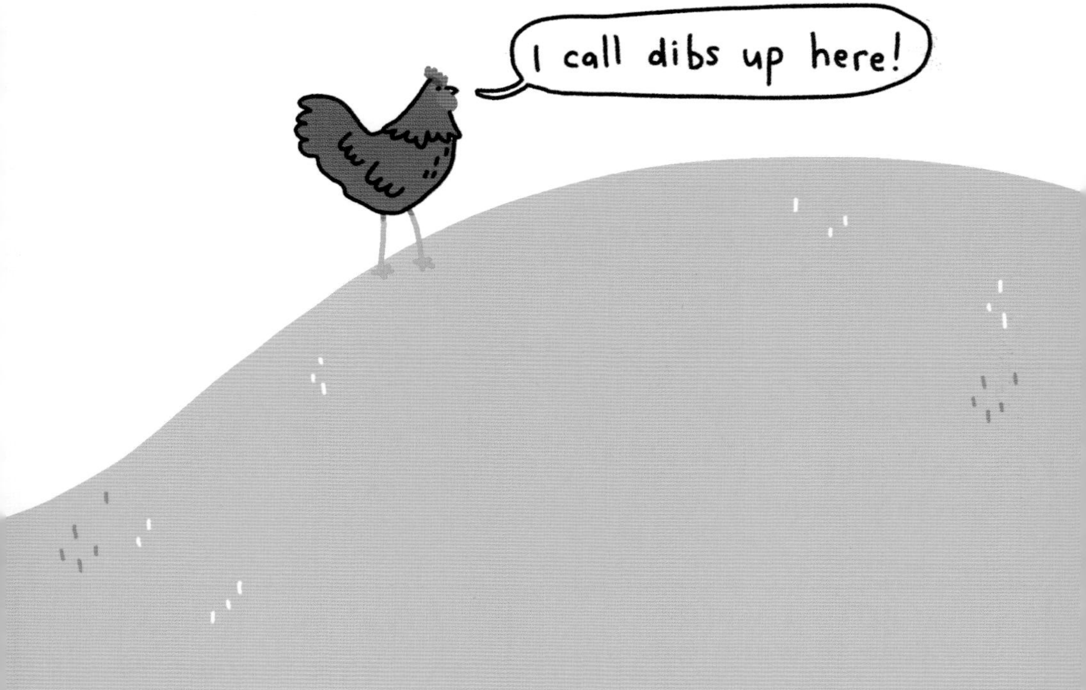
I call dibs up here!

Dr. Shimmura wondered how roosters
know when it's morning.

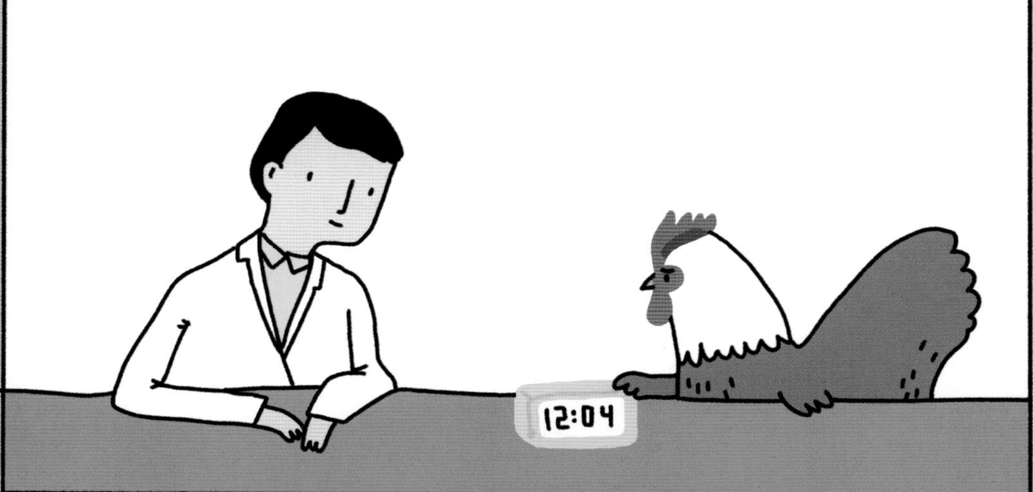
12:04

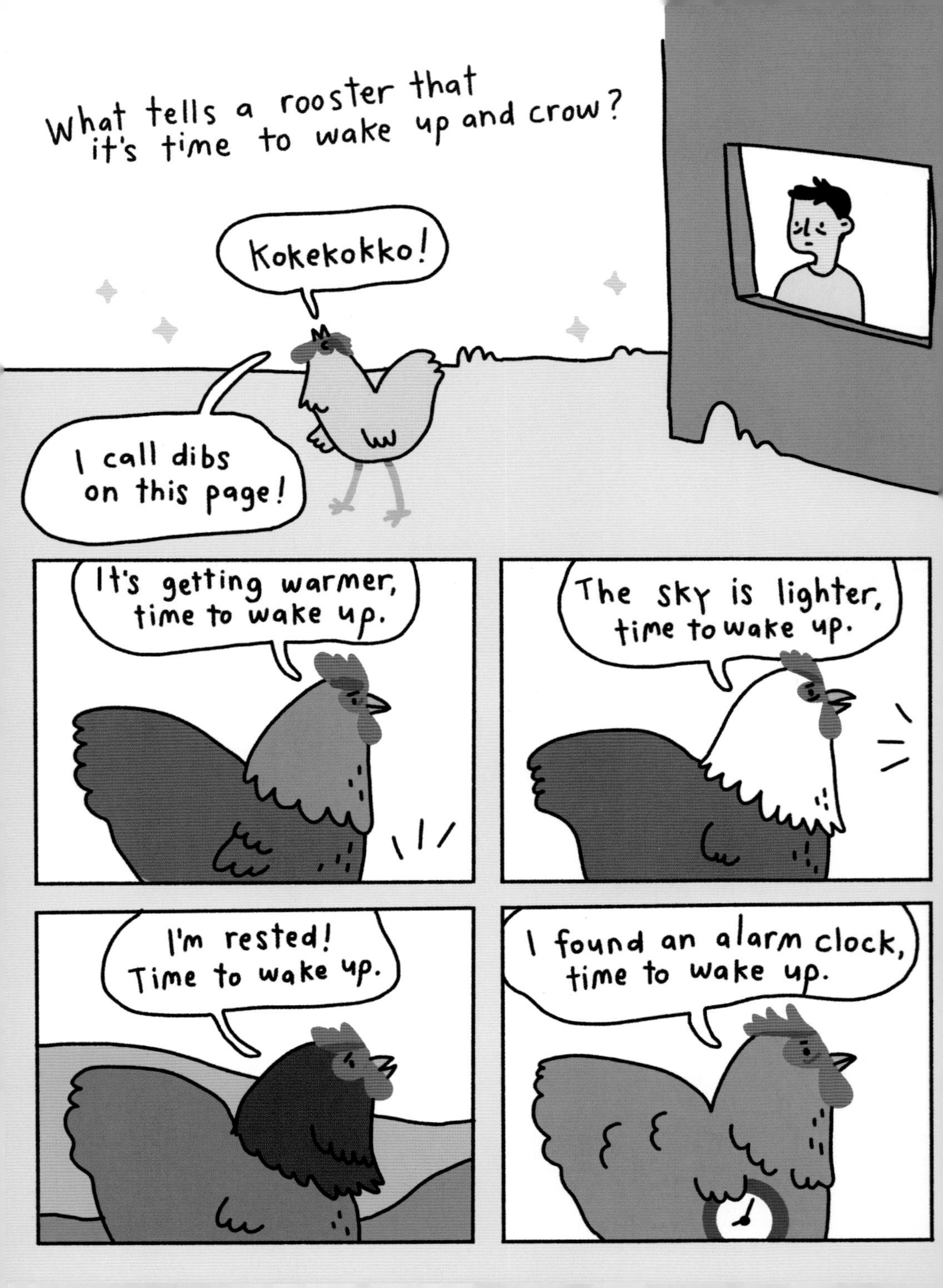
What tells a rooster that it's time to wake up and crow?
Kokekokko!
I call dibs on this page!
It's getting warmer, time to wake up.
The sky is lighter, time to wake up.
I'm rested! Time to wake up.
I found an alarm clock, time to wake up.

Roosters *also* crow when they see a bright light.

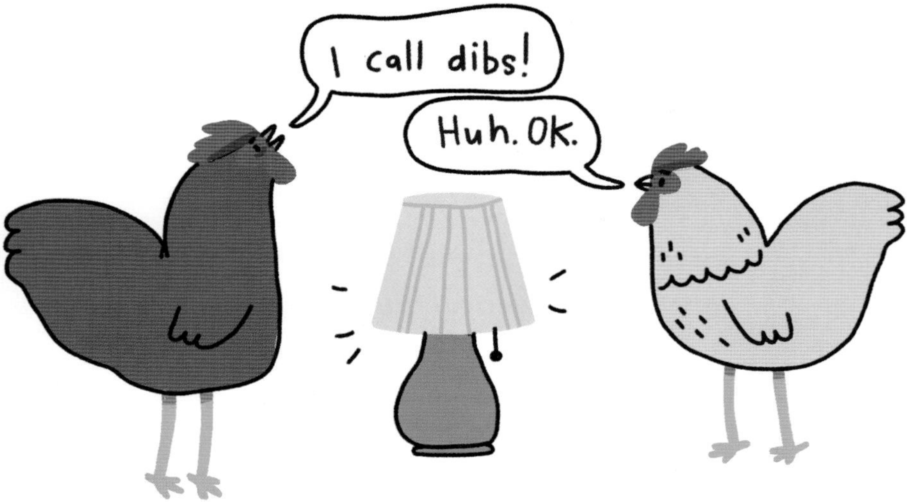
I call dibs!
Huh. OK.

Do roosters crow in the morning because they see the sun, and the sun is a huge light?

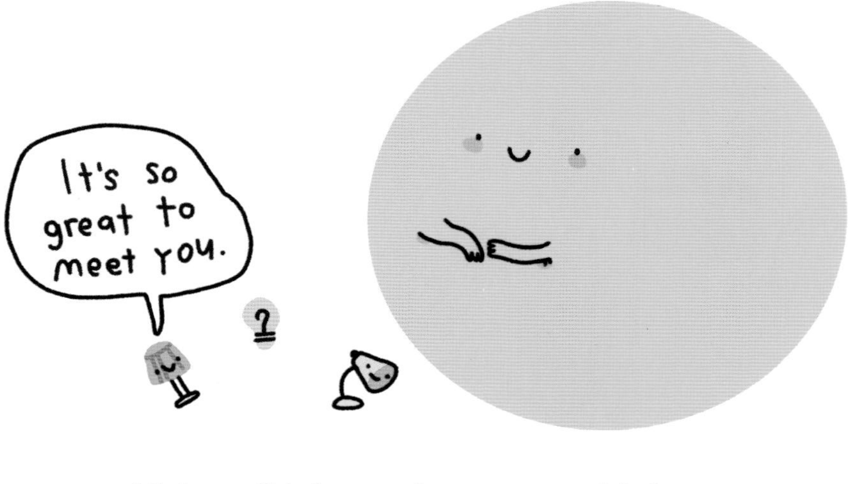
It's so great to meet you.
?

If they didn't see the sun, would they still know it was morning?

Dr. Shimmura observed roosters indoors, without natural light.

Instead of turning on artificial lights every twenty-four hours when the sun came up, the scientists put lights on a more random schedule.

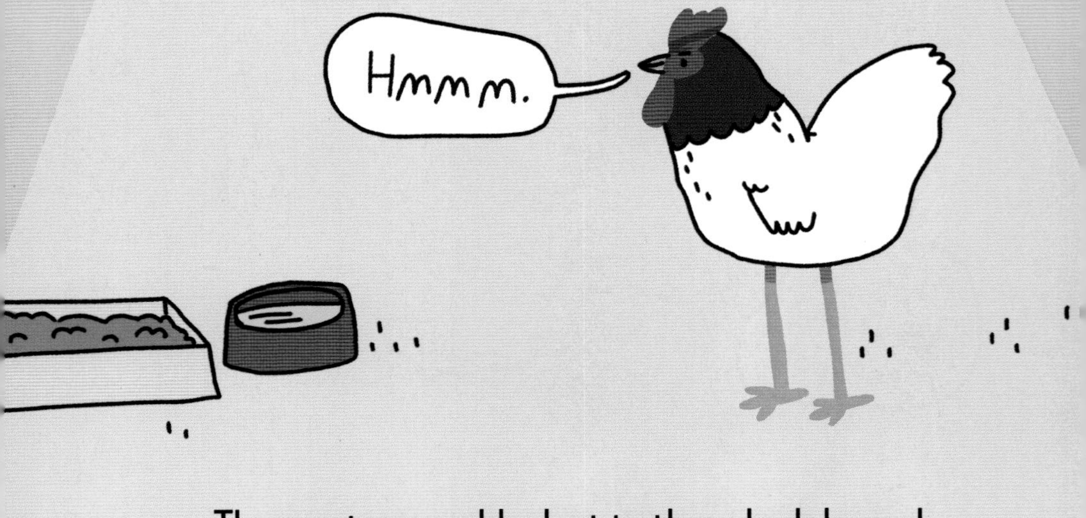
Hmmm.

The roosters would adapt to the schedule, and would crow just before the lights came on.

Even without the sun, they're able to wake themselves up at the right time, for something important.

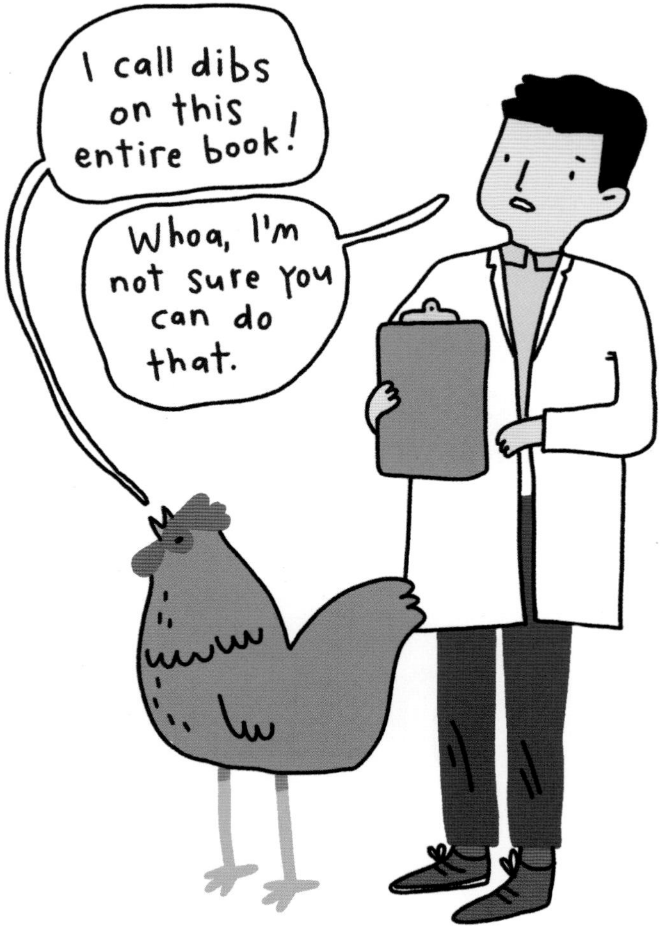
I call dibs on this entire book!
Whoa, I'm not sure you can do that.

We still don't know exactly how roosters wake up before the sun, but Dr. Shimmura's research is helping us understand them a little better.

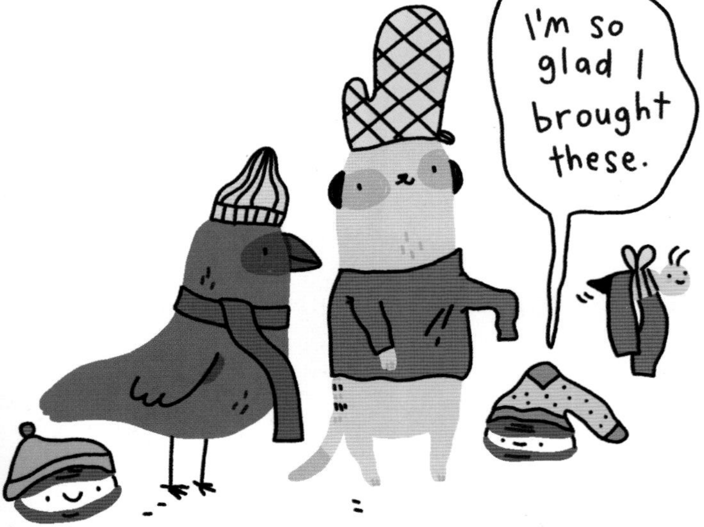
I'm so glad I brought these.

Dr. Nicholas Teets
studies Antarctic midges.

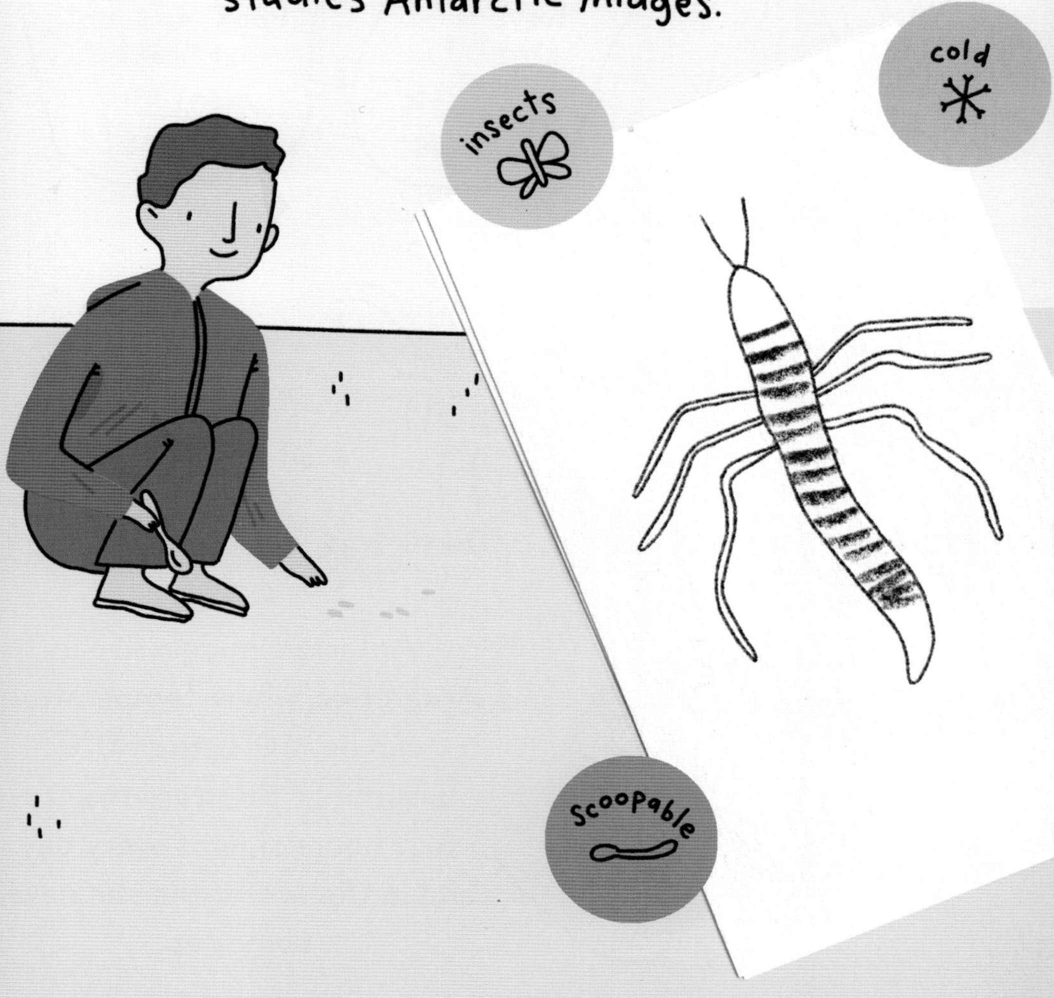
insects
cold
scoopable

ANTARCTIC MIDGES

YESSS!

I told you they would have a chapter about Antarctic midges!

I said they're not going to make a whole book and not at least mention midges!

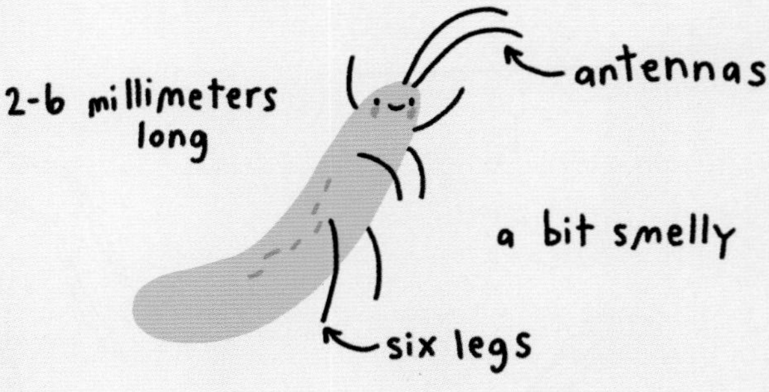

2-6 millimeters long

antennas

a bit smelly

six legs

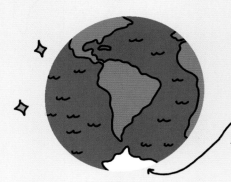

Antarctic midges live in Antarctica, where temperatures can be −10°C to −60°C. In summer there are twenty-four hours of light every day, and in the winter the sun never comes up.

Dr. Teets's team visits in the summer to collect midge specimens to study. They fly to Chile and travel by boat across the Drake Passage.

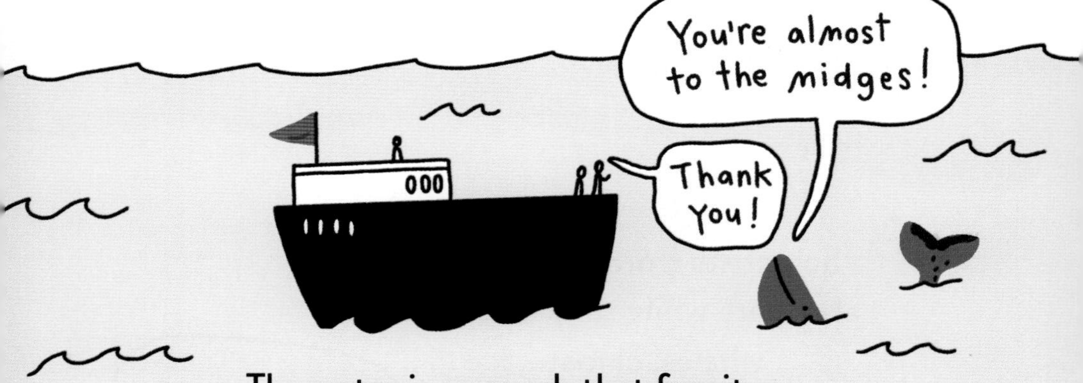
You're almost to the midges!
Thank You!

The water is so rough that furniture in the boat is attached to the floor.

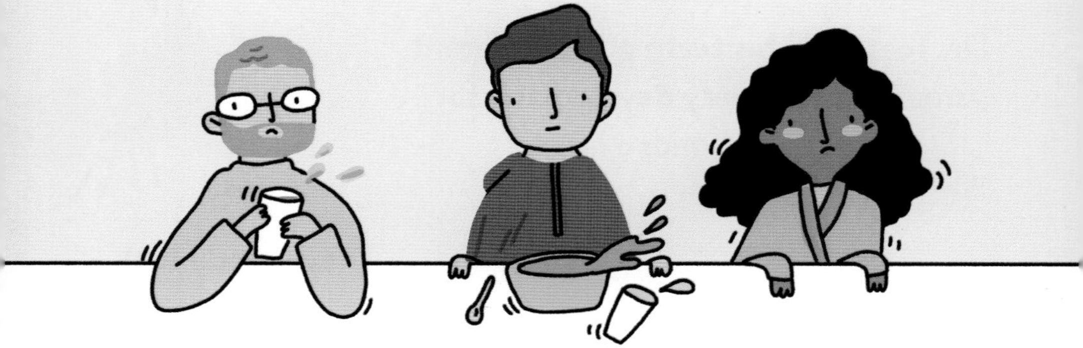

Some of the scientists get seasick.

After a three- or four-day trip, they get to Palmer Station.

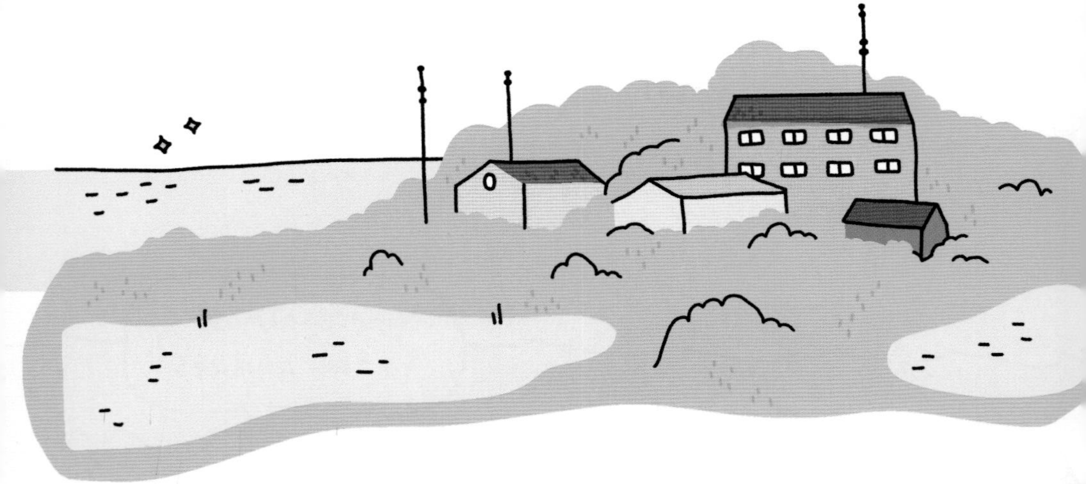

Scientists from around the world stay here while they research wind, whales, climate, ice . . .

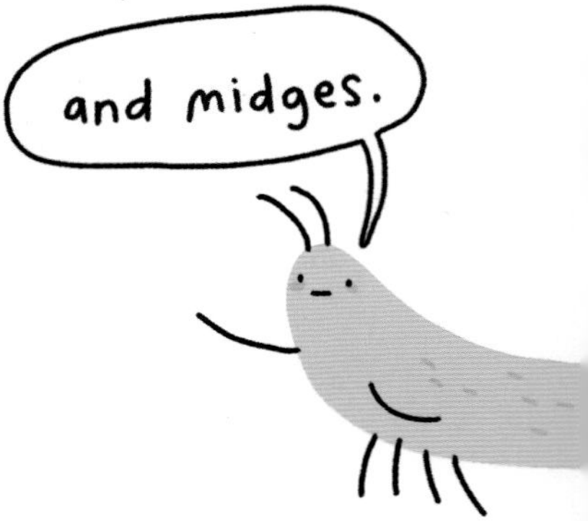
and midges.

Dr. Teets and his team go to different small islands every day, looking for midges and midge larvae.

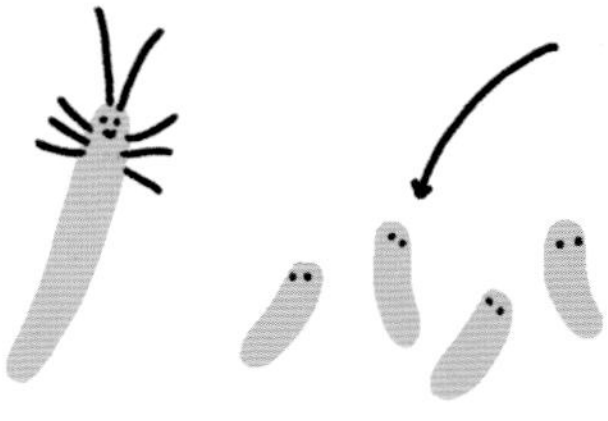

They mostly look for larvae, because they're easier to find and collect.

Midges are the only insects that live on Antarctica, and the *largest* land-based creature in Antarctica.

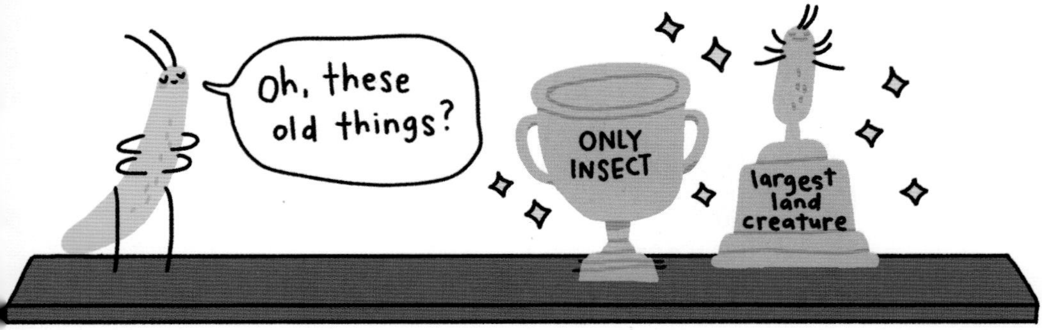
Oh, these old things?
ONLY INSECT
largest land creature

Larger animals like penguins and whales use the water to stay warm.

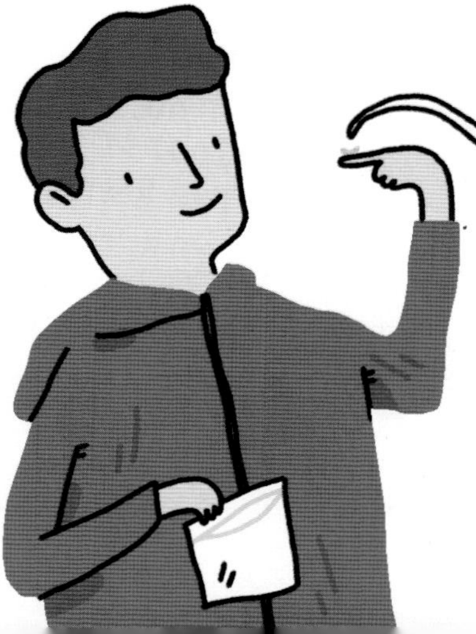

Dr. Teets is studying how these tiny and amazing! insects spend eight months of the year frozen.

Everything you need to collect midge larvae:

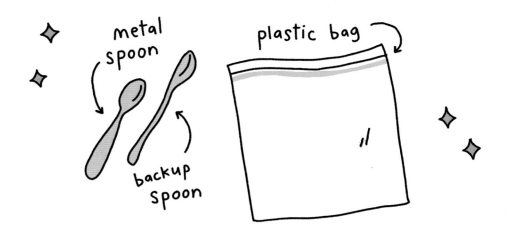

metal spoon

backup spoon

plastic bag

(The team used to use spoons from the research station's kitchen. But people asked them to stop. Now they bring their own.)

Midges live near penguin and elephant seal guano, where there are lots of nutrients.

Did you know guano is another word for poop?

GROSS! Why didn't you tell me sooner?! I've been living in this for months!

While the researchers look for midge larvae, nearby penguins shout to introduce themselves to each other.

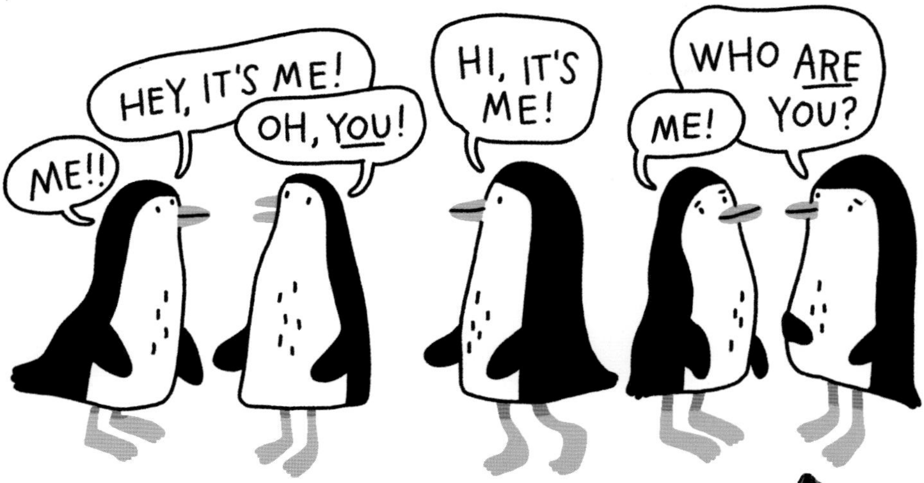
ME!!
HEY, IT'S ME!
OH, YOU!
HI, IT'S ME!
ME!
WHO ARE YOU?

If they find an adult midge, they suck it up using a tubelike straw called a pooter.

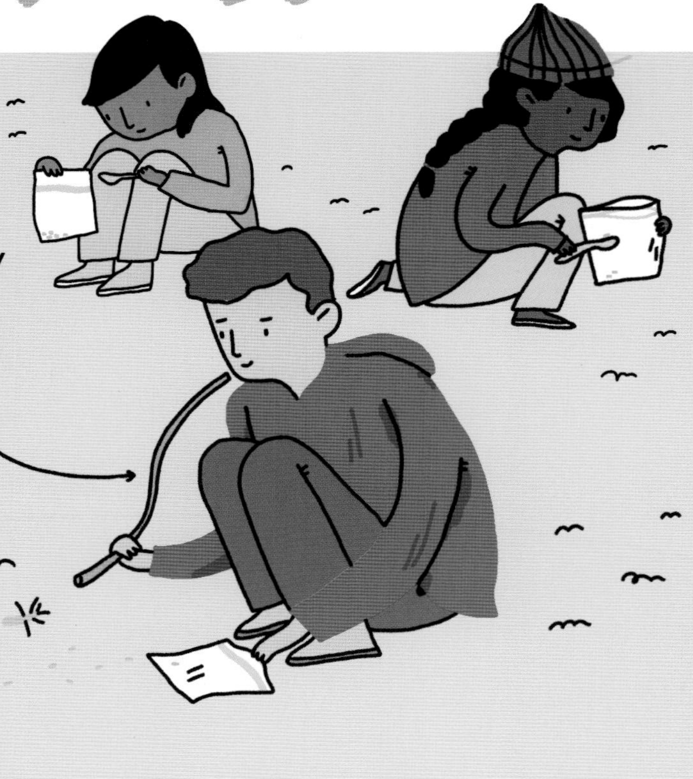

Sometimes it can get *really* loud in Antarctica.
The penguins are always shouting, and the
elephant seals burp.

Other times, it's really quiet.

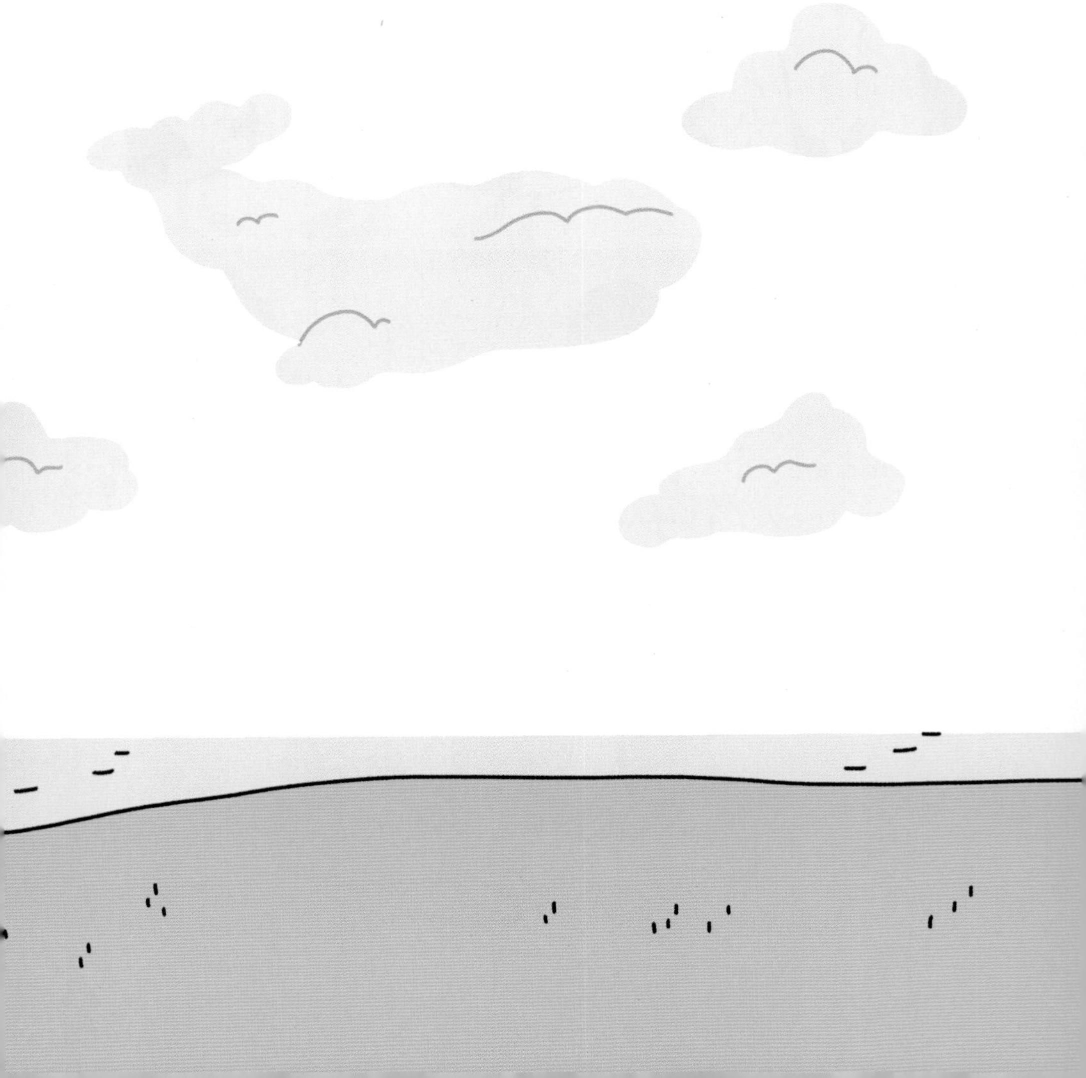

Nick has always loved animals. When he was a kid, his favorite animal was the cheetah.

After he read every book about cheetahs at his local library,

his mom drove him to other libraries so he could find more to read about them.

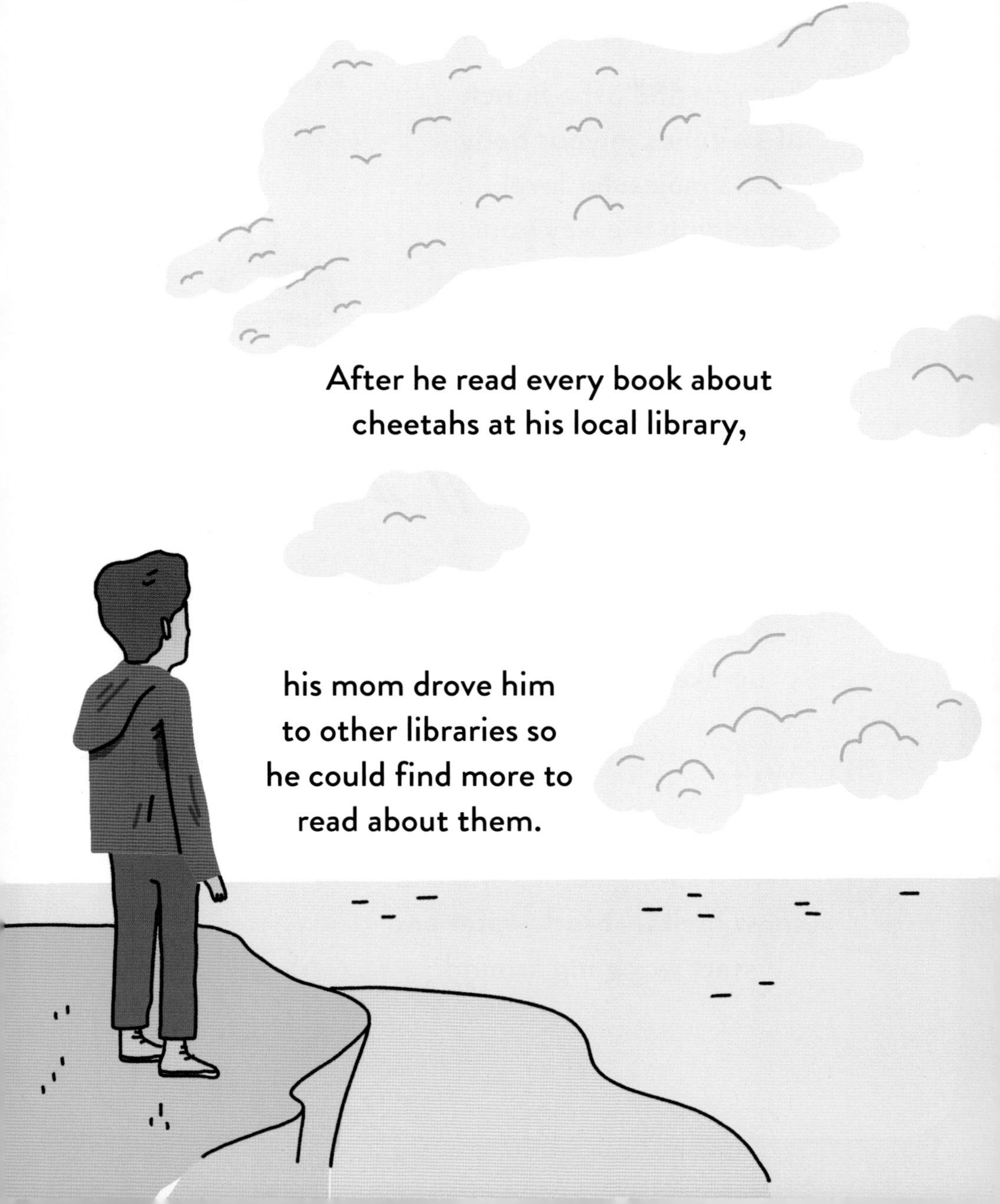

A MIDGE'S GUIDE to FREEZING

1. Turn on and off a bunch of switches in your body at a *molecular* level, changing the way your cells work. (This is the part scientists have the most questions about.)

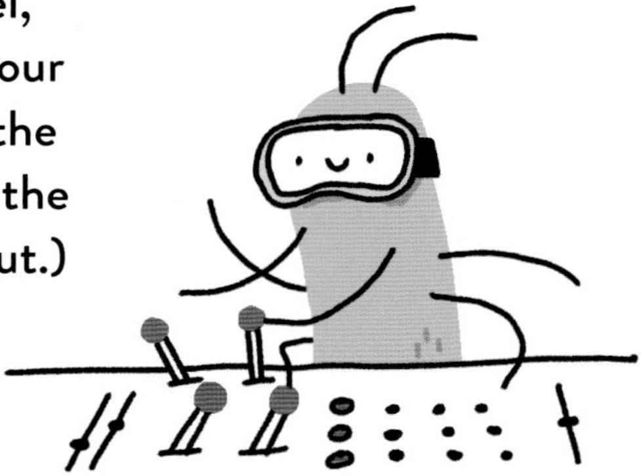

2. Lose half the water in your body, and shrink up like a raisin.

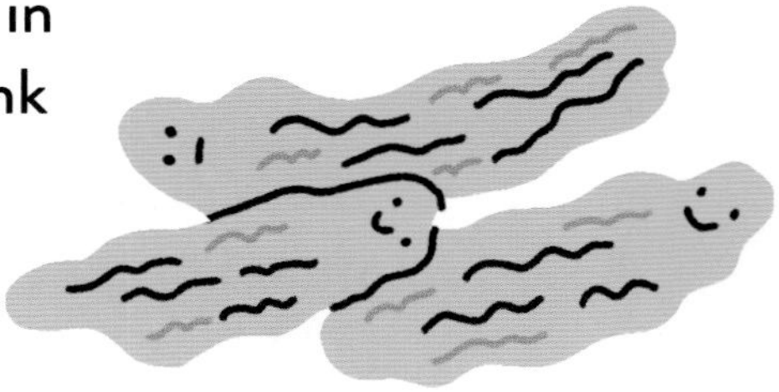

3. Wait.

4. When spring comes and the snow melts, absorb water and start wriggling around.

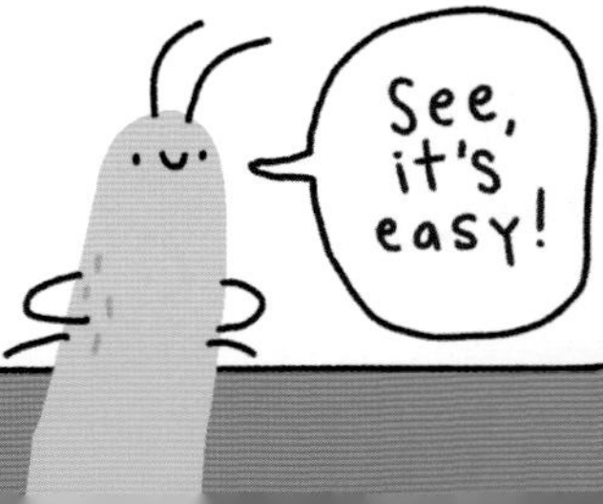
See, it's easy!

When the team has collected enough midge larvae, they pack them with ice to keep them cool and put them on a boat to study at the lab in Kentucky.

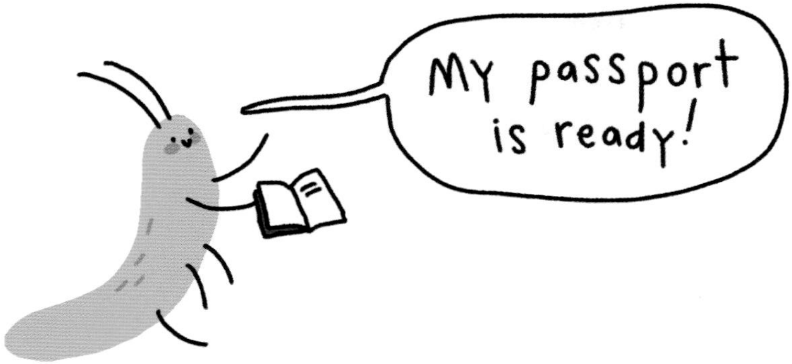
My passport is ready!

We humans might not ever be able to freeze ourselves every winter, but learning how midges do it could help us preserve organs for transplants even better.

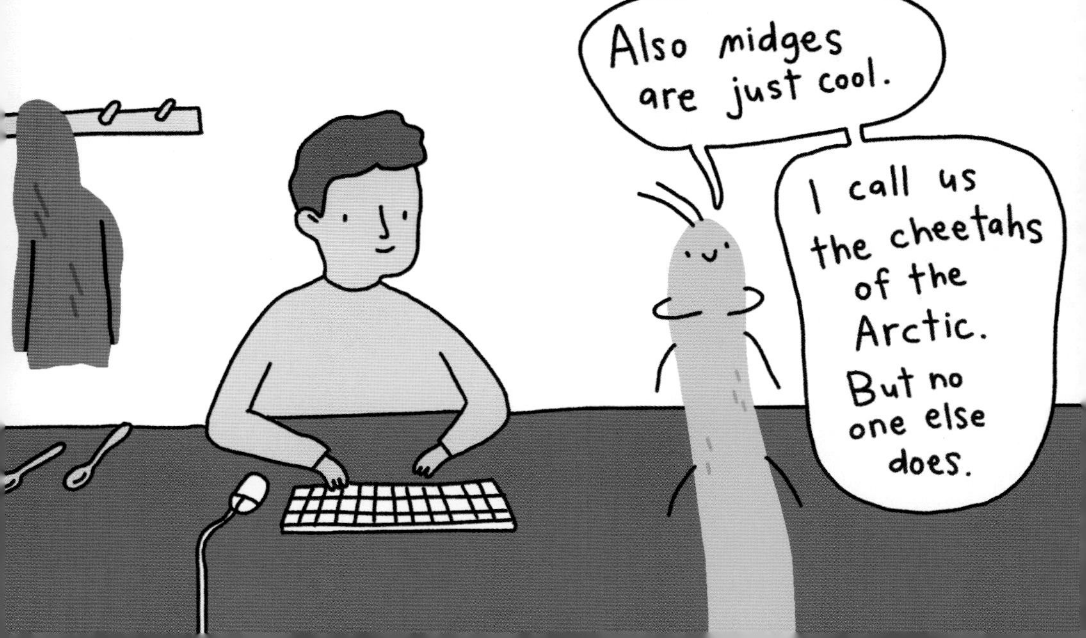
Also midges are just cool.
I call us the cheetahs of the Arctic. But no one else does.

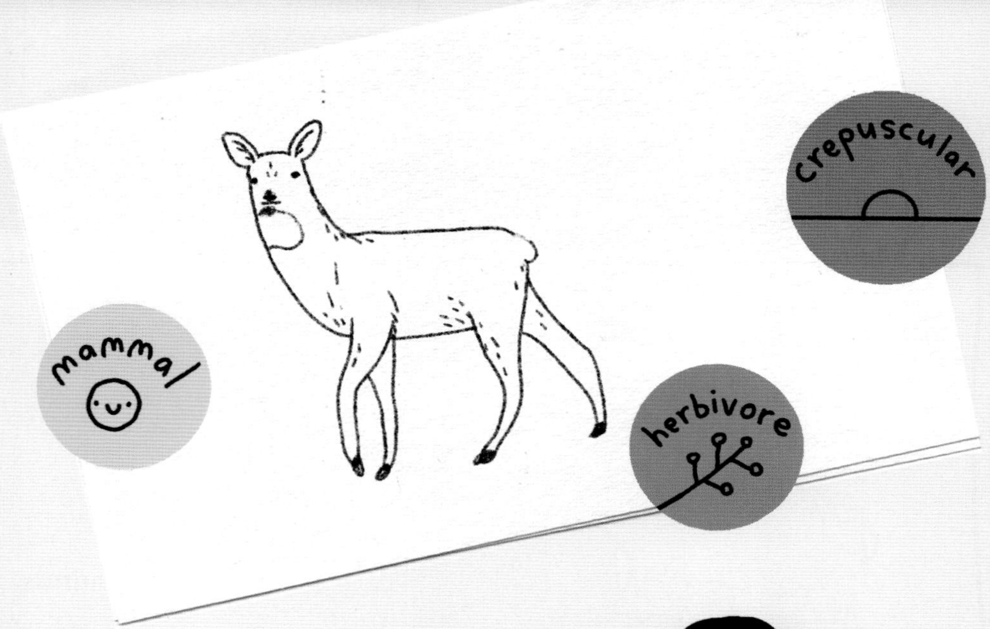
mammal
crepuscular
herbivore

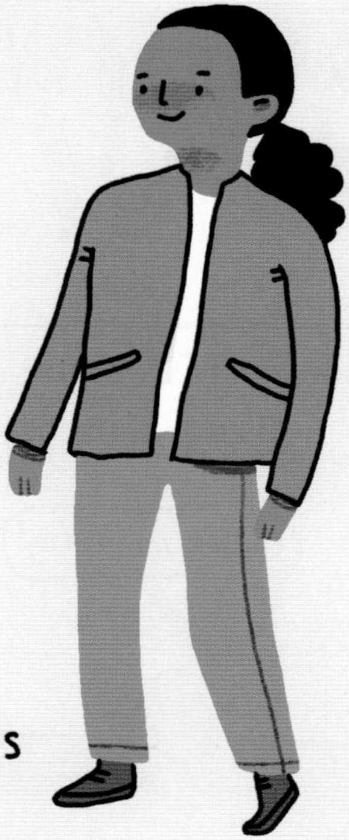

Rhiannon Kirton studies
white-tailed deer.

WHITE-TAILED DEER

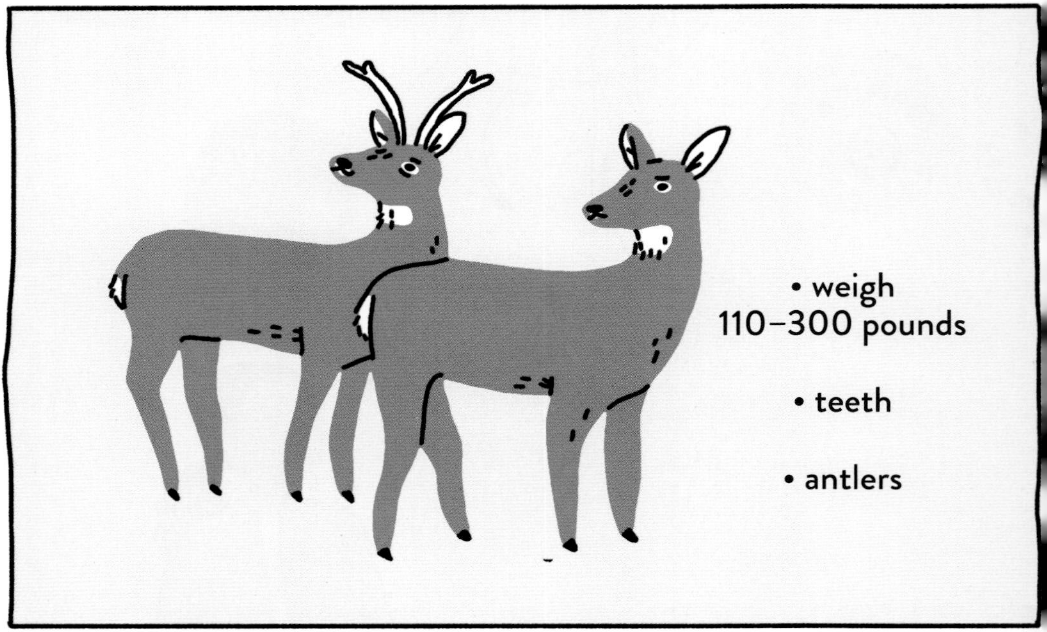

• weigh 110–300 pounds
• teeth
• antlers

White-tailed deer are *crepuscular*, which means they're active around dawn and active again at dusk.

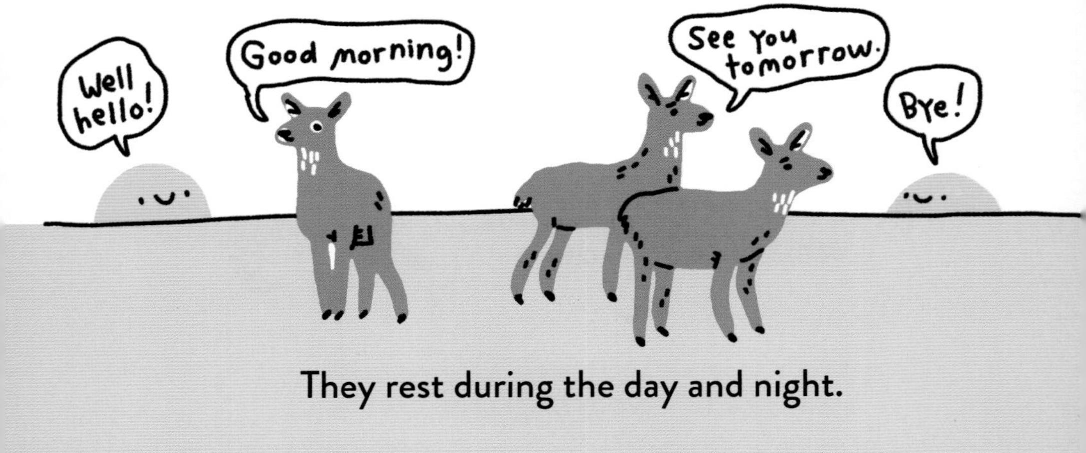

Well hello!
Good morning!
See you tomorrow.
Bye!

They rest during the day and night.

They hold their white tails up in the air when running away from predators.

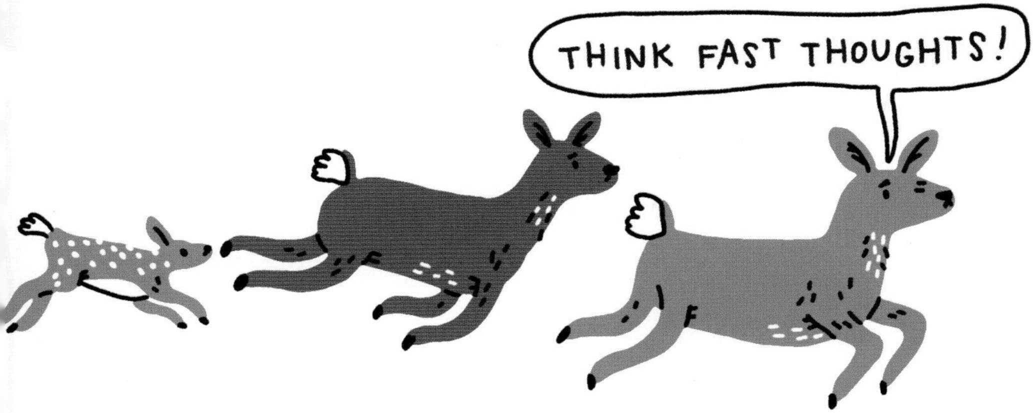
THINK FAST THOUGHTS!

Their sporty white tails make them look speedy as they run away, so their predators give up and decide not to chase them. They can run at speeds of up to thirty miles per hour.

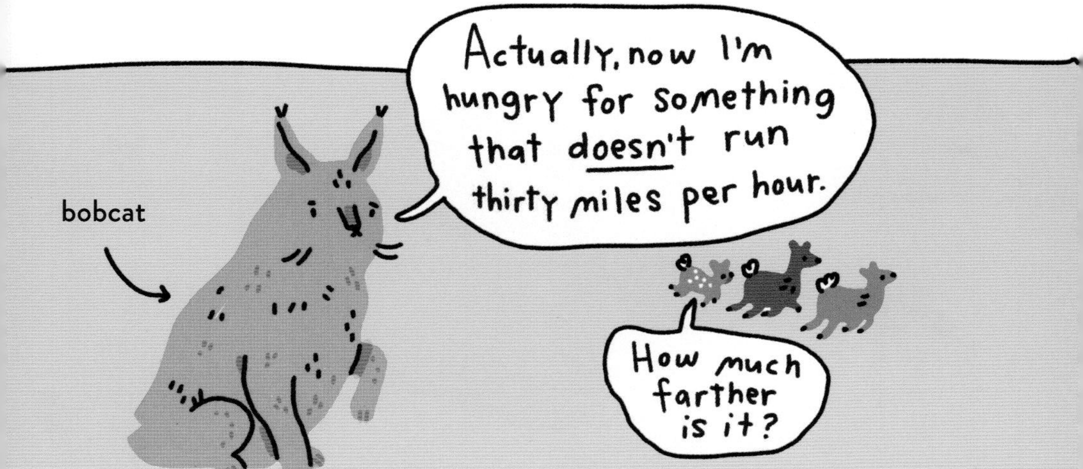
Actually, now I'm hungry for something that doesn't run thirty miles per hour.
bobcat
How much farther is it?

Coyotes, wolves, mountain lions, and bobcats used to be the white-tailed deer's main predators.

Rhiannon has always loved animals and has always loved to be outdoors. When she was growing up, she had to write a school paper on wolves.

She called a local wildlife park and asked if she could study their wolves, and they said yes.

Her mom drove her to the sanctuary, and they spent three days in a cage watching the rescued wolves, so Rhiannon could write her paper.

She even got to feed the wolves.

Rhiannon wrote her school paper on how wolves are scary in fairy tales, but they aren't actually scary once you learn more about them.

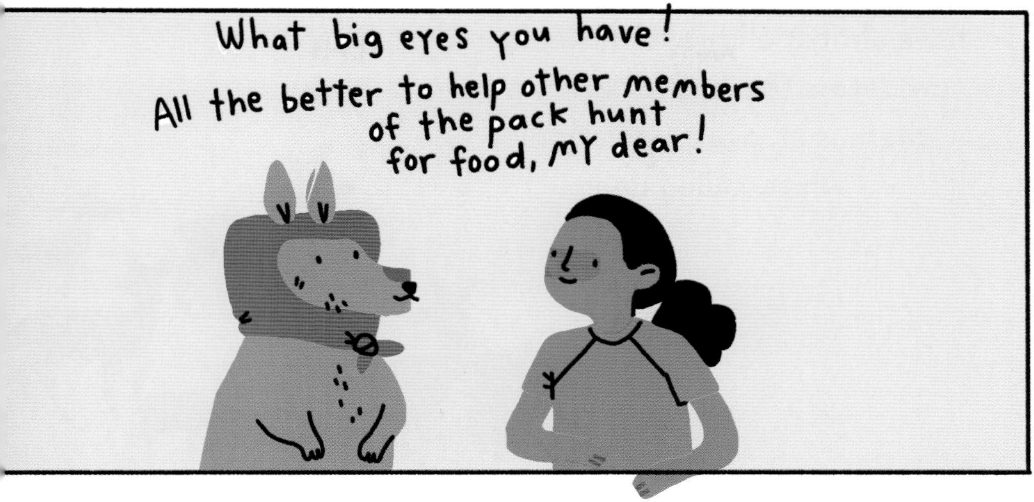
What big eyes you have!
All the better to help other members of the pack hunt for food, my dear!

Today, her work as a mammalogist helps humans understand mammals better.

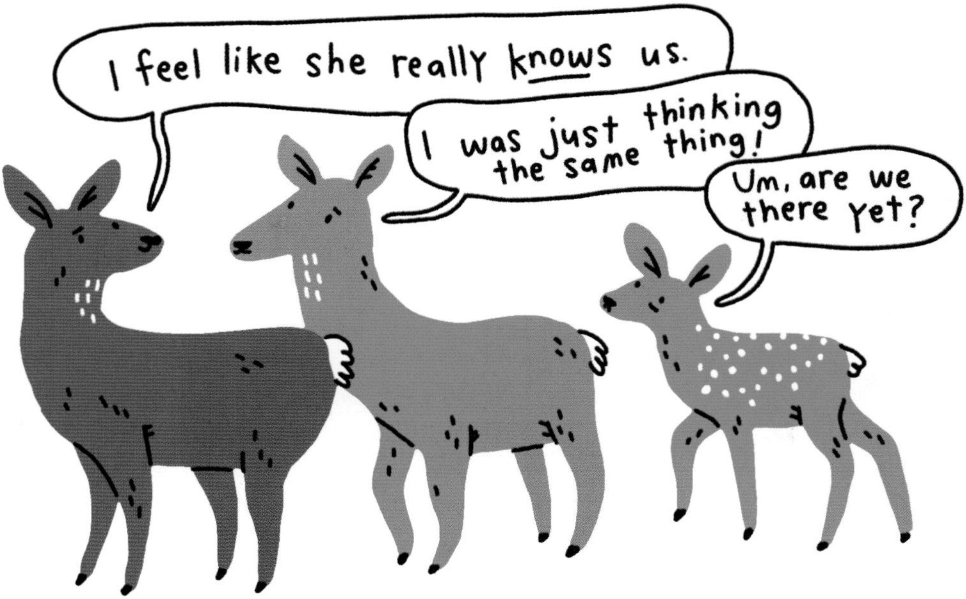
I feel like she really knows us.
I was just thinking the same thing!
Um, are we there yet?

Rhiannon studies white-tailed deer in Canada. Because humans have almost eliminated the deer's predators (except for humans), there is an overpopulation of white-tailed deer.

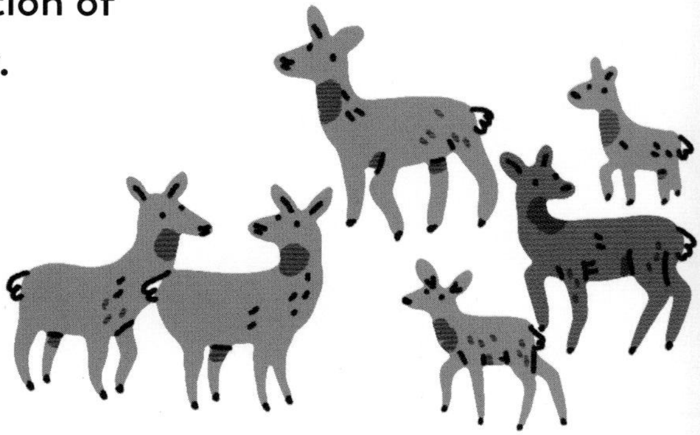

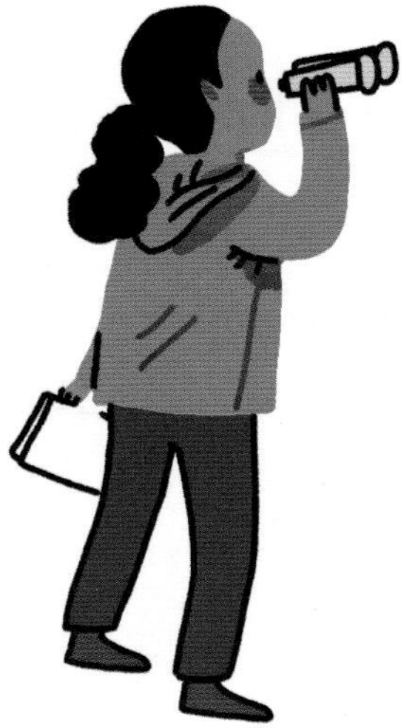

She records their location, to understand the deer population and where they live.

Rhiannon and her team have discovered a few ways white-tailed deer protect themselves during hunting season. Every year, many groups of deer travel to places where hunting isn't allowed.

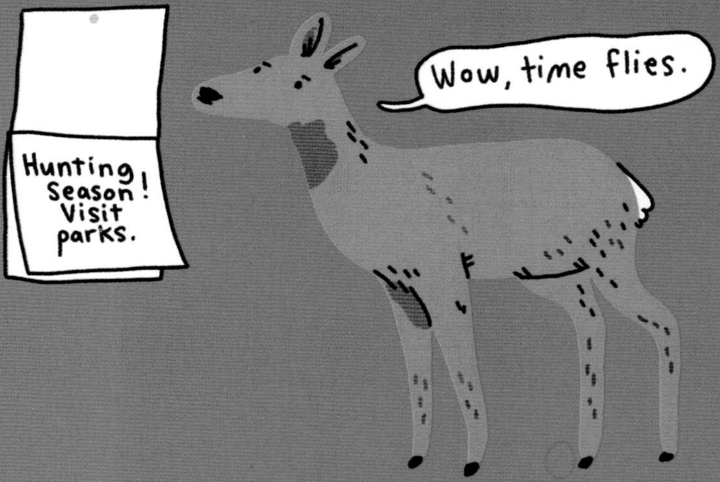
Hunting Season! Visit parks.
Wow, time flies.

And they also travel after sunset, instead of moving while it's still light out.

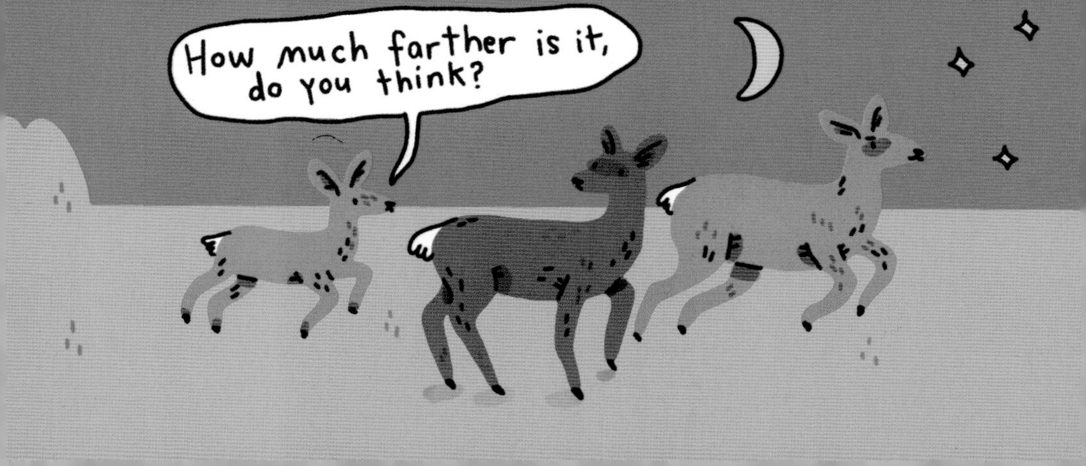
How much farther is it, do you think?

Even though deer are overpopulated right now, it's still important for scientists to learn about them and their habitat . . .

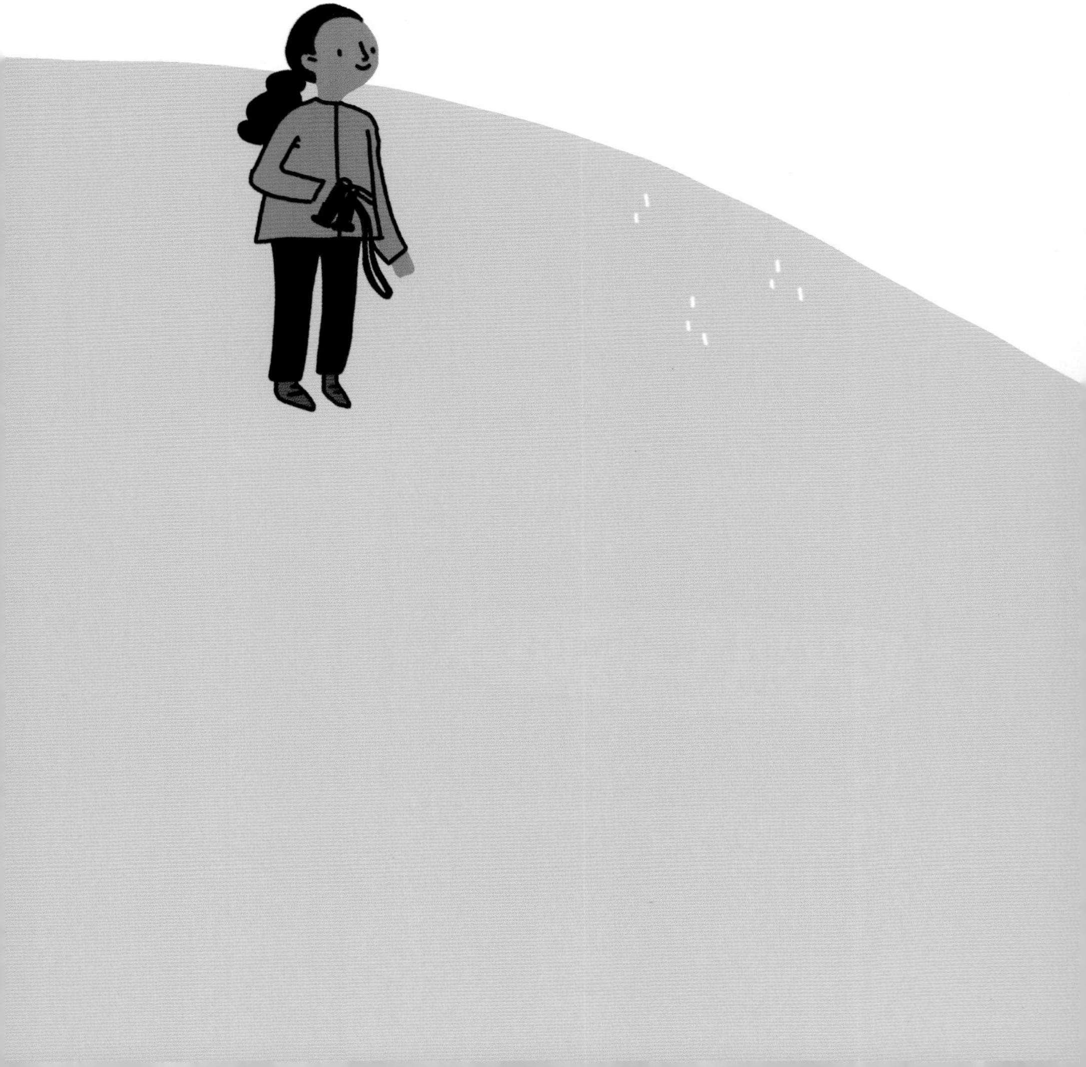

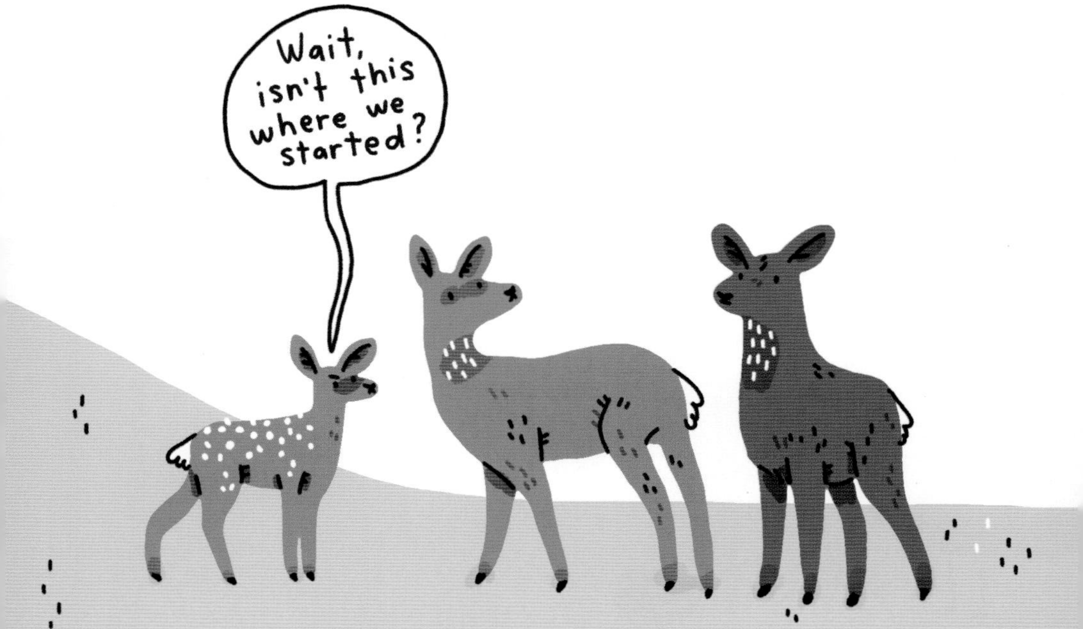
Wait, isn't this where we started?

especially when there's still
so much we don't know yet.

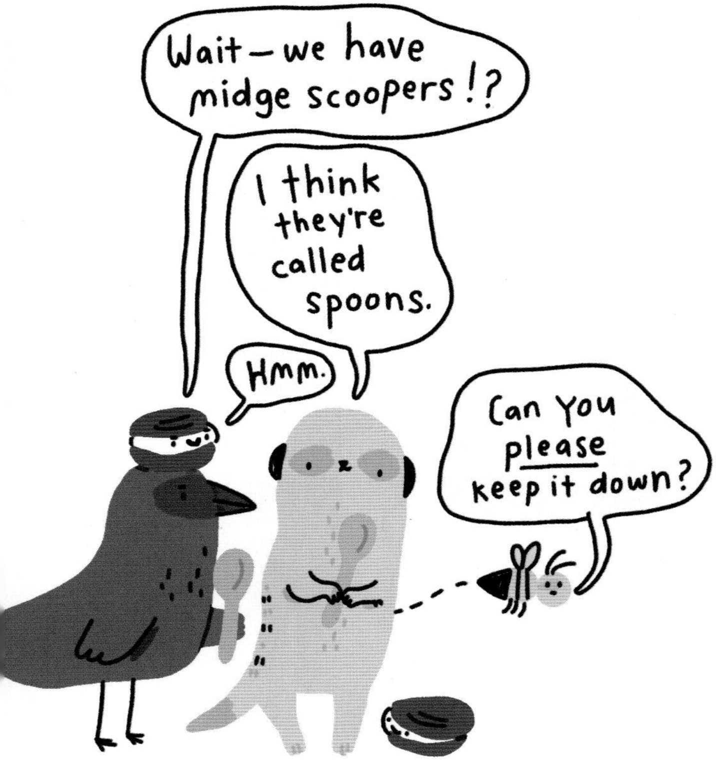

Wait—we have midge scoopers!?
I think they're called spoons.
Hmm.
Can you please keep it down?

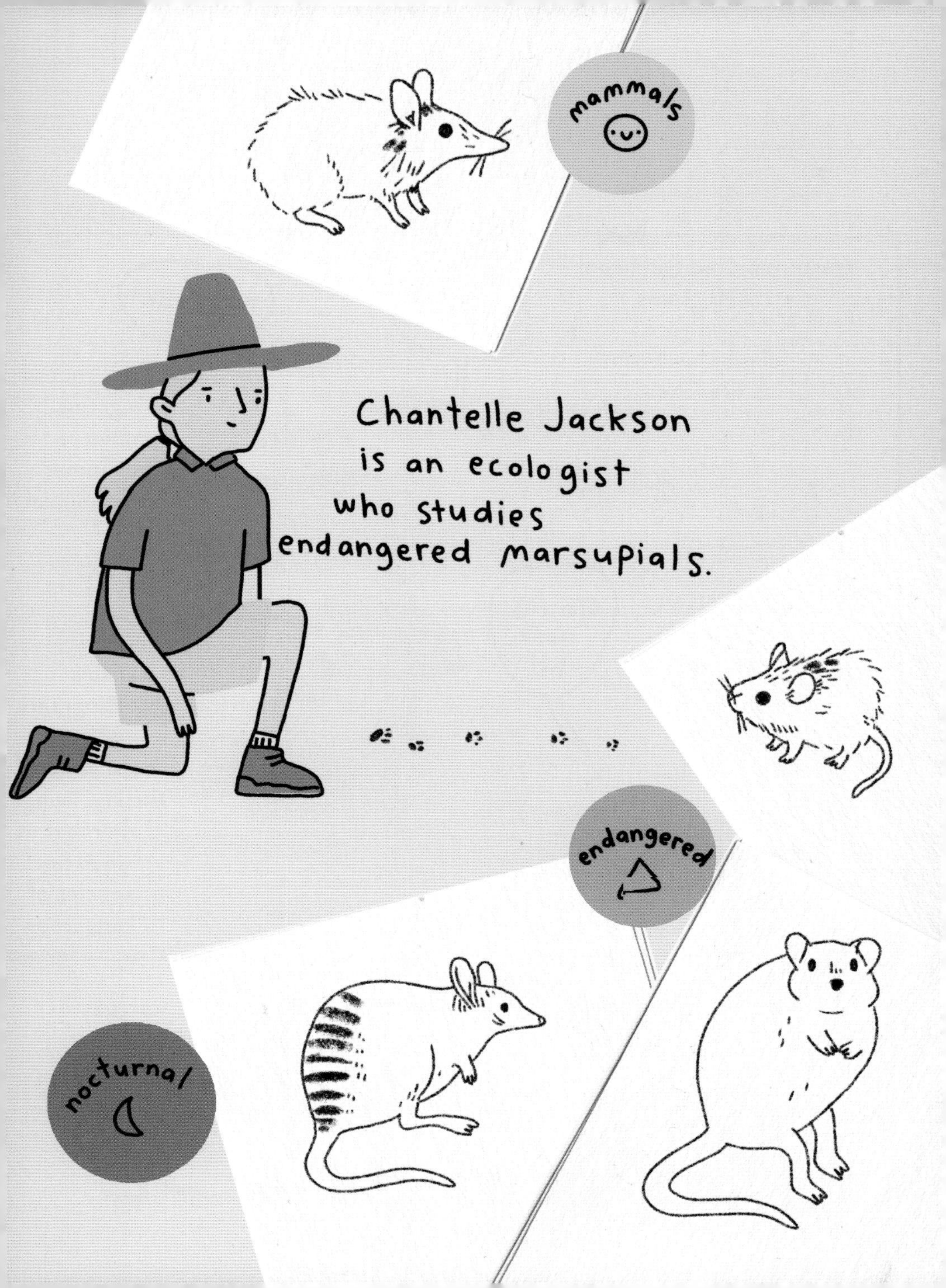
mammals
Chantelle Jackson is an ecologist who studies endangered marsupials.
endangered
nocturnal

MARSUPIALS

and a mouse

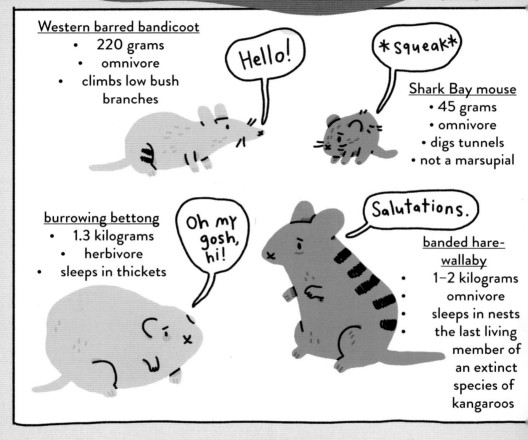

<u>Western barred bandicoot</u>
- 220 grams
- omnivore
- climbs low bush branches

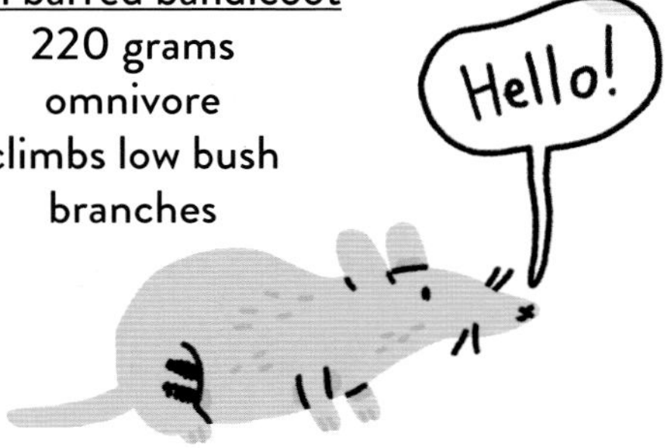
Hello!

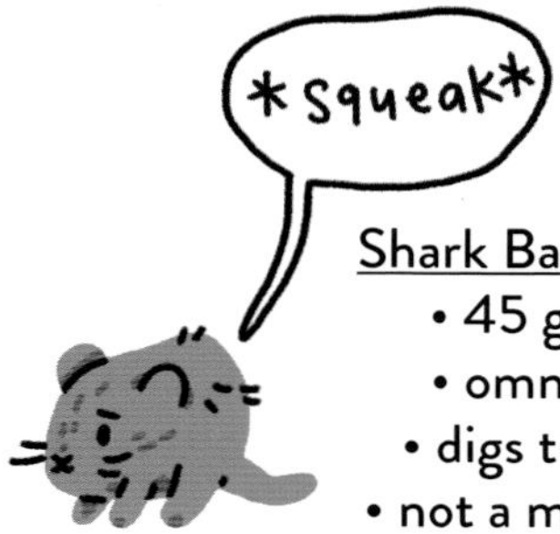
squeak

<u>Shark Bay mouse</u>
- 45 grams
- omnivore
- digs tunnels
- not a marsupial

<u>burrowing bettong</u>
- 1.3 kilograms
- herbivore
- sleeps in thickets

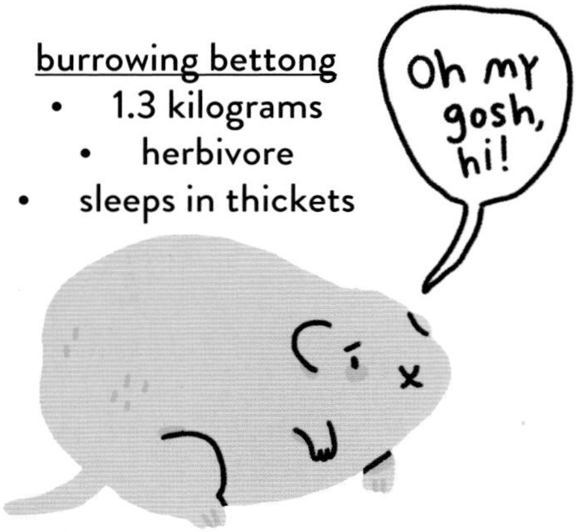
Oh my gosh, hi!

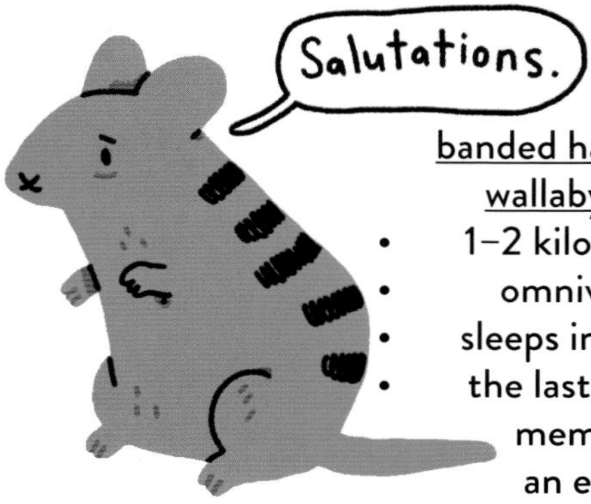
Salutations.

<u>banded hare-wallaby</u>
- 1–2 kilograms
- omnivore
- sleeps in nests
- the last living member of an extinct species of kangaroos

The four of them are nocturnal, and they eat a variety of things, including flowers, mushrooms, moss, leaves, grass, insects, and other small creatures.

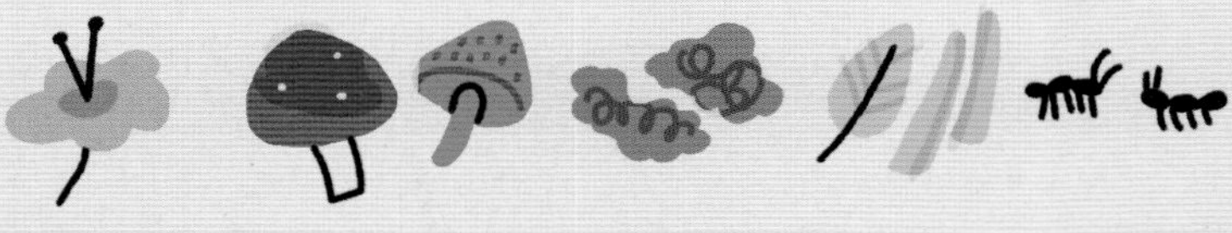

These four animals (and lots of others) used to live all around Australia until they became threatened by feral cats.

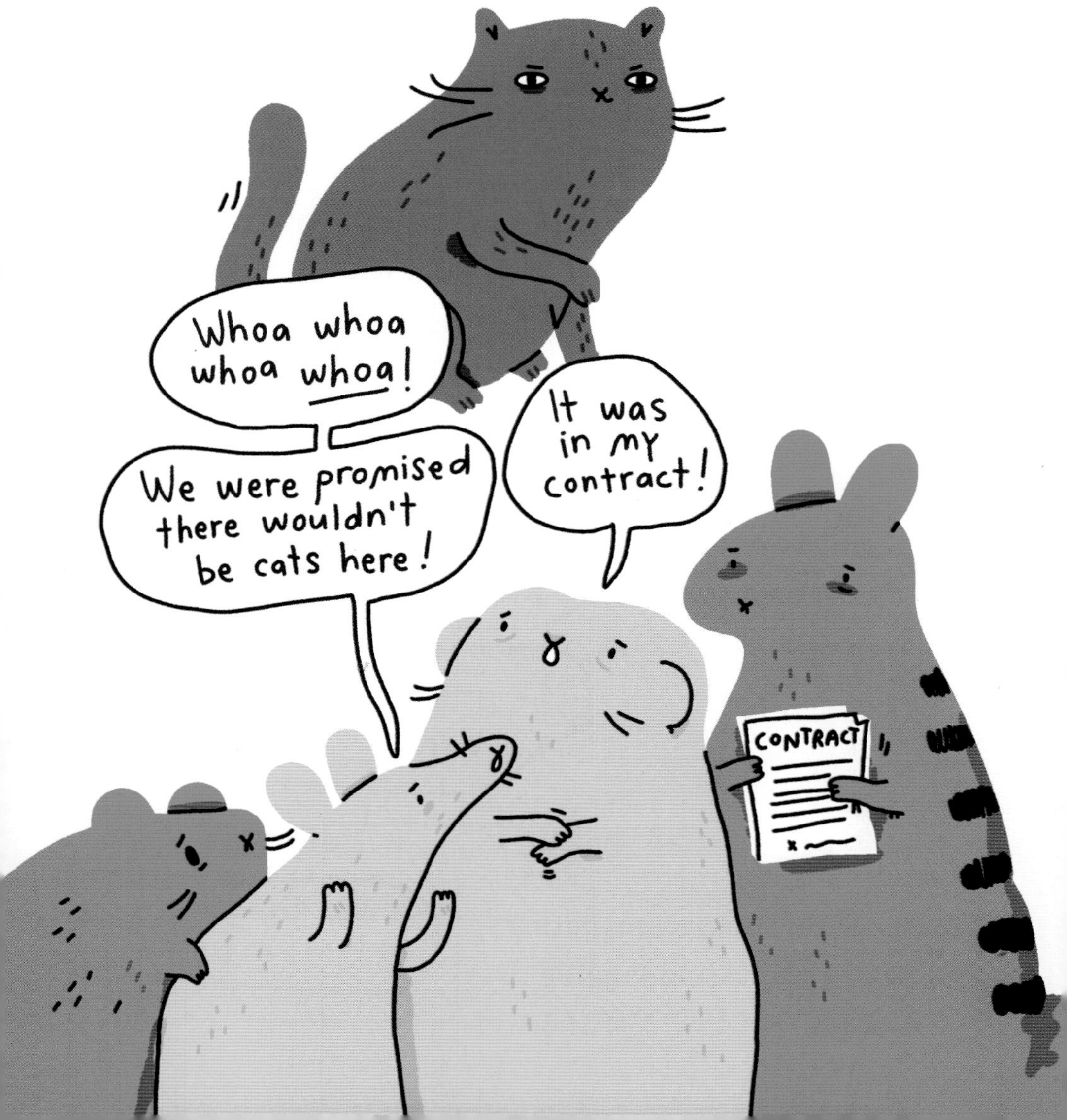
Whoa whoa whoa whoa!
We were promised there wouldn't be cats here!
It was in my contract!
CONTRACT

When large groups of Europeans moved to Australia, they brought ~~cats~~ furry domesticated predators.

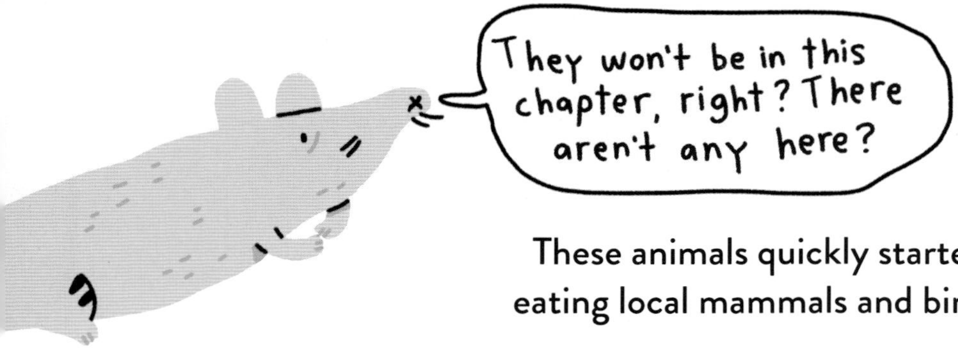
They won't be in this chapter, right? There aren't any here?

These animals quickly started eating local mammals and birds.

87 percent of mammal species in Australia *only* live in Australia. So if they go extinct there, they're gone.

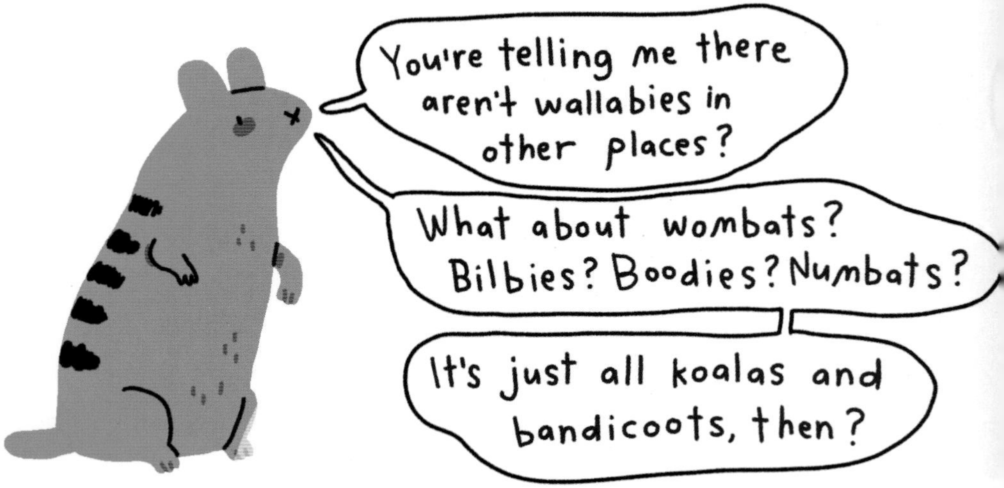
You're telling me there aren't wallabies in other places?
What about wombats? Bilbies? Boodies? Numbats?
It's just all koalas and bandicoots, then?

And the small mammals are part of the ecosystem, eating native plants and digging tunnels that help the soil.

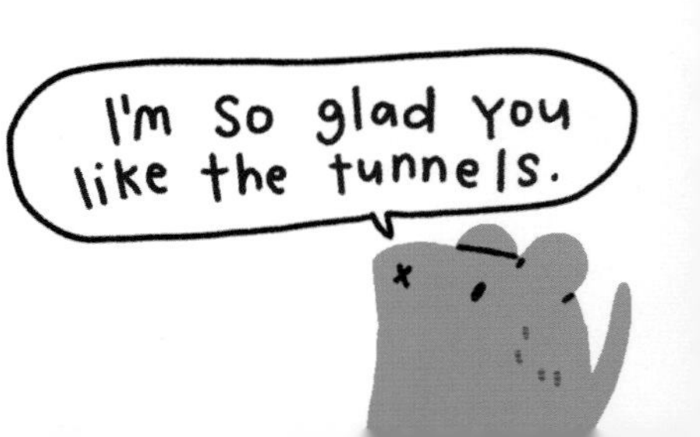
I'm so glad you like the tunnels.

Scientists have tried tracking the cat population . . .

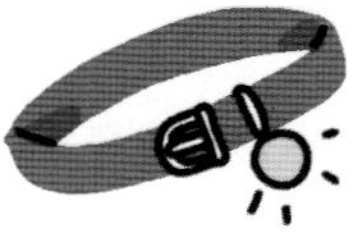

and building fences . . .

Use me to build!

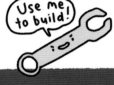

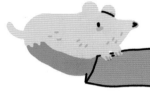

or moving native mammals to new places.

There are so many feral cats across the country today that many native species are extinct, and it's almost impossible to completely protect the ones that are still left.

What about training us in combat?
That sounds interesting.
I have an idea for a cat-proof vest!

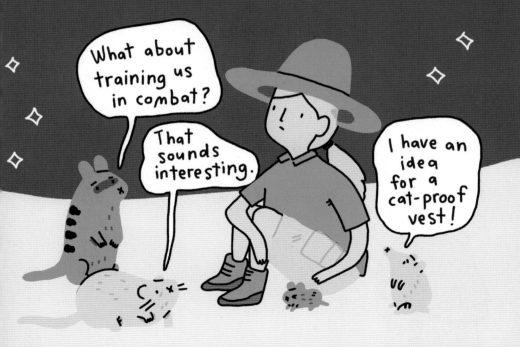

Chantelle works on Faure Island, a predator-free island habitat for these mammals.

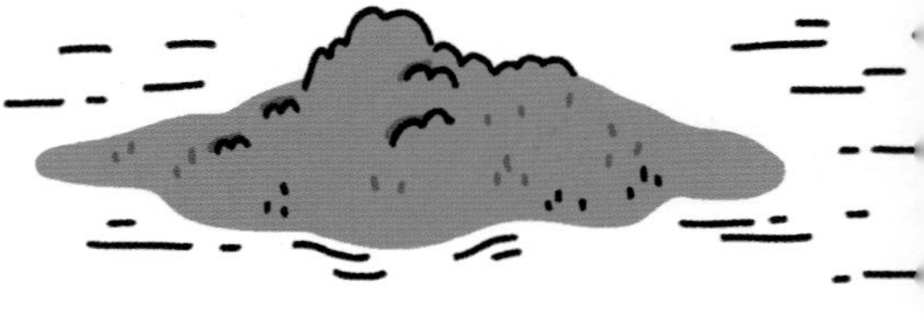

Researchers removed all cats and foxes from the area and brought over the four species that are there today.

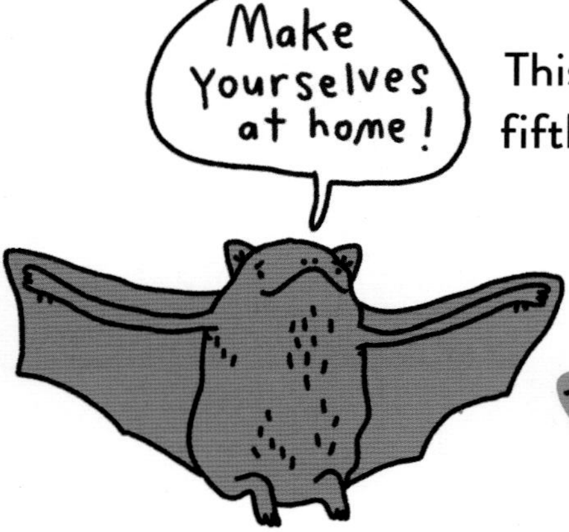
Make yourselves at home!
northern freetail bat

This bat already lived there, so it's the fifth mammal species on Faure Island.

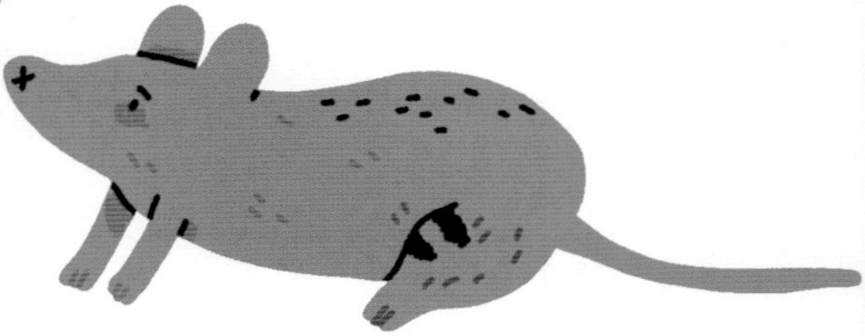

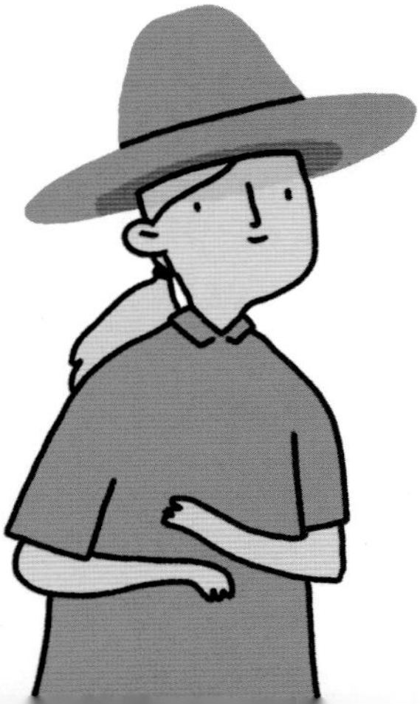

And in the water around the islands, scientists see all kinds of animals.

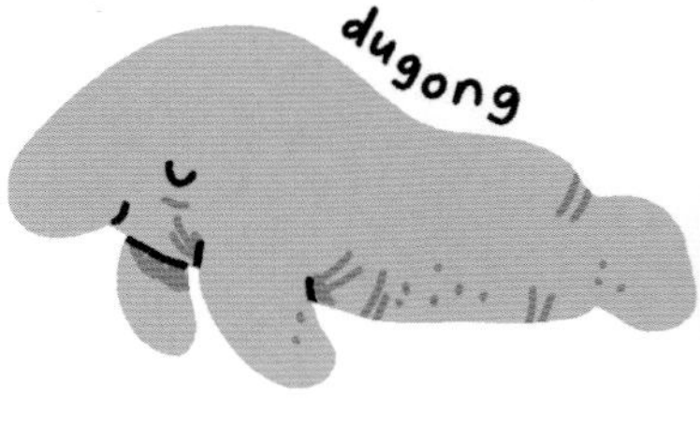
dugong

To get to Faure Island, Chantelle takes a nine-minute flight on a small plane, or an hour-long boat ride.

There's only one building on the island for researchers to store equipment.

It's called the homestead.

Everything else is just plants and animals.

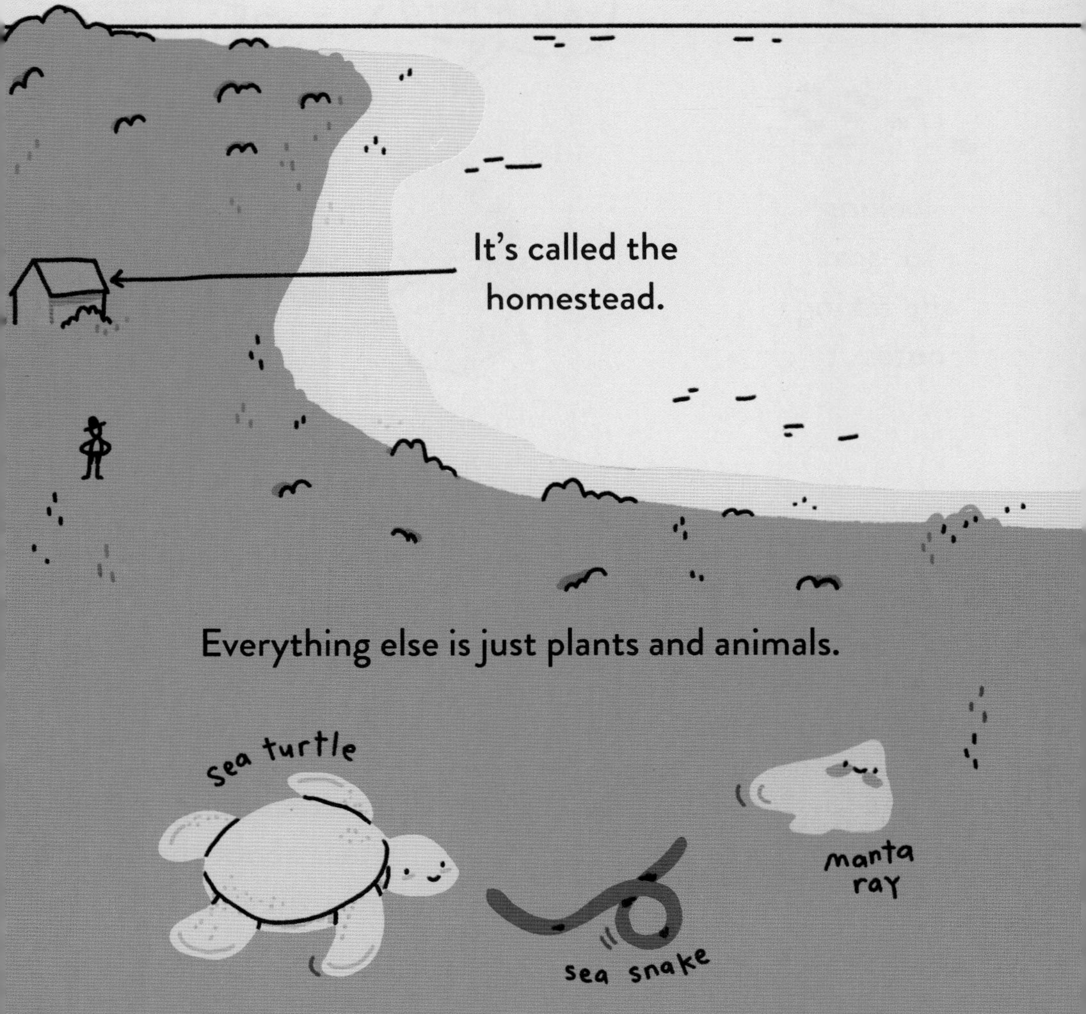
sea turtle
sea snake
manta ray

Chantelle's job is to report on how the animals are doing on the island. She works at night when they're awake, and estimates the population size by:

Yessss!

looking for scat and taking notes . . .

I have 26 kids.
Wow, congratulations!

trapping, observing, and releasing animals . . .

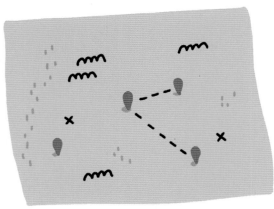

and recording details about the paths they take.

Without invasive predators and with space to eat and hide and sleep, the animals can live like they used to. There are thousands of burrowing bettongs on Faure Island.

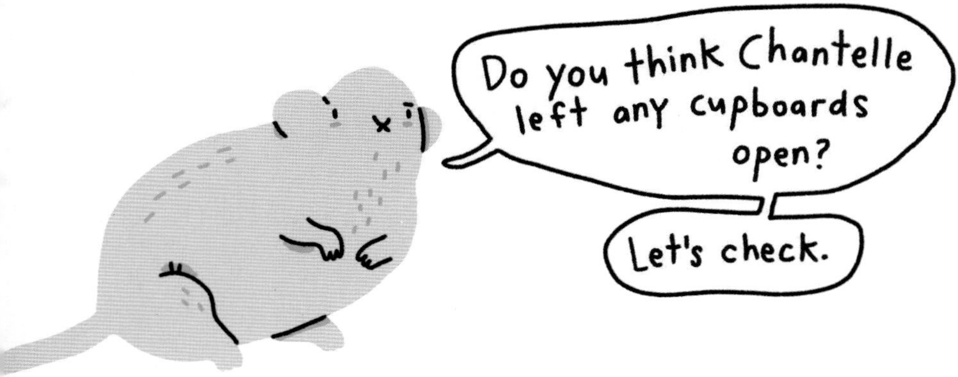
Do you think Chantelle left any cupboards open?
Let's check.

They'll sneak into the homestead if the doors aren't closed all the way.

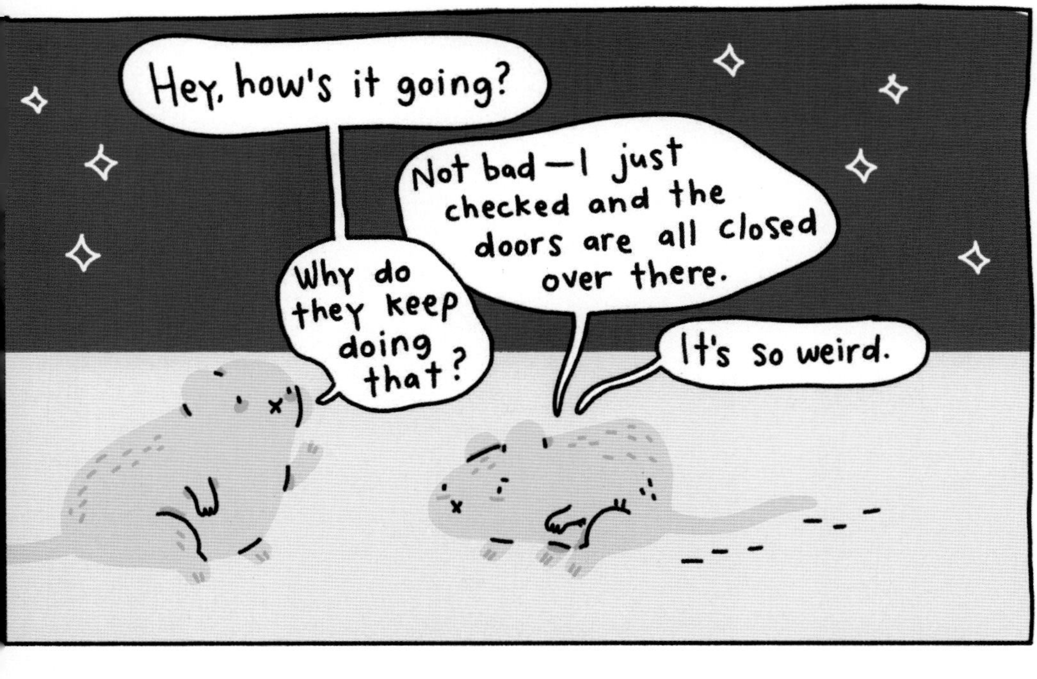
Hey, how's it going?
Not bad—I just checked and the doors are all closed over there.
Why do they keep doing that?
It's so weird.

If Chantelle turns off her flashlight at night, she can hear the burrowing bettongs scurrying closer.

When she turns it back on, there will be
five of them right by her feet.

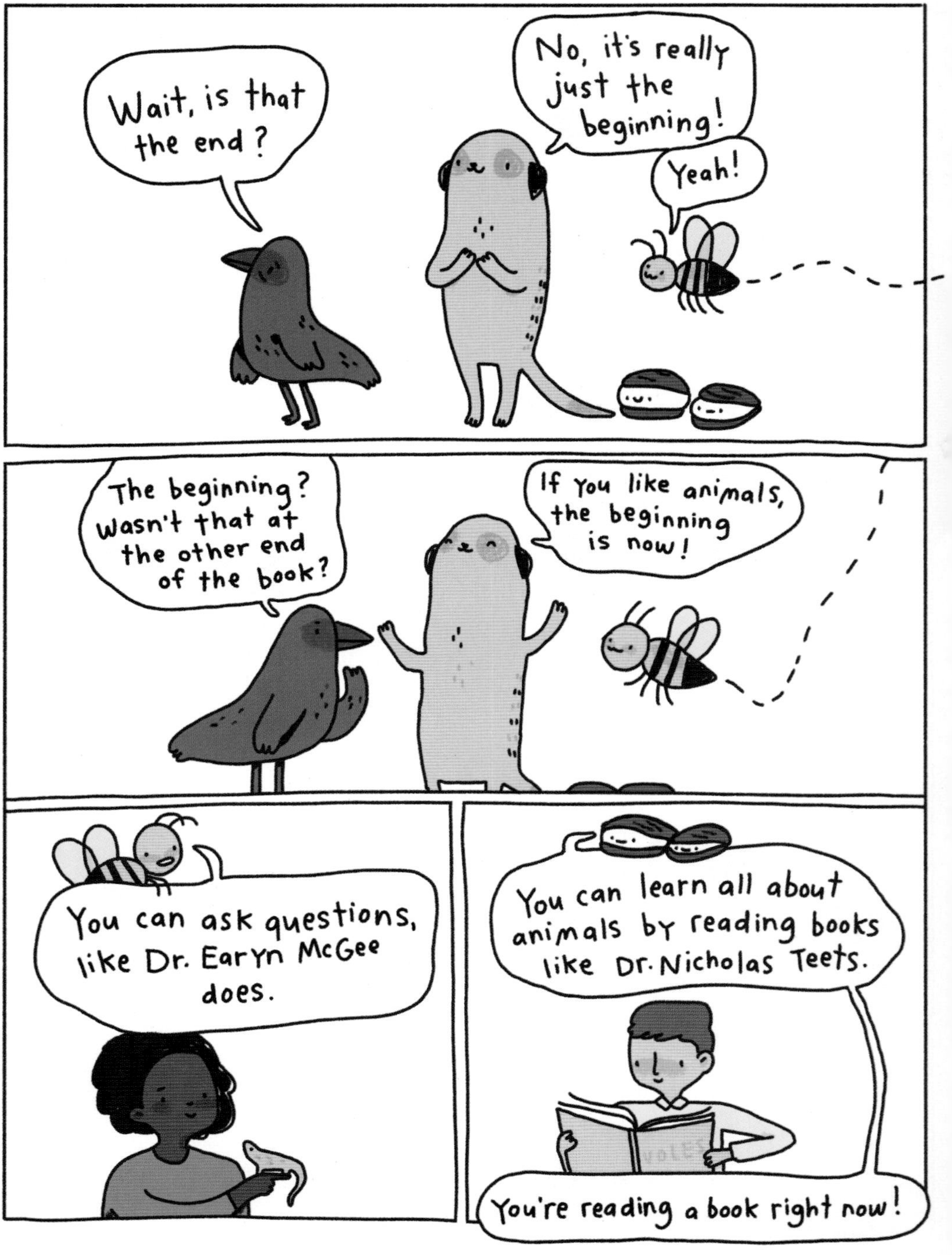
Wait, is that the end?
No, it's really just the beginning!
Yeah!
The beginning? Wasn't that at the other end of the book?
If you like animals, the beginning is now!
You can ask questions, like Dr. Earyn McGee does.
You can learn all about animals by reading books like Dr. Nicholas Teets.
VOLES
You're reading a book right now!

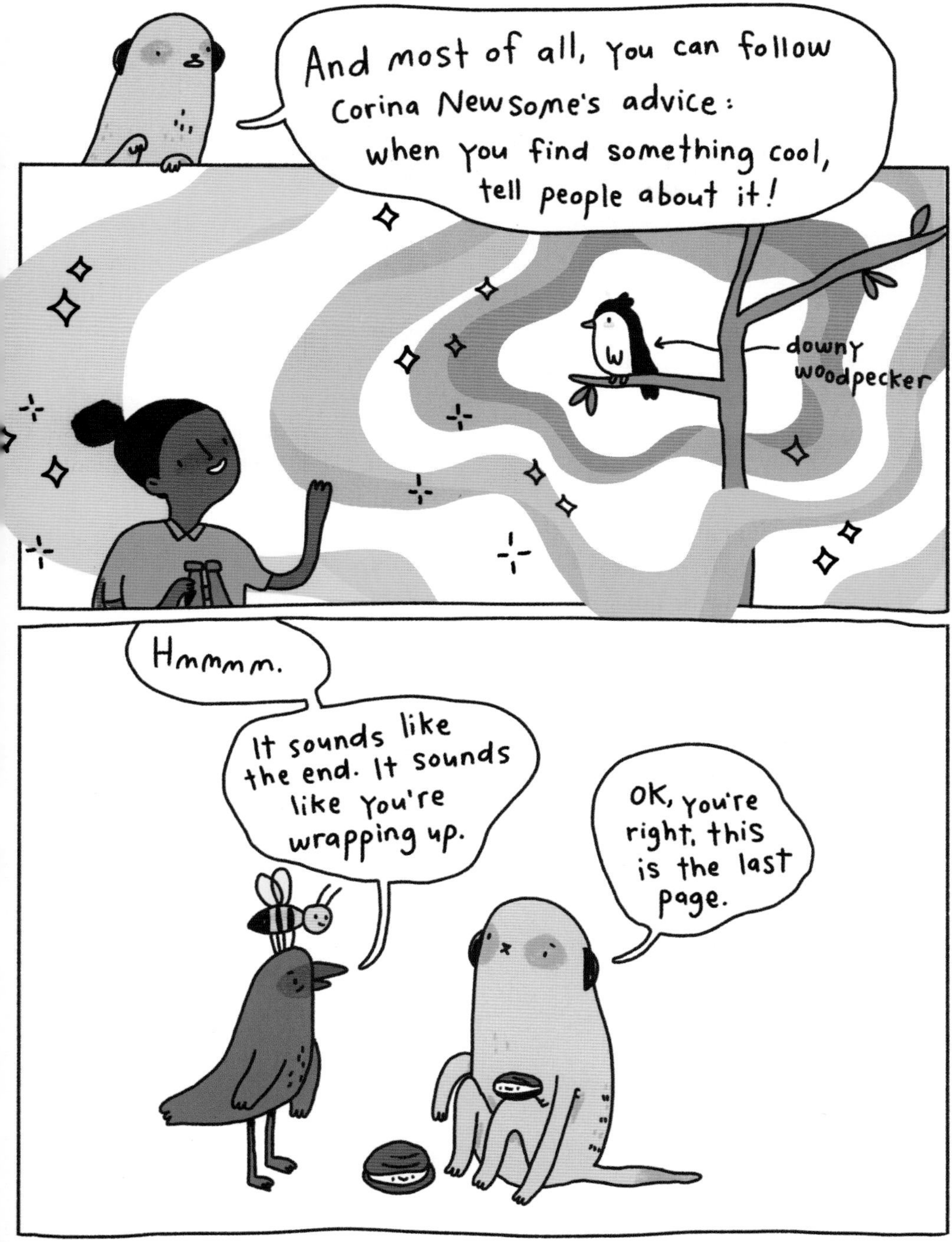

And most of all, you can follow Corina Newsome's advice: when you find something cool, tell people about it!
downy woodpecker
Hmmmm.
It sounds like the end. It sounds like you're wrapping up.
OK, you're right, this is the last page.

GLOSSARY

Bacteria
Organisms that usually consist of just one cell. Humans and animals carry millions of bacteria. Most bacteria are good for us, but some bacteria can cause diseases and make us sick.

Camouflage
The way an animal blends in with its surroundings to disguise itself. For instance, a white polar bear will be camouflaged in an Arctic habitat filled with snow.

Carnivore
An animal that eats mostly or only meat. Tigers, orcas, and civets are all carnivores.

Climate change
Changes to Earth's temperature and atmosphere are called climate change. The climate has shifted throughout our planet's history, but scientists have noticed that right now, temperatures around the world are rising higher and faster than they have before, and human activities like burning fossil fuels (such as gasoline) are some of the main causes. Even though the temperature is only a few degrees warmer in some places, it's a big change for many plants and animals.

DNA
DNA stands for "deoxyribonucleic acid." It's a tiny molecule that contains all sorts of genetic information. DNA is kind of like a recipe for living things: it decides what color eyes an animal might have or what its hair or fur will look like.

Habitat
The place where an animal or plant would be found in the wild.

Herbivore
An animal that only eats plants. Pandas and elephants are herbivores.

Invertebrate
An animal that doesn't have a backbone.

Magma
A hot liquid under and inside the Earth's crust. When magma makes it to the surface of the Earth, we call it lava.

Mammal
Mammals are covered in hair or fur, and they feed milk to their young. They also have three middle-ear bones. The largest mammal is a blue whale, and the smallest mammals are the Etruscan shrew and the bumblebee bat.

Mammalogist
A scientist who studies and observes . . . you guessed it: mammals.

Molecule
A microscopic particle that is made up of atoms, which are pretty much the smallest things there are. If something is molecular, it's related to molecules.

Nocturnal
Nocturnal animals are active at night and rest during the day.

Omnivore
An animal that eats both plants and meat (which could mean insects). Two omnivores that wanted to be mentioned here are grizzly bears and hedgehogs. Humans are also omnivores.

Parasite
A creature that gets its food or nutrients from another creature, often by attaching itself to the other creature. The creature a parasite gets its food from is called a host.

Species
A grouping of plants or animals that are all in one family. There are 350,000 different species of beetles, but all humans are one species (*Homo sapiens*).

Wetland
A wet, marshy, or swampy area.

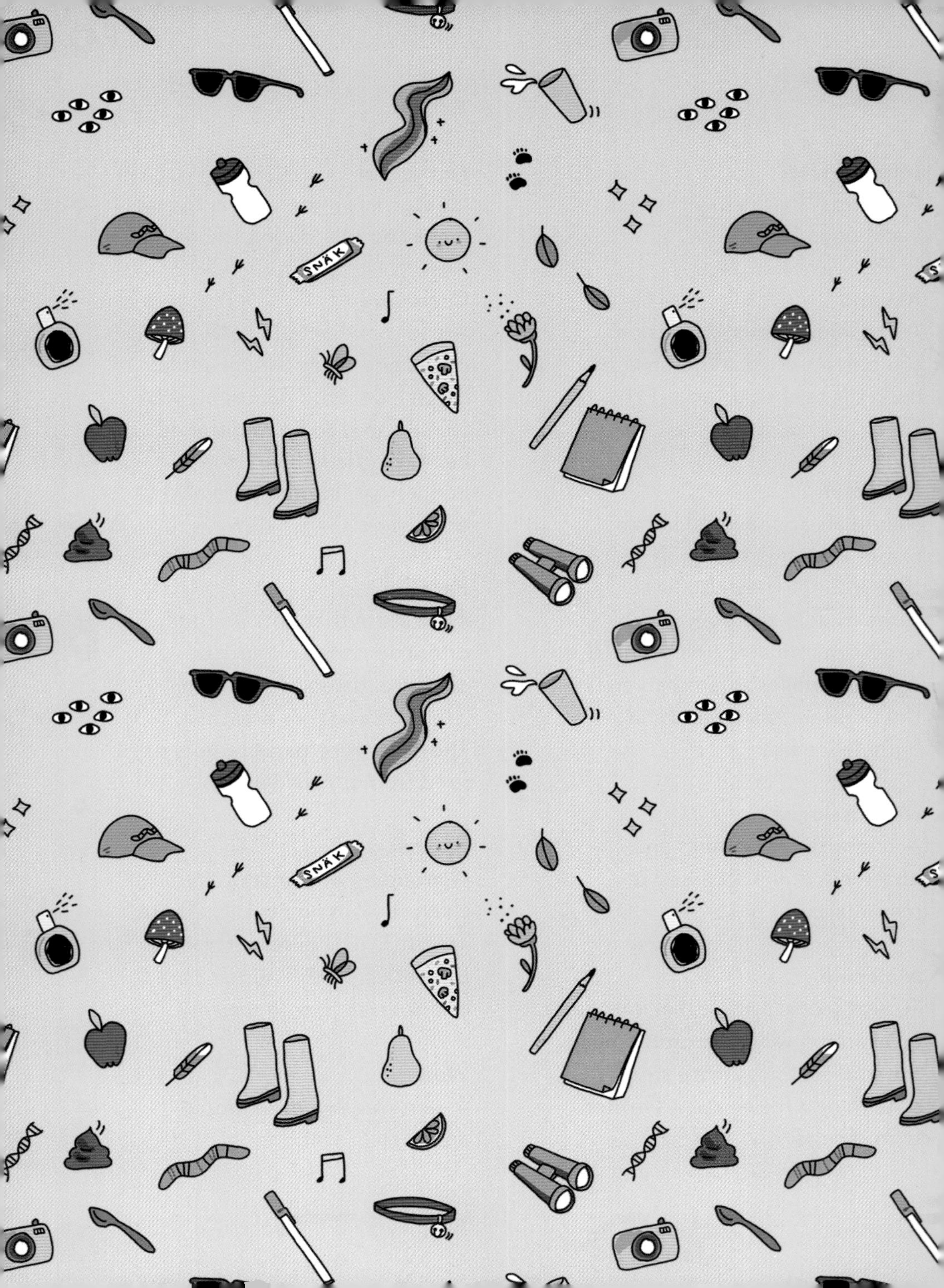
SNÄK

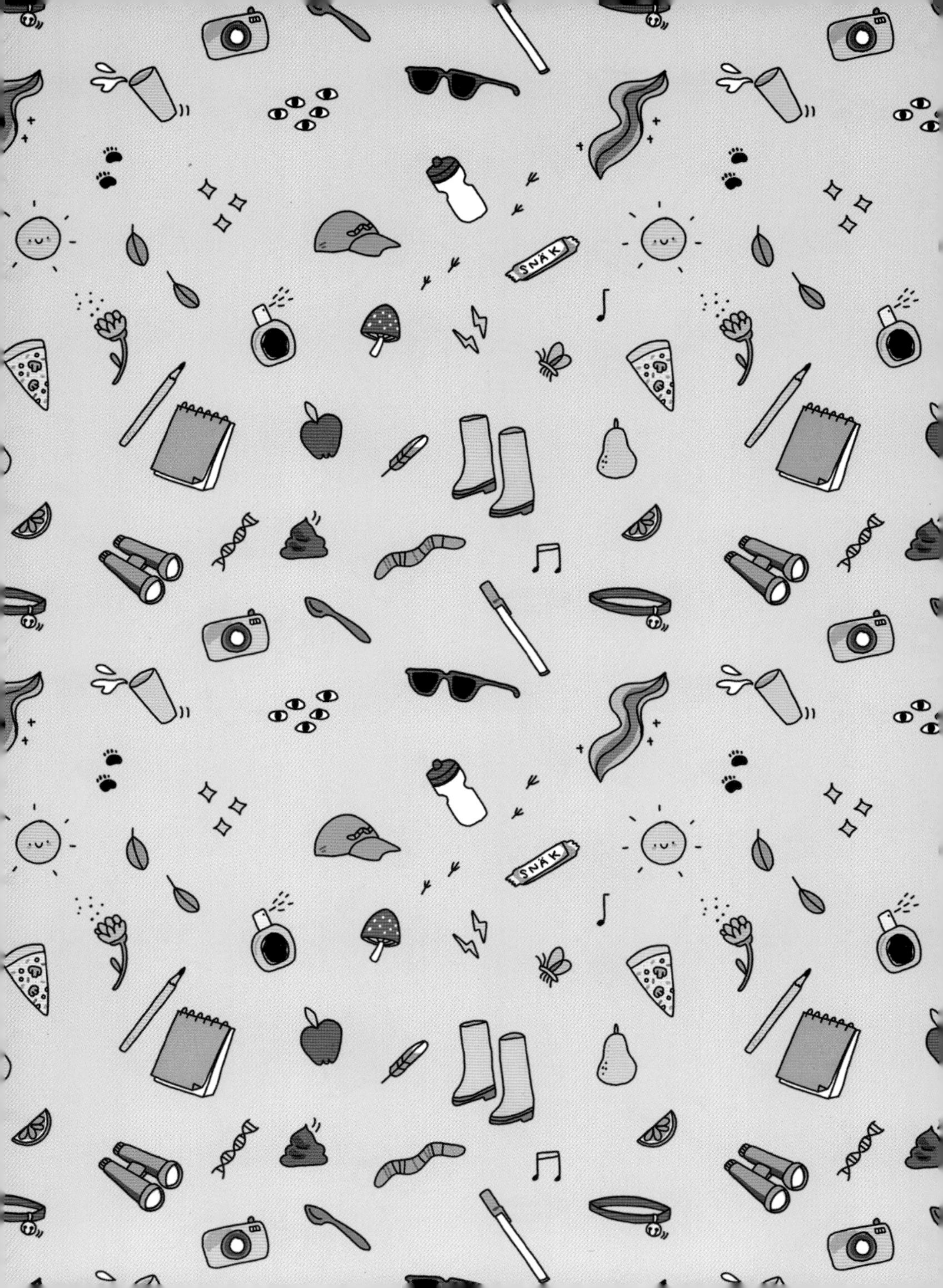
SNÄK
SNÄK

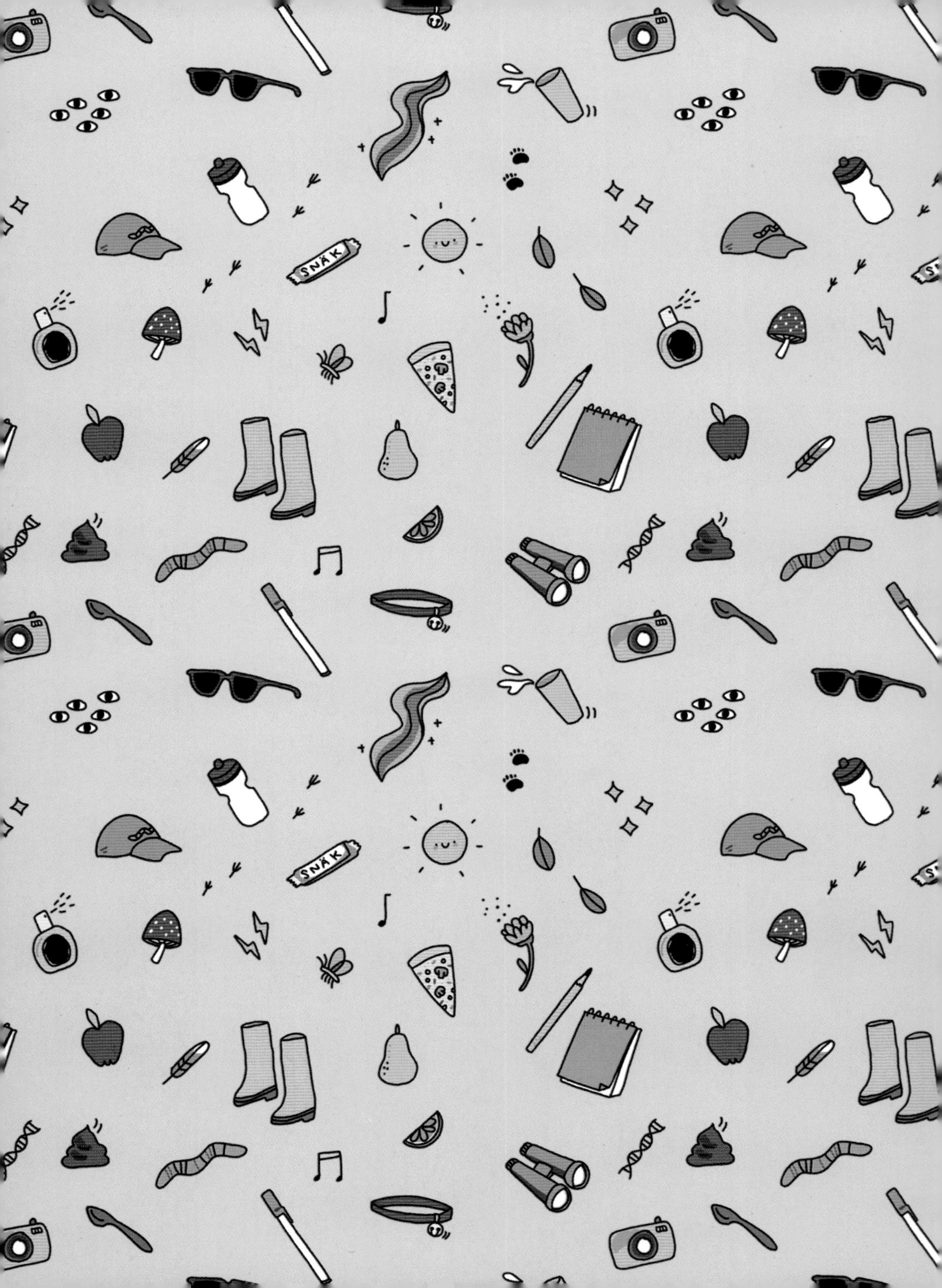
SNÄK